D1117042

The Role of Business in Fostering Peaceful Societies

This book offers a novel approach to understanding responsible business practice. Global protests against multinational companies often give the misleading impression that the interests of multinationals and of peaceful societies are at odds. By contrast, Fort and Schipani contend, not only does business benefit from a peaceful environment but it can in fact effectively foster peace through adopting responsible and open working methods. Firms that promote economic development, that allow external evaluation of their affairs and that build a sense of community both within the company and in their local areas make a great contribution to building a more harmonious culture. Relevant for academics and practitioners, the book shows how companies can encourage collaborative working across borders, discourage corruption and create citizenship and problem-solving practices which tend to reduce violence and increase social harmony.

TIMOTHY L. FORT is Associate Professor of Business Law and Business Ethics at the University of Michigan Business School and Co-Area Director of Corporate Governance and Corporate Social Responsibility at The William Davidson Institute.

CINDY A. SCHIPANI is Chair of Law, History and Communication, Professor of Business Law at the University of Michigan Business School and Co-Area Director of Corporate Governance and Corporate Social Responsibility at The William Davidson Institute.

The Role of Business in Fostering Peaceful Societies

TIMOTHY L. FORT
University of Michigan Business School and
The William Davidson Institute

and

CINDY A. SCHIPANI
University of Michigan Business School and
The William Davidson Institute

CAMBRIDGE
UNIVERSITY PRESS

PUBLISHED BY THE PRESS SYNDICATE OF THE UNIVERSITY OF CAMBRIDGE
The Pitt Building, Trumpington Street, Cambridge, United Kingdom

CAMBRIDGE UNIVERSITY PRESS
The Edinburgh Building, Cambridge CB2 2RU, UK
40 West 20th Street, New York, NY 10011–4211, USA
477 Williamstown Road, Port Melbourne, VIC 3207, Australia
Ruiz de Alarcón 13, 28014 Madrid, Spain
Dock House, The Waterfront, Cape Town 8001, South Africa

http://www.cambridge.org

First published 2004

Printed in the United Kingdom at the University Press, Cambridge

Typeface Sabon 10/13 pt.   *System* LATEX 2$_\varepsilon$ [TB]

A catalogue record for this book is available from the British Library

ISBN 0 521 83262 4 hardback

To Kaela and Lana
To Kurina and Steven

Contents

Tables

Acknowledgements

Joint Acknowledgements

We would like to thank Professor Jan Svejnar, Everett E. Berg Professor of Business Administration and Director of The William Davidson Institute at The University of Michigan Business School for his support of the Corporate Governance and Sustainable Peace Conferences, especially when these ideas were in their infancy. The conferences provided the initial spark for this book.

In addition, we would like to express gratitude to The William Davidson Institute, the Aspen Institute's Business and Society Program and Dr. Erika O. Parker for their co-sponsorship of the Corporate Governance and Sustainable Peace Conferences. This work benefited greatly from the initial airing of ideas at those conferences.

We would also like gratefully to acknowledge the support of our colleagues, Professor George Siedel and Professor Dana Muir at the University of Michigan Business School. Both George and Dana participated in the conferences and have supported us in this work in so many ways.

Finally, we would like to thank Shannon Droz, Krysia Johnson, Avec G. Gomez Lee, Elizabeth Peirce and Jill Van Dalen for valuable research assistance, and Connie Allen for all of her administrative assistance in pulling this book together.

Professor Schipani's Personal Acknowledgements

I would also like to note that this work would not have been possible without the support and encouragement of a number of people. I would like to thank my coauthor, Professor Timothy Fort, for everything he brought to this project. It has been a tremendous experience working with him on this endeavor from beginning to end. Tim's creativity and energy knows no bounds.

This work would not be complete without noting the inspiration from the music of Bruce Springsteen and the E Street Band. Throughout the course of this project I attended over thirty of their concerts and each concert provided additional ideas and energy for this project. I hope this work in some way, supports Bruce Springsteen's "Land of Hope and Dreams."

Finally, I am most grateful for the love and support of my family without whom this work would not have been possible – my parents, my sisters, my husband and my daughters. My husband, Bob Van Til and daughters, Kaela and Lana have supported this project day to day and have been my deepest inspiration. I hope that this work in some way contributes to a more peaceful world in which my daughters can grow and thrive.

Professor Fort's Personal Acknowledgements

I would like to acknowledge the indispensable work of my coauthor Cindy Schipani. Cindy has the wisdom and good sense to keep my flights of fancy anchored in scholarly research and to carefully ground our theory.

Music is a repository for my inspiration as well. Ralph Vaughn Williams's *Dona Nobis Pacem* and, in particular, the setting of Walt Whitman's "Beat, Beat Drums" is a painful, searing, reminder of the disruptive angst of war. Listening to it prods me to stay up a little later at night to try to contribute something that might mitigate the prevalence of bloodshed.

My gratitude to my wife, Nancy Nerad, is infinite. Impatient with academic meanderings, she bolstered me at every turn to make this contribution as writing that might really make a difference to the world. My multicultural children – Kurina Mei Ke Nerad Fort whom we adopted from China and Steven Yohanes Nerad Fort whom we adopted from Ethiopia – remind me of the opportunities to grow from openness both as children of their native lands and, more profoundly, as my daughter and my son.

Publication Acknowledgements

We would like to acknowledge and to thank two scholars with whom we previously published joint work and who graciously allowed us to use that work in this book.

Professor Terry Dworkin collaborated with Professor Schipani on chapter 5 of this book in an article entitled "Gender Voice and Correlations with Peace." Professor Fort collaborated with Professor Thomas Dunfee on an article entitled "Corporate Hypergoals, Sustainable Peace, and the Adapted Firm," portions of which appear in chapter 4 of this book. Both of these articles were originally published in vol. 36 of the *Vanderbilt Journal of Transnational Law*.

We would like further to acknowledge the *Vanderbilt Journal of Transnational Law*. In addition to the above-referenced articles, this book draws on three other articles initially published with the *Vanderbilt Journal of Transnational Law*: "Corporate Governance in a Global Environment: The Search for the Best of All Worlds," appearing in vol. 33, "The Role of the Corporation in Fostering Sustainable Peace," appearing in vol. 35, and "Adapting Corporate Governance for Sustainable Peace," appearing in vol. 36. Portions of the Conclusion were originally published in *Corporate Environmental Strategy*, vol. 10 as an article entitled "Scandals and Sustainable Security." An earlier version of this article was also presented by Professor Fort as the Prudential Lecture in Business Ethics at Rutgers University in 2002. Finally, we would like to acknowledge, the *Columbia Journal of Environmental Law*. The chapter entitled "Ecological Challenges of War: The Natural Environment and Disease" appeared in vol. 29.

Introduction

GOVERNMENTS typically provide stability and security. Armies patrol borders and police maintain order in streets. Judicial systems relocate violent criminals from neighborhoods to jails. To be sure, these responsibilities remain those of the political sector. Yet, in a complex world defined by cross-cutting commercial relationships in addition to geopolitical boundaries, governments are not the only organizations impacting social affairs. With communication technologies and travel capability making global interaction the norm, the institutions responsible for globalization impact a variety of relationships. Corporations shrink the world by commercially linking regions and people that might not otherwise be linked. This book suggests that in doing so, corporations may be able to orient their affairs to contribute to peace.

The claim that business might contribute to peace is not without controversy. As further discussed in chapter 1, there have been many protests against the unfairness of globalization. One view is that corporations are selfish organizations that undermine a sense of citizenship.[1] From this perspective, the notion that business may build peace is startling.

For example, the media and nongovernmental organizations (NGOs) recently focused on a particularly controversial interaction of economic profitability and violence involving the mining of diamonds in Sierra Leone, Angola, and the Democratic Republic of the Congo.[2] According to some reports, terrorist units have used funds from the sale of conflict diamonds to purchase weapons and other materials essential for carrying on violent campaigns.[3] The United Nations has attributed human rights abuses to the Revolutionary United Front (RUF) through its claim that the RUF has coerced children and young teenagers into their fighting forces.[4] Some NGOs accused De Beers, the South African diamond company, of not being concerned with RUF practices.[5] De Beers disputes this charge.[6] The controversy

1

also affected Belgian businesses that cut and polish the gems[7] as well as retail giant Tiffany & Co. Tiffany & Co. has responded with a two-page letter to consumers explaining how it has been actively involved with industry groups seeking ways to mark the source of diamonds to prevent conflict diamonds from entering the streams of commerce.[8] The controversy resulted in "The Kimberley Protocol," which attempts to formulate a system to track the origin of diamonds to advise consumers of the source of the gems.[9]

Assessing responsibility for the abuses in the diamond trade is an interesting exercise.[10] Even without determining the relative merits of the various charges, it is worth noting how corporations can be held accountable by popular institutions for both direct and indirect involvement in commercial affairs. As further discussed in chapter 1, controversy has also followed the actions of McDonald's Corporation,[11] Wal-Mart Stores, Inc.,[12] and major Western banks.[13] Corporate sensitivity to popular institutions is one reason why companies such as General Electric Company, Microsoft Corporation, Pfizer Inc., AOL Time Warner, Inc., DaimlerChrysler AG, Cisco Systems, Inc., E.I. duPont de Nemours and Company and Merck & Co., Inc., just to name a few, have adopted extensive community involvement programs.[14] Moreover, some corporations, as detailed in this book, have received awards from foreign policy institutions (for example from the US Secretary of State) for undertaking activities promoting geopolitical harmony.[15]

If there is a connection between business and peace, then several interesting things follow. First, fairly standard ethical business practices may reduce bloodshed. Second, the legal rules undergirding corporate governance may be reconsidered to include peace as a governance *telos*. Third, businesses could become a more important dimension of foreign policy. Consider, for instance, the potential benefits of business practices supporting peace in regions such as Bosnia, Ethiopia, Afghanistan, or Indonesia.

Studies, such as the *The Pew Global Attitudes Project, Views of a Changing World*,[16] show that although globalization raises fears, corporations and international trade are viewed generally positively worldwide.[17] This is true even though corporations and trade may be responsible for the globalization that makes people uneasy. This difference may be attributed to a type of collective cognitive dissonance that causes people to separate corporations as the suppliers of goods they need from their perceptions of the insidious effects of globalization. Even if this explanation is true, however, positive views of corporations and trade provide a foundation for a credible business effort to contribute to a positive goal, such as sustainable peace. Given the importance of reduced bloodshed in a world where access to severely destructive weapons is available to many actors in society, this book offers a way in which the power and efficacy of multinational corporations can contribute to increased global stability and security.

The evidence from *The Pew Report* suggests that corporations have a foundation of credibility to build upon. This offers an opportunity for multinational businesses to build on that credibility. Corporations cross borders. They bring people together for work. They provide important goods and services. If they are able to do this while alleviating concerns about globalization – such as the rich-poor disparity or degradation of working conditions – they can contribute to a sense of satisfaction among constituents that may reduce flashpoints over perceived mistreatment and unfairness. This book elaborates on how corporations might consider this by drawing upon empirical studies that suggest traits linked to peace and stability and linking those traits to potential business practices. In short, we suggest that businesses have credibility around the world and therefore have the potential for contributing to beneficial social practices. This book develops an argument for how corporations can build upon their existing credibility to contribute to what is perhaps the most important corporate social responsibility issue of our time – that of contributing to sustainable peace.

To develop this argument, this book is organized into six chapters, divided into three parts. Part One sets forth an argument for the plausibility of connecting business and peace. Part Two aligns the argument with current governance and ethical scholarship and practice and argues that there are at least four contributions corporations can make to sustainable peace. Part Three considers the issues of gender and ecology to provide a deeper, illustrative look at how business can contribute to sustainable peace.

Part One begins in chapter 1 by considering economic arguments regarding why businesses might be able to contribute to peace as well as why it would be reasonable for businesses to consider stability in orienting their business practices. This chapter provides an empirical study linking corruption to violence. This linkage suggests that corporations can reduce the possibility of violence by reducing, if not eliminating, corruption in daily work.

Part One continues in chapter 2 by situating the argument in the larger context of a balance of power framework. This chapter examines the literature that argues that democracy, which is a domestic expression of balance of power, is, as frequently asserted, a form of political organization likely to lead to peace and stability. Contemporary political theories suggest that we no longer live in a world with neat divisions of jurisdiction among nation-states, but instead live in an environment where multinational corporations exert independent influence. If this is true, and if it is also true that democracy is a preferable mechanism of organizing society for purposes of achieving sustainable peace, then it becomes important to consider whether corporations can enhance democracy. Our answer is that there are management techniques and moral imperatives that suggest that corporations do effective work while activating voice within their organizations. Because voice is a central attribute of democracy, corporations can make a practical contribution to a larger social goal of stability by being mediators of justice within a new sense of balance of power.

Part Two begins in chapter 3 by examining the current status of corporate governance to determine which models of governance tend to predominate. Following the foundational assessment provided in chapter 2, the corporate governance regimes of Germany, Japan and the USA are further examined. These countries were chosen for examination, in part, both because they are economically powerful countries and also because they have proven to be models followed by other nation-states. This chapter concludes that contemporary governance could accommodate business practices that would facilitate the goal of sustainable peace. In an important sense, this chapter demonstrates that our proposal, while novel, is one that is within the tradition of extant governance regimes and therefore feasible.

Part Two continues with an examination of the goal of peace from the perspective of moral theory in chapter 4. That is, this chapter argues that a teleological goal of businesses attempting to achieve sustainable peace is within the traditions of leading business ethics theories as well as within an integrative possibility of the ways corporations strategically orient their practices. Thus, ethically and strategically, businesses are on firm ground in contributing to sustainable peace. This analysis continues with an articulation of four contributions corporations can make to sustainable peace. Corporations can make these contributions by fostering economic development, exercising track two diplomacy, adopting external evaluation principles, and nourishing a sense of community.

Part Three begins in chapter 5 by providing an illustrative case in point regarding the importance of gender and voice. This chapter examines worldwide data and finds that countries with practices evidencing higher degrees of gender equity tend to resolve disputes more peacefully than other countries. Conversely, those countries experiencing low degrees of gender equity appear to be more prone to violence. The chapter concludes with a number of practical steps corporations can take to reduce the mistreatment of women. These contributions involve setting clear standards as well as the establishment of programs that may beneficially alter the work (and social) environment.

Part Three continues in chapter 6 with another case example: ecology. This chapter examines how ecological issues impact violence. This issue is analyzed both from the perspective of competition for natural resources as well as from the perspective of how ecological issues may exacerbate already existing ethnic rivalries. This chapter also considers current studies that demonstrate how fierce the competition for oil and water may become in light of current supplies and forecasted demands.

Competition for natural resources (oil and water, for instance), is often thought of as one between nation-states. And, to a large extent, this is an appropriate way to frame the competition. It is important, however, to note that nation-states are not the only entities competing for these resources. Companies also compete. When companies compete, they sometimes do so under the auspices of nation-states and, at other times, independently. In either case, *how* corporations compete is important. Moreover, following research of scholars such as Thomas Homer-Dixon, this chapter examines how the allocation of resources (or the dumping of pollutants) tends to exacerbate ethnic rivalries. That is, the distribution of resources and pollutants is not spread evenly but often reflects established political and social divisions. Thus, ecological dimensions of business behavior can have an impact on the exacerbation of rivalries that can result in violence. Part Three ends with our concluding remarks.

Notes

1. See generally Benjamin Barber, Jihad vs McWorld: How Globalism and Tribalism are Reshaping the World (1995).
2. Global Witness, *Conflict Diamonds*, at 1–2, at http://www.globalwitnes.org/campaigns/diamonds/downloads,confilct.pdf.
3. Ibid.
4. See, e.g. United Nations Mission in Sierra Leone (UNAMSIL), *Sierra Leone – UNAMSIL Background*, at http://www.un.org/ Depts/dpko/unamsil/UnamsilB.htm; US Bureau of Democracy, Human Rights, and Labor, *Sierra Leone: Country Reports on Human Rights Practices – 2000*, at http://www.state.gov/g/drl/rls/hrrpt/2000/af/755.htm.
5. News Advisory, *NGOs Call for an End to Diamond Bloodshed on Valentine's Day*, US Newswire, February 12, 2001, available at 2001 WL 4139876.
6. Eugenie Samuel, *Diamond Wars*, New Scientist, May 25, 2002, at 6.
7. David Buchan, et al., *The Deadly Scramble for Diamonds in Africa*, Fin. Times, July 10, 2000, at 6.
8. Letter from Tiffany & Co., "Conflict Diamonds: We Want You to Know" (copy of letter on file with authors).
9. DeBeers, *Leading the Way in Tackling Conflict Diamonds*, at http://debeers.com/html/corp_resp/leading.html.
10. See Thomas W. Dunfee and Timothy L. Fort, *Corporate Hypergoals, Sustainable Peace, and the Adapted Firm*, 36 Vand. J. Transn'l. L. 563 (2003) (providing an example of one such attempt to characterize the issues of the diamond trade with a view toward corporate strategic practices. Parts of this Introduction are drawn, with permission of the authors, from this article.)
11. See e.g. Laurie Goodstein, *For Hindus and Vegetarians, Surprise in McDonald's Fries*, N.Y. Times, May 20, 2001, at A1 (cited and discussed in ch. 1 of this book).
12. Toby Helm, *Bush Protests Off to Early Start*, London Daily Telegraph, May 22, 2001, at B1.
13. Anthony Faiola, *Argentine Peso Quickly Sinks After Government Lets it Float; Protests Against Economic Changes Turn Violent in Capital*, Wash. Post, January 13, 2002, at A23.
14. See David Hess, Nikolai Rogovksy, and Thomas W. Dunfee, *The Next Wave of Corporate Community Involvement: Corporate Social Initiatives*, 44 Calif. Mgmt. Rev. 110 (2002) (reporting on a number of

corporate community programs and assessing the relative merits and strategies underlying them).

15. See e.g. US Deptartment of State, *2000 Award for Corporate Excellence*, at http://www.state.gov/e/eb/cba/bs/ace.

16. THE PEW GLOBAL ATTITUDES PROJECT, VIEWS OF A CHANGING WORLD (2003).

17. Ibid.

I | *The plausibility of connecting business and peace*

1 | *The role of business in fostering sustainable peace*

O N May 20, 2001, a front-page *New York Times* news story reported that Hindus in scattered areas of the world protested McDonald's decision to cook its French fries in beef fat, despite announcing in 1990 that it would cook its fries only in vegetable oil.[1] As a result, "[T]he news ricocheted to India, where restaurant windows were smashed, statues of Ronald McDonald were smeared with cow dung, and Hindu nationalist politicians called for the chain to be evicted from the country."[2] The controversy is not the first McDonald's has faced. A well-toned Prince Philip of Great Britain stated, "You people [McDonald's] are destroying the rainforests of the world by grazing your cheap cattle."[3] And even as McDonald's CEO, Jack Greenberg, acknowledged and defended McDonald's record, the company faces challenges on issues from undermining local farmers, threatening local culture, using genetically modified organisms in its food, relying on hormonally treated beef, opposing local unionization, distributing unsafe toys to children, and employing child labor.[4] Such a seemingly ubiquitous problem-causing image may be why another journal not known for its left-leaning views, *The Economist*, jokingly began a recent story with "Scientists at the McDonald's Centre for Obesity Research suggest that eating a hamburger a day actually reduces cholesterol levels."[5] This appeared in a story suggesting that the scientific community is beholden to the corporations funding its research.[6]

On the other hand, in addition to the employment McDonald's restaurants bring to local areas, their influence on economic affairs and perhaps even peace, have been trumpeted as well. In a more serious vein – at least somewhat so – *The Economist* uses the price of a McDonald's hamburger in different countries as a way to assess distortions in the exchange rate of currencies.[7] Thomas Friedman, the National Book Award-winning *New York Times* columnist, has advanced a theory called "The Golden Arches Theory of Conflict Prevention," claiming "no two countries that both had McDonald's had fought a war against each other since each got its McDonald's."[8] Friedman amended this theory slightly in light of the 1999 conflict between NATO and Yugoslavia, where all countries had McDonald's restaurants. Indeed, he contended the turning point of that conflict occurred when NATO bombed the power grids and, therefore, eliminated the benefits of a networked global economy for the people, including the convenience of consuming a Big Mac.[9] Thus, although there is now, according to Friedman, an exception to the Golden Arches Theory, the power of globalization works to mitigate the extent of conflict.[10] These examples illustrate the complexity involved in assessing the ways multinational corporations may or may not foster beneficial relationships with the people they encounter. From these limited comments regarding McDonald's, one could hypothesize several potential theories.

(1) Multinational corporations cause unrest, protest, and bitterness.
(2) Multinational corporations are convenient scapegoats because of their power and their facelessness.
(3) The influence of multinational corporations is so fundamental that they undermine even seemingly objective analyses of contemporary issues (such as scientific analysis).
(4) The influence of multinational corporations is so fundamental that they have the potential to build a *Pax E-Commercia*[11] that philosophers such as Kant[12] only hoped to realize.

In short, the relationship between corporate action and an ideal such as sustainable peace seems to be ambiguous. Within the ambiguity, however, there may lie patterns of relationships that can be elucidated. To date, very little attention has been devoted to this topic.[13] It is hoped that this book will contribute to a dialogue on these issues in light of the following observations.

As demonstrated below, there is a plausible, conceptual relationship among corporate governance, business ethics, and sustainable peace. Accordingly, the following section is concerned with developing this connection in terms of recognizing the protests against as well as the benefits of globalization, the reciprocal benefits between stable geopolitical entities and economic activity, and specific historical events that collectively add to the ambiguity, but which may also foreshadow patterns to be illuminated.

I. Connecting governance, ethics, and peace

The first question to be asked is whether there is a plausible connection among corporate governance, ethics, and peace. As demonstrated below, the answer to that question is yes, both empirically and conceptually.

A. *An initial empirical connection*

Transparency International (TI) is a nongovernmental organization which attempts to document the level of corruption that exists within countries today.[14] As its chairman, Peter Eigen, states, "[T]he scale of bribe-paying in international corporations in the developing countries of the world is massive . . . [and] . . . the results include growing poverty in poor countries, persistent undermining of the institutions of democracy, and mounting distortions in fair international commerce."[15] In attempting to determine perceptions of the level of corruption in countries, TI conducted 779 interviews with representatives of companies doing business in emerging markets.[16] In conjunction with this index devoted specifically to bribe-taking, TI also utilized other indices to create a "Corruption Perceptions Index."[17] The rankings of these ninety countries provide an indication of levels of corruption that exist today. The chart is reproduced below:

Table 1.1 *The 2000 Corruption Perceptions Index*[18]

Country Rank	Country	2000 CPI Score	Surveys Used	Standard Deviation	High-Low Range
1	Finland	10.0	8	0.6	9.0–10.4
2	Denmark	9.8	9	0.8	8.6–10.6
3	New Zealand	9.4	8	0.8	8.1–10.2
	Sweden	9.4	9	0.7	8.1–9.9
5	Canada	9.2	9	0.7	8.1–9.9
6	Iceland	9.1	7	1.1	7.3–9.9
	Norway	9.1	8	0.7	7.6–9.5
	Singapore	9.1	11	1.0	6.2–9.7

(*cont.*)

Table 1.1 (*cont.*)

Country Rank	Country	2000 CPI Score	Surveys Used	Standard Deviation	High-Low Range
9	Netherlands	8.9	9	0.6	8.1–9.9
10	United Kingdom	8.7	9	0.6	7.3–9.7
11	Luxembourg	8.6	7	0.7	7.4–9.3
	Switzerland	8.6	8	0.3	8.1–9.1
13	Australia	8.3	10	1.0	6.7–9.3
14	USA	7.8	10	0.8	6.2–9.2
15	Austria	7.7	8	0.7	6.2–8.5
	Hong Kong	7.7	11	1.2	4.3–8.6
17	Germany	7.6	8	0.8	6.2–8.4
18	Chile	7.4	8	0.9	5.7–8.4
19	Ireland	7.2	8	1.9	2.5–8.5
20	Spain	7.0	8	0.7	5.9–8.0
21	France	6.7	9	1.0	4.3–7.7
22	Israel	6.6	8	1.3	4.3–7.9
23	Japan	6.4	11	1.3	4.3–7.8
	Portugal	6.4	9	0.9	5.3–8.1
25	Belgium	6.1	9	1.3	4.3–8.8
26	Botswana	6.0	4	1.6	4.3–8.2
27	Estonia	5.7	4	1.6	4.4–8.1
28	Slovenia	5.5	6	1.1	4.1–7.3
	Taiwan	5.5	11	1.4	2.5–7.2
30	Costa Rica	5.4	4	1.9	3.8–8.1
	Namibia	5.4	4	0.8	4.3–6.1
32	Hungary	5.2	10	1.2	3.9–8.1
	Tunisia	5.2	4	1.5	3.8–7.1

(*cont.*)

Table 1.1 (*cont.*)

Country Rank	Country	2000 CPI Score	Surveys Used	Standard Deviation	High-Low Range
34	South Africa	5.0	10	0.9	3.8–6.6
35	Greece	4.9	8	1.7	3.7–8.1
36	Malaysia	4.8	11	0.6	3.8–5.9
37	Mauritius	4.7	5	0.8	3.9–5.6
	Morocco	4.7	4	0.7	4.2–5.6
39	Italy	4.6	8	0.6	4.0–5.6
	Jordan	4.6	5	0.8	3.8–5.7
41	Peru	4.4	5	0.5	3.8–5.0
42	Czech Republic	4.3	10	0.9	3.3–6.2
43	Belarus	4.1	3	0.8	3.4–4.9
	El Salvador	4.1	4	1.7	2.1–6.2
	Lithuania	4.1	4	0.3	3.8–4.4
	Malawi	4.1	4	0.4	3.8–4.8
	Poland	4.1	11	0.8	2.8–5.6
48	South Korea	4.0	11	0.6	3.4–5.6
49	Brazil	3.9	8	0.3	3.6–4.5
50	Turkey	3.8	8	0.8	2.1–4.5
51	Croatia	3.7	4	0.4	3.4–4.3
52	Argentina	3.5	8	0.6	3.0–4.5
	Bulgaria	3.5	6	0.4	3.3–4.3
	Ghana	3.5	4	0.9	2.5–4.7
	Senegal	3.5	3	0.8	2.8–4.3
	Slovak Republic	3.5	7	1.2	2.2–6.2

(*cont.*)

Table 1.1 (*cont.*)

Country Rank	Country	2000 CPI Score	Surveys Used	Standard Deviation	High-Low Range
57	Latvia	3.4	3	1.3	2.1–4.4
	Zambia	3.4	4	1.4	2.1–5.1
59	Mexico	3.3	8	0.5	2.5–4.1
	Colombia	3.2	8	0.8	2.5–4.5
60	Ethiopia	3.2	3	0.8	2.5–3.9
	Thailand	3.2	11	0.6	2.4–4.0
63	China	3.1	11	1.0	0.6–4.3
	Egypt	3.1	7	0.7	2.3–4.1
	Burkina Faso	3.0	3	1.0	2.5–4.4
65	Kazakhstan	3.0	4	1.2	2.1–4.3
	Zimbabwe	3.0	7	1.5	0.6–4.9
68	Romania	2.9	4	1.0	2.1–4.3
69	India	2.8	11	0.7	2.3–4.3
	Philippines	2.8	11	1.0	1.7–4.7
	Bolivia	2.7	4	1.3	1.7–4.3
71	Côte-d'Ivoire	2.7	4	0.8	2.1–3.6
	Venezuela	2.7	8	0.7	2.1–4.3
74	Ecuador	2.6	4	1.0	2.1–4.3
	Moldova	2.6	4	0.9	1.8–3.8
	Armenia	2.5	3	0.6	2.4–3.5
76	Tanzania	2.5	4	0.6	2.1–3.5
	Vietnam	2.5	8	0.6	2.1–3.8
79	Uzbekistan	2.4	3	0.9	2.1–3.7
80	Uganda	2.3	4	0.6	2.1–3.5

(*cont.*)

Table 1.1 (*cont.*)

Country Rank	Country	2000 CPI Score	Surveys Used	Standard Deviation	High-Low Range
81	Mozambique	2.2	3	0.2	2.4–2.7
82	Kenya	2.1	4	0.3	2.1–2.7
	Russia	2.1	10	1.1	0.6–4.1
84	Cameroon	2.0	4	0.6	1.6–3.0
85	Angola	1.7	3	0.4	1.6–2.5
	Indonesia	1.7	11	0.8	0.5–3.2
87	Azerbaijan	1.5	4	0.9	0.6–2.5
	Ukraine	1.5	7	0.7	0.5–2.5
89	Yugoslavia	1.3	3	0.9	0.6–2.4
90	Nigeria	1.2	4	0.6	0.6–2.1

Similar to TI's Corruption Perception Index, the Heidelberg Institute for International Conflict Research produces an index related to conflict around the world.[19] This index uses a variety of sources and twenty-eight variables to define the types of conflict involved and the methods used by parties to those conflicts to resolve them.[20] "Conflict" is defined as:

[T]he clashing of overlapping interests (positional differences) around national values and issues (independence, self-determination, borders and territory, access to or distribution of domestic or international power); the conflict has to be of some duration and magnitude of at least two parties (states, groups of states, organizations or organized groups) that are determined to pursue their interests and win their case. At least one party is the organized state. Possible instruments used in the course of a conflict are negotiations, authoritative decisions, threat, pressure, passive or active withdrawals, or the use of physical violence and war.[21]

Conflicts, therefore, could involve any number of issues. The intensity of those conflicts, however, is even more important. According to the

Heidelberg Institute, there are four levels of conflict: (1) latent conflicts, which are completely nonviolent; (2) crisis conflicts, which are mostly nonviolent; (3) severe crisis conflicts, where there is sporadic use of force; and (4) war, where there is systemic, collective use of force.[22]

From 1989 to 1999, this index showed that there were 146 conflicts in the world and that eighty-two of them were addressed either through war or through mostly violent means.[23] More interestingly, however, is an examination of the particular countries engaged in conflict and the intensity of the conflict. If the frequency of how conflicts are addressed is compared with the TI index, we find that since 1975 in those countries with the least amount of corruption – that is, those in the top quadrant of TI's Corruption Perception Index – only 14 percent of conflicts were addressed by mostly violent means or by warfare. Countries in the second quadrant of TI's index used mostly violent means or warfare to address 26 percent of their conflicts. In the third quadrant, that figure rose to 44 percent and in the bottom quadrant, which represents the countries with the most severe corruption, it escalated to 60 percent.

This does not necessarily mean that corruption causes violence. There are many reasons why nations go to war or why individuals and groups resort to violence within borders.[24] There may be explanations as to why nations that are the least corrupt do not resort to violence to address disputes. For instance, in examining the TI chart, the countries in the top quadrant are, essentially, functioning democracies. Thus, it could well be that a functioning democracy provides the means for disputes to be resolved in a peaceful manner.[25]

On the other hand, according to *Fortune* magazine's 100 Largest Economic Table, only three of the TI top quadrant – Iceland, Luxembourg, and New Zealand – were not large economic units.[26] This might

Table 1.2 *Corruption Perception and Conflict Resolution Comparison*

Transparency International Quadrant	Resolution of Conflicts by Violence
Quadrant #1 (least corrupt)	14%
Quadrant #2	26%
Quadrant #3	44%
Quadrant #4	60%

suggest that wealth precludes the need for corruption, or countries that are already wealthy can afford the luxury of carefully complying with the law. This would be more persuasive if not for the fact that other countries not faring as well on TI's index, such as China and Mexico, were ninth and thirteen respectively on the *Fortune* list.[27] Regardless of whether corruption causes violence or whether corruption is an indicator of something more fundamentally askew in a country, the data above show that it is at least plausible that corruption and violence are in some way linked. Corporations engaged in corruption seem at least to be in the midst of a social milieu that is prone to bloodshed. If this correlation is plausible, then the question becomes whether corporations might have a role to play in rectifying this situation.

B. A normative rationale for action

With the exception of those industries that have a specific reason to profit from war, rarely will business advocate warfare for reasons of profitability.[28] They may, of course, legitimately be concerned with other national goals that require warfare, and their businesses may profit from that warfare.[29] The economic leverage and political weight that such industries may wield in making decisions leading to military conflict should not be diminished.[30] Yet, the narrower question of whether companies not engaged directly in producing military hardware benefit from warfare should be considered. It is reasonable to believe that they do not.

The cost of violent conflict is large. One study shows that "every major famine in recent years has taken place in a war zone."[31] Famine exists, in large part, because of the inability to deliver foodstuffs within a war zone. These difficulties may arise either because of the danger inherent in navigating between warring armies, or because the armies in control of certain areas wish to prevent delivery.[32] As recently as 1994, 42 million people were displaced as a result of warfare,[33] and the impact on other social institutions, such as those supporting medical care and the legal system, can be large as well. This kind of disintegration can have a direct economic impact, as was the case in Kashmir, where the number of tourists dropped from 722,000 in 1988 to 10,400 in 1992.[34] Moreover, with 80 percent of the population of Kashmir dependent upon agriculture, that food rationing became necessary shows the kind of social and economic hardship that can be experienced when conflict grips a region.[35] Even those defense industries that benefited from the conflict could conceivably have redirected their productivity toward manufacturing, which could have been used to combat poverty rather than build armies.[36] Kashmir is not an isolated case. Similar kinds of economic displacement and hardship have been chronicled in Yugoslavia,[37] Sudan,[38] Peru,[39] Mozambique,[40] Iraq,[41] and East Timor.[42]

These cases are important because they suggest that there can be a business cost to warfare. Of course, there may also be a social and humanitarian cost as well; it is hard to think of a modern war that does not include human suffering.[43] More generally, however, there exists a dialectically supporting relationship between business and sustainable peace: business needs stability to thrive, and peace can be sustained through the relationships businesses build.

C. Benefits for commerce resulting from stability: three economic reasons

Perhaps the best way to understand the benefits that accrue to businesses through stability and peace is to look at the subject through the eyes of three influential economists: F.A. Hayek, Amartya Sen, and Hernando DeSoto. Although each of these economists has significant ties to the USA, their global breadth (Hayek being Austrian, Sen being Indian, and DeSoto being Peruvian) makes them a diverse trio through which the importance of peace to economic enterprise can be seen. Three important benefits for business can be identified through their analyses.

1. Virtues, stability, and trade (Hayek)
F. A. Hayek provides an important argument for linking ethics and trade.[44] Hayek argues that integrity virtues, such as promise-keeping and honesty, as well as production of high-quality goods and services and enforcement of voluntary contracts, are essential to help business flourish.[45] The reason they are important is not necessarily because these virtues are ennobling – Hayek does not pass judgment on this issue – but because they allow for an extended order based on efficient trading.[46] Hayek suggests that the way to establish global ethical values and more peaceful international relations, is to encourage international trade, because then potential trading partners can see the

benefit of practicing these kinds of relationship-sustaining virtues.[47] In this conceptual understanding, ethics and trade are mutually re-inforcing. Integrity virtues lead to more trade, and more trade demon-strates the efficacy of practicing these virtues, at least over the long run. In the short run, however, there are always risks of individuals seeking the advantages of trade without practicing virtues that would sustain trade, which is why a governance system is required.[48] Unfor-tunately, it is not enough simply to rely on individuals to practice these virtues.

It can be inferred from this that business is more likely to flour-ish when societies practice integrity virtues that foster harmonious re-lationships. As demonstrated above, however, those countries most prone to addressing conflicts through violent means are also those countries in which corruption is most prevalent. In other words, they do not reconcile disputes harmoniously. Moreover, some have noted that a technologically connected global economic system is vulner-able not so much to cross-border wars, but to the actions of in-dividuals empowered to wreak havoc on the system. Thought of another way, globalization requires even more attention to the prac-tice of virtues that lead to harmony, because the reaction against perceived injustices can be violent. For instance, the chief of net-work designs for Sun Microsystems, Geoff Baehr, has been quoted as follows:

My biggest worry, and it cannot be overstated, is that this entire infrastruc-ture is very vulnerable to attack, not just from a computer hacker, but from someone getting into the telephone switches. In this world the attacker can go to the telephone front, go home and have a sandwich, and come back and attack again.[49]

Globalization provides the opportunity to link society, but also pro-vides the "super-empowered individuals who hate America more than ever because of globalization and who can do something about it on their own" with the ability to disrupt the system.[50] It would seem to be a simple truism that a technologically linked world is dependent on a certain level of stability simply to be able to keep the telephone lines open. Indeed, Friedman notes that a stable political and economic en-vironment is the precursor to encouraging entrepreneurship.[51] Thus, if virtues are a component to justice, then flourishing commerce benefits from virtuous behavior and is threatened by non-virtuous behavior.

2. Creativity and growth (Sen)

A second, related benefit to business from stability and peace is its enhancement of the possibility of freedom and freedom's benefits, ranging from alleviating marginalization to flourishing markets. The leading spokesperson for this viewpoint is the economist Amartya Sen.[52] Rather than focusing on the numerical increase in trade as an indicator of development, Sen looks at the process that allows individuals, particularly the poor, to reach the potential they would have not been able to achieve had they remained in poverty.[53] An important reason for this emphasis is that, as Sen notes, the increase in "overall opulence" in today's global economy produces "elementary freedoms" to a large number of individuals simultaneously, perhaps even to the majority of people on the globe.[54] The satisfaction of material needs allows individuals to unleash their potential. That creativity further enriches the market. In this sense, freedom results from individuals being free from constraints imposed by the grinding harness of poverty and from "tyranny, poor economic opportunities as well as systematic social deprivation, neglect of public facilities as well as intolerance or other activity of repressive states."[55] Rather than focusing solely on economics, this can be done by integrating values and economics. According to Sen:

The exercise of freedom is mediated by values, but the values in turn are influenced by public discussions and social interactions, which are themselves influenced by participatory freedoms. . . . It is important not only to give markets their due, but also to appreciate the role of other economic, social, and political freedoms in enhancing and enriching the lives that people are able to lead.[56]

Friedman underscores the consequential validity of this approach by noting that "when you put assets in the hands of the poor in a politically distorted environment, such as Liberia or Burma, not much happens. But when you put assets in the hands of the poor in reasonably stable and free environments a lot will happen."[57] From this, one can believe that it is possible that participatory freedoms empower individuals who can engage the market and enjoy its benefits. Values and business opportunities are thus enhanced, and thereby provide a way to combat marginalization of the poor and reduce the threat of violent reaction borne of desperation.

3. Stability from legal structures can unleash capital (DeSoto)

Not only does the focus on the development of freedom lead to an emphasis on governance so that freedoms can be achieved by unleashing human potential, but proper legal governance regimes can free trapped capital as well. The spokesperson for this viewpoint is economist Hernando DeSoto.

DeSoto argues that the major difficulty that most of the world's poor have in obtaining the benefits of capitalism exists because countries do not have the legal infrastructure for registering proper title to real estate.[58] This lack of legal infrastructure, for instance, makes it virtually impossible for the poor to make use of the assets they have, such as their homes, to become entrepreneurs.[59] The West, he argues, takes its property law system for granted so much so that it typically ignores the history of legal development where gradually governments provided reliable property documentation for ownership where title was otherwise obscured.[60] Thus, the poor have houses built on land where there are no recorded ownership rights. As a result, lenders have no reliable collateral to support loans that could be used to start a business.[61]

The latent economic potential of this situation is immense. DeSoto calculates that in Haiti, for instance, 68 percent of those living in the city and 97 percent of people in the countryside reside in homes where there is no clear legal title.[62] In Egypt, the same problem arises for 92 percent of city dwellers and 83 percent of the people in the countryside.[63] DeSoto estimates that the total assets held by the poor in the Third World and former communist countries that cannot be accessed because of defective property registration systems is at least $9.3 trillion.[64]

The institution of property registration systems in the West, De Soto argues, required legitimizing the extant, albeit informal, rules of customs practiced by the population to provide productive economic activity, a greater good to society.[65] The connection of this process to peace is that, by doing so, the chances for social confrontation, particularly over scarce resources, are reduced and economic growth is encouraged. DeSoto argues, "everyone will benefit from globalizing capitalism within a country, but the most obvious and largest beneficiary will be the poor."[66] As already intimated, this benefit may have direct consequences for sustainable peace. Klaus Schwab of the World Economic Forum recognizes that "if we do not invent ways to make globalization more inclusive . . . we have to face the prospect of a resurgence of the acute social confrontations of the past, magnified at the international level."[67]

It follows that failure to avoid social confrontations is itself a threat to business. A mutually supporting atmosphere where members of society are engaged in a market economy rather than marginalized to the point of resentment connects business and peace. The Western property system allows for the production of surplus value beyond what a home would otherwise represent because it is possible to tap into the economic potential of the real estate itself.[68]

The difficulty for the legal system is that if it does not keep pace with such basic natural impulses as that of building a home, it will frustratingly marginalize individuals so that they remain outside of the economic system. If this occurs, individuals will invent their own extralegal substitutes for property protection.[69] This occurs now in Third World and former communist countries, but it was also the case in the West.[70]

Rather than maintain a system that was out of touch with the norms of the people they governed, Western nations gradually began to recognize these arrangements as legitimate and found ways to absorb these contracts into the legal system.[71] The law maintains its legitimacy by staying in touch with the norms that guide daily life.[72] If the law fails to do so, those operating by extra-legal contracts will not enter the economic and legal system.[73] "What governments in developing countries have to do is listen to the barking dogs [marking local territory] in their own communities and find out what their law should say. Only then will people stop living outside it."[74]

D. *The reciprocal relationship between business and peace*

Business has an interest in peaceful relations for several reasons. One of the implications of the foregoing discussion is that in order to foster sustainable peace, businesses will need to do more than attend to profitability. The causes of war are more multifaceted than any one business or set of businesses can eliminate, but businesses can play a role in mitigating those causes when they attend to human issues. Thus, although development of wealth is an appropriate interest of business, Sen also argues that "the usefulness of wealth lies in the things that it allows us to do – the substantive freedoms it helps us to achieve."[75]

Indeed, it is more of an ideological mantra to assume that human beings are selfish than it is a fact of human life.[76] A goal of achieving freedom is itself a moral determination and its consequential efficacy is demonstrated by Sen's finding that "no famine has ever taken place in the history of the world in a functioning democracy."[77]

The notion of democracy is that people have a voice in the laws that govern them. Not only does attention by business to the development of freedom reinforce the processes by which peace is achieved, but the internal dynamic by which domestic policies are created requires attention to DeSoto's "barking dogs," in order to understand the informal, but very real contracts that people enter into and the appropriation of which serves to legitimize government.[78] Thus, there is a reciprocal, even cybernetic, relationship between business and peace, where business is benefited by the stability peace brings and achievement of that stability requires business to engage in issues of human development, to encourage legal development of institutions such as property, and to nurture, as Hayek would argue, integrity virtues.

II. The benefits of business to peace

In addition to the reciprocal relationship between business and peace identified above, business may contribute to stability in other ways. Recently, a symposium identified just and sustainable economic development as one of the ten practices necessary for abolishing war.[79] There is considerable support in history for this sentiment. Philosophers such as Montesquieu have argued that by trading, nations make it more unlikely that they will go to war.[80] Immanuel Kant held a similar view[81] that has been carried into the present as well.[82]

There is, however, another view. Donald Kagan, for instance, argues that any hope for lasting peace based on the emergence of a free market economy or on the basis of the history of democratic nations not fighting one another is misguided.[83] Kagan warns that the "only thing more common than predictions about the end of war has been war itself."[84] Moreover, anthropologist Lawrence Keeley's studies show that while groups may not trade in the midst of war, they do trade before and after war.[85] Not only was this true "before civilization," the USA and Japan actively traded prior to the attack on Pearl Harbor, and all of the combatants of World War I traded with each other before and after hostilities.[86]

Nevertheless, even after undertaking his study, Keeley recommends that engagement between countries is more likely to lead to the kind of relationships where they are less likely to go to war.[87] In addition, others have noted that, although there has always been trade and there have always been multinational nongovernmental organizations, there is something unique about this particular time and place, because "what is new is [transnational factors and organizations'] number and variety and, more significant, their challenge to the control that state actors have over world affairs."[88]

From all of this, it can be discerned that business can contribute to peace in at least four ways: (1) by fostering economic development; (2) by exercising track two diplomacy; (3) by adopting external evaluation principles such as transparency and supporting a legal system, i.e., a "rule of law"; and (4) by nourishing a sense of community both within the company and in the areas where the company is located. In looking at these alternatives, it should be stressed that they are considered in light of the most basic definition of peace: the absence of war. As Robert Pickus has argued, evils such as oppression and starvation have their own names, but "something precious is lost when the word 'violence' is blurred."[89] Departing from Pickus, who further would preserve the term "violence" for mass, organized warfare, the term "violence" as used herein refers to the willful killing of people. This more narrow definition of the term provides a sufficiently concrete and precise understanding of the evil sought to be avoided so as to maintain an appropriate focus on the means by which businesses can constructively mitigate its prevalence.[90]

This section will focus on the ways corporations can contribute to peace by fostering economic development and through track two diplomacy. Chapter 4 will return to these issues and provide further analysis of the ways in which corporations can adopt external evaluation principles and nourish a sense of community.

A. Economic opportunity and growth

Just as there is a correlation between corruption and violence, "there is a highly positive correlation between underdevelopment and armed conflict."[91] It has also been found, not surprisingly, that war creates poverty.[92] Complaints regarding poverty are frequently involved in wars:

In many of the conflicts and revolutions in Latin America during the 1960s through the 1990s, a crucial element was the struggle of the poor for justice. This was true in Nicaragua, El Salvador, and Guatemala, in Haiti, Jamaica, and the Dominican Republic, in Chile, Brazil, and Columbia. Poverty was an important ingredient in the struggle against apartheid in South Africa, the people power revolution in the Philippines, the troubles in Northern Ireland, the overthrow of the Shah of Iran, and the Palestinian question in Israel.[93]

Another interpretation of the correlation between corruption and violence is that the correlation exists because corrupt governments frequently dominate poor countries.[94] It is because of this connection that economic assistance provided to emerging countries is typically tied to reform. Incentives such as those provided by the International Monetary Fund and the World Bank typically provide access to First World funds and markets in return for budgetary, and sometimes political, reform.[95]

There is the possibility that poverty contributes to warfare more than does corruption. If this is true, then it would make sense to spur economic development, even at the price of corruption, in order to reduce poverty. There is, undoubtedly, some truth to this claim. As already mentioned, there are studies demonstrating a high positive correlation between underdevelopment and violence.[96] Tying violence to corruption, however, may be a more helpful indicator of a social structure likely to beget more violence. If this hypothesis is also true, then multinational expansion should be justified not only upon the capacity to alleviate poverty, but to do so in a way that also mitigates corruption. Again, the link between corruption and violence requires additional research, but there are at least three initial reasons to support the hypothesis that they be linked in some way.

First, in Amartya Sen's assessment of poverty, he describes poverty in terms of a "capability deprivation."[97] He argues that some deprivations are intrinsically important.[98] He further contends that there are other influences on capability deprivation than low income, and that the relationship between low income and low capability is variable among different communities.[99] Factors influencing this variability include the age of a particular person, gender and social roles, location insofar as that location is prone to disruption due to natural disasters, famine, or violence, and the epidemiological atmosphere.[100] Moreover, the relative deprivation in terms of income can lead to an absolute deprivation in terms of capability because "being relatively poor in a rich country can be a great capability handicap, even when one's absolute income is high in terms of world standards."[101] In part, this relative deprivation occurs where the desire to avoid "social exclusion" creates a demand for the poor in a rich country to devote resources to the acquisition of goods, such as televisions and automobiles, that would not occur in a poor country, where such goods are not as widespread.[102] A consequential example of this, Sen writes, lies in comparing premature mortality. For example, African-American men possess significantly higher income than Chinese, Indian, Sri Lankan, Costa Rican, and Jamaican men, but have "remarkably higher death rates."[103] Another possible reason for these death rates might be the significantly higher levels of violence that occur in African-American communities.[104]

From this, Sen does not deduce that inequality should be eradicated. Rather, Sen notes that such attempts can "lead to loss for most – sometimes even for all."[105] He does, however, argue that insufficient attention has been directed to ways in which equality can be manifested; capabilities of the poor are influenced by factors more complex than comparisons of income.[106] In particular, Sen emphasizes the need for social participation and public discussion in making economic policy in order to inform economic policy of the complex dynamics that foster frustration and dampen human development.[107]

Second, anthropologists provide helpful clues as to why low income is itself not explanatory. One reason is that pre-modern societies were relatively poorer than today's world, yet they were also less violent. Anthropologist Leslie Sponsel, for instance, argues that by studying the accumulated specimens of fossil hominids in museums and universities, one can conclude that "nonviolence and peace were likely the norm throughout most of human pre-history and that intra-human killing was probably rare."[108] Although eschewing the notion of a prehistoric, peace-loving hominid, anthropologist Lawrence Keeley similarly concludes that, adjusted for population sizes, humans during the twentieth century killed at a rate twenty times higher than at any time during the hunter-gatherer era.[109] Yet, there is no evidence that these societies were materially more prosperous than the world is today.

Sen's explanation for relative capability deprivation provides a possible explanation for this. Although hunter-gatherer societies were often hierarchical, this hierarchy was frequently based on stable environments. This is not to say that pre-modern societies did not experience catastrophes – they did – but rather catastrophes more frequently occurred as the result of natural influences such as earthquakes or volcanoes than by disruption of political and economic arrangements.[110] Change, however, produces stress that can accentuate capability deprivation in two important ways. The first way is in the sense of a loss of the capability to control one's life. The free market, for all its merits, directly undermines this capability.[111] Unfortunately, globalization introduces stress, threat, and social change:

The bigger, faster and more influential the herd becomes, "the more individual citizens start to feel that the locus of economic control and political decisionmaking on economic matters is shifting from the local level, where it can be controlled, to the global level, where no one is in charge and no one is minding the store. When all politics is local, your vote matters. But when the power shifts to these transnational spheres, there are no elections and there is no one to vote for."[112]

This phenomenon creates disempowerment, or to use Sen's phrase, a "capability deprivation," because it deprives individuals within a community of a sense of stability and control in their lives. That no one person is responsible does not mitigate the effect because "the most arbitrary powers in history always hid under the claim of some impersonal logic – God, the laws of nature, the laws of the market – and they always provoked a backlash when morally intolerable discrepancies become glaringly visible."[113]

One final anthropological example demonstrates the moral difficulties, as well as the capability deprivations, produced by economic change and material distributions. When Hawaii encountered the West, through the interaction with British Commander James Cook, the practice of *kapu*, or taboo, was part of the religious system by which the Islands kept themselves in *pono*, or balance.[114] *Kapu* derived from the *Kumulipo*, the Hawaiian creation myth, and was part of an extremely hierarchical social system so rigid that if the shadow of an *Ali'i Nui*, or noble, fell on a common person, the person had to be put to death.[115] Nevertheless, the *Moi*, or king, had strict responsibility to govern for the common good; for example, if the land was not fertile, Hawaiian religion deemed it a judgment by the gods of the lack of the *Moi*'s purity.[116]

Once Westerners showed that *kapu* rules, such as the prohibition for men and women to eat together, could be violated without retribution and, further, that *kapu* rules could be used by *Ali'i Nui* to restrict new Western goods to themselves, the notion of *kapu* was transformed. Rather than something that was part of a system that required reciprocal duties from all elements of society, it became something that was simply a rule, like "no trespassing," that was imposed on the poor without a concomitant obligation to treat them well.[117] By making this kind of transformation, *kapu* rules created a capability deprivation for the common people. In other words, *kapu* rules were divorced from their communal context and simultaneously made less transparent, the combination of which created a relative disparity that was different from simple material disparity.

Thus, it may be concluded that it is not simply low income that contributes to unrest, but that the ordering of social institutions, particularly in times of stress and change, can disempower individuals and thereby increase their capability deprivation. The disordering of social institutions thus can create the seeds of exploitation, alienation, and deprivation for which there are fewer "weapons" for the disadvantaged to use in claiming resources necessary for development. Disordering can also create a moral disparity by which those in power may be more inclined to use violence as a way to avoid discussion regarding whether the distribution of capabilities is fair. It is not simply inequality that is a problem, nor is it poverty. Instead, what threatens violence is a governance mechanism that has become corrupt because it fails to allow individuals to influence the rules that govern them.

B. Track two diplomacy

Track two diplomacy is unofficial interaction among non-state actors with the goal of creating an environment in which political leaders are freer to reach accords.[118] Certainly, an economic enterprise that provides benefits to two different countries embroiled in a dispute contributes to an environment where the leaders of the countries can point to the mutual economic advantages of resolving a conflict as a reason to avoid escalation. It could also occur when a businessperson who has credibility and access conveys messages between governments without going through formal diplomatic channels. In each of these scenarios, corporations can build relationships that cross boundaries in a way that might not be accomplished through the traditional political means. Corporations, therefore, may be able to provide channels for communication that might not otherwise have existed.[119]

There is another important insight implicit in this understanding of track two diplomacy.[120] Just as informal diplomacy or fostering of economic relations can create the atmosphere for political leaders to take risks, there is also an opportunity for multinational corporations to "arrest the dehumanization process between the groups in conflict, and gradually to educate the population about the human dimension of the pain and loss all sides suffer from the conflict. It is a difficult cognitive and group psychological process."[121] This insight is particularly relevant to corporations because, as demonstrated below, corporations can perform this role within the boundaries of one country where there are disputes among various groups. Thus, not only may corporations play a role in defusing conflicts between nation-states by building relationships to enable political leaders to negotiate with a government that might otherwise be considered a violent enemy, but corporations, through employment, trade, and outreach, can also "humanize" adversaries within countries to mitigate the possibilities of violence. We return to issues of track two diplomacy in chapter 4.

Conclusion

If the analysis is correct, then the meaning of the so-called "backlash" against globalization is more comprehensible. One argument for the need for corporations to pay attention to the needs of corporate constituents, after all, is that there is a backlash against globalization. Protests such as those in Seattle,[122] Davos,[123] and Quebec provide evidence of this backlash.[124] Similar protests against capitalism were also raised in India by Gandhi,[125] as well as in China against British industries in the nineteenth century.[126]

It may be tempting to dismiss these protests as symbolic and ineffective. Yet the technology that allows so much of globalization to occur also provides the mechanism for others to disrupt it. For instance, that a teenager in the Philippines can hack into computer systems and disrupt computers around the world[127] illustrates the vulnerability of a networked system. Similarly, chemical and biological weapons are small enough to fit into backpacks,[128] and therefore can be used to disrupt globalization in countless ways.

The crux of the matter is that globalization can create a sense of disempowerment as well as empowerment. Disrupting existing social structures in exchange for material development can provide the opportunity for disempowerment of common people and corruption of those with authority to gain access to wealth and thus suppress accountability to the common good. In a manner similar to what occurred in Hawaii, this dynamic is based on the ability to control societies and to reduce accountability. Maintaining such a system is easier when there is less transparency of transactions. All of these dynamics foster corruption as well as limit the viability of nonviolent conflict resolution, for the simple reason that the lack of transparency helps hide unfairness. There are also social and moral, in addition to economic, dimensions that transform a relative lack of wealth into an unjust social structure. The unjustness of a social structure calls for governance reform. This is not to call for the establishment of a global governance system. Instead, corporations could arrange their governance regimes in ways correlated with attributes of peaceful societies.

Thus, to the extent that business may both impact and benefit from sustainable peace, it becomes important to consider the role of business in a geopolitical world. Chapter 2 addresses this issue by providing a foundational underpinning for the role of business in emerging theories of balances of power in which corporations are important actors independent from nation-states. Further, in light of contemporary political theory suggesting that democratic institutions contribute to sustainable peace, chapter 2 also considers how corporations may play a part in fostering democratic institutions.

Notes

This chapter is reprinted in large part from Timothy L. Fort and Cindy A. Schipani, *The Role of the Corporation in Fostering Sustainable Peace*, 35 VAND. J. TRANSN'L L. 389 (2002). Reprinted with permission.

1. Laurie Goodstein, *For Hindus and Vegetarians, Surprise in McDonald's Fries*, N.Y. TIMES, May 20, 2001, at A1.
2. Ibid.
3. Moises Naim, *McAtlas Shrugged*, FOREIGN POL'Y, May–June, 2001, at 26, available at 2001 WL 11393490.
4. Ibid., at 26–32.
5. *Going for gold*, ECONOMIST, May 19, 2001, at 15.
6. Ibid.

7. Naim, above n. 3, at 31.
8. THOMAS L. FRIEDMAN, THE LEXUS AND THE OLIVE TREE 248 (2000).
9. Ibid., at 252–53.
10. Ibid., at 253.
11. This term, with its Internet twist, is from Timothy L. Fort and James J. Noone, *Gifts, Bribes and Exchanges in Pre-Market Economies: Lessons for Pax E-Commercia*, 33 CORNELL INT'L L.J. 515 (2000).
12. See IMMANUEL KANT, *Perpetual Peace: A Philosophical Sketch*, in POLITICAL WRITINGS (Hans Reiss ed., H.B. Nisbet trans., 2d ed., 1991).
13. The following authors are among the first systematically to reflect on these issues. See Juliette Bennett, *Public Private Partnerships: The Role of the Private Sector in Preventing Funding Conflict*, 35 VAND. J. TRANSN'L L. 711 (2002); Terry Morehead Dworkin, *Whistleblowing, MNCs, and Peace*, 35 VAND. J. TRANSNAT'L L. 457 (2002); Scott Greathead, *The Multinational and the "New Stakeholder": Examining the Business Case for Human Rights*, 35 VAND. J. TRANSN'L L. 719 (2002); Linda Lim, Keynote Address, *Terrorism and Globalization: An International Perspective*, in 35 VAND. J. TRANSN'L L. 703 (2002); Donald O. Mayer, *Corporate Governance in the Cause of Peace: An Environmental Perspective*, 35 VAND. J. TRANSN'L L. 585 (2002); Jeffrey Nesteruk, *Conceptions of the Corporation and the Prospects of Sustainable Peace*, 35 VAND. J. TRANSN'L L. 437 (2002); Eric W. Orts, *War and the Business Corporation*, 35 VAND. J. TRANSN'L L. 549 (2002); Steven R. Salbu, *The European Union Data Privacy Directive and International Relations*, 35 VAND. J. TRANSN'L L. 655 (2002); Lee A. Tavis, *Corporate Governance and the Global Social Void*, 35 VAND. J. TRANSN'L L. 487 (2002); Interview by B. Joseph White with Madeleine Albright, US Secretary of State, *The Business of Peace*, 35 VAND. J. TRANSN'L L. 697 (2002).
14. For more information on Transparency International, see the organization's website, at http://www.transparency.de.
15. Peter Eigen, *The Transparency International Bribe Payers Survey*, at www.transparency.de/documents/cpi/1999/bps.html.
16. Ibid.
17. Ibid. "The index defines corruption as abuse of public office for private gain, and measures the degree to which corruption is perceived to exist among a country's public officials and politicians. Scores range from ten (no corruption) to zero (highly corrupt). Transparency International considers a

score of 5.5 the borderline number between countries with and without a serious problem." Transparency International 2002, http://www.Transparency.com. Transparency International notes that there are countries that would likely rank even lower than those indicated in its 2000 Corruption Perceptions Index, but insufficient polling data in many countries makes it difficult to assess. Transparency International, *The 2000 Corruption Perceptions Index*, at http://www.transparency.de/documents/cpi/2000/cpi2000.html.

18. Transparency International, *The 2000 Corruption Perceptions Index*, above n. 17.
19. Heidelberg Institute for International Conflict Research, at http://www.conflict.com/hiik/manual_en.html.
20. Ibid.
21. Ibid.
22. Ibid.
23. Ibid.
24. Michael Cranna, *Introduction*, in THE TRUE COST OF CONFLICT xv, xvii (Michael Cranna ed., 1994).
25. CONNIE PECK, SUSTAINABLE PEACE: THE ROLE OF THE UN AND REGIONAL ORGANIZATIONS IN PREVENTING CONFLICT 17 (1998).
26. *The Fortune Global 500, 100 Largest Economic Table*, FORTUNE, August 5, 1996, at F1.
27. Ibid.
28. Michael Cranna, *What is to be Done? Policy Initiatives for the International Community*, in THE TRUE COST OF CONFLICT 197 (Michael Cranna ed., 1994).
29. Dwight D. Eisenhower, *Farewell Radio and Television Address to the American People* (January 17, 1961), in PUBLIC PAPERS OF THE PRESIDENTS OF THE UNITED STATES, 1960–61 1038 (1978).
30. The US government spent an estimated $280.8 million for defense functions in the year 2000. 145 CONG. REC. S3835 (daily ed., April 12, 1999) (statement of Senator Specter). The US GDP in 2000 was $9.963 trillion. UNITED STATES FACT BOOK, at http://www.cia.gov/cia/publications/factbook/geos/us.html.
31. Cranna, above n. 24, at xv.
32. William DeMars, *War and Mercy in Africa*, WORLD POL'Y J., Summer 2000, at 110, available at 2000 WL 20783587; Stephan Williams, *Sudan: In from the Cold*, AFRICAN BUS., July–August, 2001, at 42, available at 2001 WL 11994463.
33. Nils Bhinda, *The Kashmir Conflict*, in THE TRUE COST OF CONFLICT 55, 63 (Michael Cranna ed., 1994).
34. Ibid.

35. Ibid.
36. Ibid., at 70, 74.
37. Angela Burke and Gordon Macdonald, *The Former Yugoslavia Conflict*, in THE TRUE COST OF CONFLICT 155 (Michael Cranna ed., 1994).
38. Nicholas Shalita, *The Sudan Conflict*, in THE TRUE COST OF CONFLICT 135 (Michael Cranna ed., 1994).
39. David Shave, *The Peru Conflict*, in THE TRUE COST OF CONFLICT 113 (Michael Cranna ed., 1994).
40. Shaun Vincent, *The Mozambique Conflict*, in THE TRUE COST OF CONFLICT 81 (Michael Cranna ed., 1994).
41. Gregory Quinn, *The Iraq Conflict*, in THE TRUE COST OF CONFLICT 25 (Michael Cranna ed., 1994).
42. Ian Robinson, *The East Timor Conflict*, in THE TRUE COST OF CONFLICT 1 (Michael Cranna ed., 1994).
43. MICHAEL I. HANDEL, MASTERS OF WAR: CLASSICAL STRATEGIC THOUGHT 24 (3d ed., 2001).
44. See generally F.A. HAYEK, THE FATAL CONCEIT: THE ERRORS OF SOCIALISM (1988).
45. Ibid., at 12, 70.
46. Ibid., at 12, 70–71.
47. Ibid., at 38–47.
48. Ibid., at 12.
49. FRIEDMAN, above n. 8, at 398.
50. Ibid.
51. Ibid., at 356.
52. See generally AMARTYA SEN, DEVELOPMENT AS FREEDOM (1999).
53. Ibid., at 3.
54. Ibid., at 3–4.
55. Ibid., at 3.
56. Ibid., at 9.
57. FRIEDMAN, above n. 8, at 356.
58. See generally HERNANDO DESOTO, THE MYSTERY OF CAPITAL: WHY CAPITALISM TRIUMPHS IN THE WEST AND FAILS EVERYWHERE ELSE (2000).
59. Ibid., at 6.
60. Ibid., at 8.
61. Ibid., at 6.
62. Ibid., at 33.
63. Ibid.
64. Ibid., at 35. As an analogy, DeSoto talks about the untapped potential of a mountain lake.

Consider a mountain lake. We can think about this lake in its immediate physical context and see some primary uses for it, such as canoeing and fishing. But when we think about this same lake as an engineer would by focusing on its capacity to generate energy as an additional value beyond the lake's natural state as a body of water, we suddenly see the potential created by the lake's elevated position. The challenge for the engineer is finding out how he can create a *process* that allows him to convert and fix this potential into a form that can be used to do additional work. In the case of the elevated lake, that process is contained in a hydroelectric plant that allows the lake water to move rapidly downward with the force of gravity, thereby transforming the placid lake's energy potential into the kinetic energy of tumbling water. This new kinetic energy can then rotate turbines, creating mechanical energy that be used to turn electromagnets that further convert it into electrical energy. As electricity, the potential energy of the placid lake is now fixed in the form necessary to produce controllable current that be further transmitted through wire conductors to faraway places to deploy new production. . . . Capital, like energy, is also a dormant value. Bringing it to life requires us to go beyond *looking* at our assets as they are to actively *thinking* about them as they could be. It requires a process for fixing an asset's economic potential into a form that can be used to initiate additional production.

Ibid., at 44–45.
65. Ibid., at 194–95.
66. Ibid., at 189.
67. Ibid., at 213.
68. Ibid., at 51.
69. Ibid., at 71.
70. Ibid., at 102.

Law began adapting to the needs of common people, including their expectations about property rights, in most West European countries during the nineteenth and early twentieth centuries. By that time, the Europeans had concluded that it was impossible to govern the Industrial Revolution and the presence of massive extralegality through minor ad hoc adjustments. Politicians finally understood that the problem was not people but the law, which was discouraging and preventing people from becoming more productive.

Ibid.
71. Ibid., at 106.
72. Ibid., at 108.

73. Ibid., at 172.
74. Ibid., at 168.
75. SEN, above n. 52, at 14.
76. Ibid., at 118 (stating that "the presumption of ubiquitous selfishness is hard to defend empirically"); see also Timothy L. Fort and James J. Noone, *Banded Contracts, Mediating Institutions, and Corporate Governance: A Naturalist Analysis of Contractual Theories of the Firm*, 62 LAW & CONTEMP. PROBS. 163 (1999) (providing an overview of anthropological indicators that human beings are more social than individual).
77. Ibid., at 16.
78. DeSoto, above n. 58, at 178.
79. JUST PEACEMAKING: TEN PRACTICES FOR ABOLISHING WAR (Glen Stassen ed., 1998). The ten practices are:

  1   Support Nonviolent Direct Action;
  2   Take Independent Initiative to Reduce Threat;
  3   Use Cooperative Conflict Resolution;
  4   Acknowledge Responsibility for Conflict and Injustice and Seek Repentance and Forgiveness;
  5   Advance Democracy, Human Rights and Religious Liberty;
  6   Foster Just and Sustainable Economic Development;
  7   Working with Emerging Cooperative Forces in the International System;
  8   Strengthen the UN and International Efforts for Cooperation and Human Rights;
  9   Reduce Offensive Weapons and Weapons Trade;
10   Encourage Grassroots Peacemaking Groups.

80. See Philip M. Nichols, *Regulating Transnational Bribery in Times of Globalization and Fragmentation*, 24 YALE J. INT'L L. 257, 263 (1999).
81. See generally KANT, above n. 12.
82. Nichols, above n. 80, at 263. Nichols, for instance, cites evidence supporting the position that those countries that choose to trade rather than to erect barriers to trade tend to go to war less frequently. Ibid.
83. See generally DONALD KAGAN, ON THE ORIGINS OF WAR AND THE PRESERVATION OF PEACE (1995).
84. Ibid., at 1. Past theories of war's obsolescence were much the same as today's theories. Ibid. In 1792 Joseph Priestley argued that:

[T]he present commercial treaties between England and France, and between other nations formerly hostile to each other, seem to show that mankind begin to be sensible of the folly of war, and promise a new and important era in the state of the world in general, at least in Europe.

Ibid. Thomas Paine expressed a similar belief in his pamphlet, *The Rights of Man*, which appeared in the same year: "If commerce were permitted to act to the universal extent it is capable, it would extirpate the system of war." Paine also believed, following Montesquieu and Kant, that "the substitution of republics for monarchies would guarantee lasting peace." Ibid. "In 1848, John Stuart Mill sang the praises of commerce, which was 'rapidly rendering war obsolete, by strengthening and multiplying the personal interests which act in natural opposition to it ... [T]he great extent and rapid increase of international trade ... [is] the principal guarantee of the peace of the world.'" Ibid., at 2.

85. See generally LAWRENCE KEELEY, WAR BEFORE CIVILIZATION (1996).
86. Ibid., at 117–22.
87. Ibid., at 181.
88. Robert Pickus, *New Approaches*, in APPROACHES TO PEACE: AN INTELLECTUAL MAP 235 (W. Scott Thompson and Kenneth M. Jensen eds., 1991).
89. Ibid., at 231.
90. Ibid.
91. J. Lewis Rasmussen, *Peacemaking in the 21st Century: New Rules, New Roles, New Actors*, in PEACEMAKING IN INTERNATIONAL CONFLICT: METHODS & TECHNIQUES 31 (I. William Zartman and J. Lewis Rasmussen eds., 1999).
92. JOSEPH MILBURN THOMPSON, JUSTICE AND PEACE: A CHRISTIAN PRIMER 58 (1997).
93. Ibid.
94. *100 Largest Economic Table*, above n. 26, at F-1.
95. David I. Oyama, *World Watch*, WALL ST. J., August 29, 2001, at A6; *India: IMF Reviewing Conditionalities*, HINDU, August 30, 2001, at 1; see also DAVID CORTRIGHT, THE PRICE OF PEACE (1997) (analyzing the various incentives governments can use to encourage reforms that contribute to peace). As an example, Cortright cites to the economic incentives provided by the USA to Czechoslovakia from 1990 to 1992, which included IMF and World Bank resources, market access in the form of MFN status, economic assistance, investment guarantees and credits, and transfer of technology in return for guarantees on the use of such technology. Ibid., at 105.

96. Rasmussen, above n. 91, at 31.

97. SEN, above n. 52, at 87.

98. Ibid.

99. Ibid., at 87–88.

100. Ibid., at 88.

101. Ibid., at 89.

102. Ibid.

103. Ibid., at 96.

104. Dan Eggen, *Death Penalty Foes Fault Justice Study*, WASH. POST, June 19, 2001, at A3.

105. SEN, above n. 52, at 93.

106. Ibid., at 107–08.

107. Ibid., at 110.

108. Leslie E. Sponsel, *The Natural History of Peace: The Positive View of Human Nature and Its Potential*, in A NATURAL HISTORY OF PEACE 95, 103 (Thomas Gregor ed., 1996).

109. KEELEY, above n. 85, at 93.

110. But see Peter Gray and Kendrick Oliver, *The Memory of Catastrophe*, HIST. TODAY, February, 2001, at 915, available at 2001 WL 11232953.

111. Ervin Staub writes that:

    [S]trongly established hierarchical arrangements are potentially harmful, especially in complex, heterogeneous human societies with varied subgroups that can turn against each other. Among primates, a stable dominance hierarchy reduces violence, and this can happen in small human groups as well. Under stable conditions, hierarchical, obedience-oriented or monolithic societies may be as peaceful as pluralistic ones. But when stress, threat, life problems, or social change bring forth leadership that moves the group toward violence against others, a multiplicity of beliefs and values makes it more likely that opposition will arise that inhibits this movement.

    Ervin Staub, *The Psychological and Cultural Roots of Group Violence and the Creation of Caring Societies and Peaceful Group Relations*, in APPROACHES TO PEACE: A READER IN PEACE STUDIES 135 (David P. Barash ed., 1999).

112. FRIEDMAN, above n. 8, at 191 (quoting Stephen J. Kobring).

113. Ibid. (quoting Yaron Ezrahi).

114. ALASDAIR MACINTYRE, AFTER VIRTUE 105 (1981); see also Fort and Noone, above n. 11, at 528.

115. See VALERIO VALERI, KINGSHIP AND SACRIFICE: RITUAL AND SOCIETY IN ANCIENT HAWAII (Paula Wissing trans., 1985) (discussing the

Hawaiian religious system); see also Marshall Sahlins, Islands of History (1985).

116. Lilikala Kame'eleihiwa, Native Land and Foreign Desires, Ko Hawai'i 'aina ame Na Koi Pu'umake a ka Po'e Haole: A History of Land Tenure Changes in Hawaii From Traditional times until the 1948 Mahele Including an Analysis of Hawaiian Ali'i Nui and American Calvinists 104–15 (1992); see also Timothy L. Fort, *Corporate Makahiki: The Governing* Telos *of Peace*, 38 Am. Bus. L.J. 301, 342–43 (2001).

117. See Sahlins, above n. 115, at 242; see also Fort, above n. 116, at 348–49.

118. See Joseph V. Montville, *Transnationalism and the Role of Track-Two Diplomacy*, in Approaches to Peace: An Intellectual Map 262–63 (W. Scott Thompson and Kenneth M. Jensen eds., 1991).

119. Fort and Noone, above n. 11, at 518 n.18.

120. Montville, above n. 118, at 262.

121. Ibid., at 263.

122. David Postman, *Resistance Takes Fast Track – Protestors Training Now for Sit-ins, Blockades*, Seattle Times, September 10, 1999, at A1 (describing the protests in Seattle at the meeting of the World Trade Organization).

123. David Gresing, *Shades of Seattle Riot as Clinton Addresses Elite Economic Forum*, Chi. Trib., January 30, 2000, at C13 (describing the protests in Davos at the meeting of influential business leaders held there annually).

124. Anthony De Palma, *In the Streets, Fervor, Fears and A Gamut of Issues*, N.Y. Times, April 22, 2001, at A4.

125. See Louis Fischer, The Life of Mahatma Gandhi 162–76 (1950).

126. See Jonathan D. Spence, The Search for Modern China 117–64 (1990).

127. *Computer Virus Hits 14 Agencies*, Chi. Trib., May 10, 2000, at A1.

128. *Nerve Gas Kills 6 in Tokyo; Thousands Sickened in Suspected Terrorist Plot*, Chi. Trib., March 20, 1995, at N1.

2 | *Balances of power and mediators of justice*

ORPORATIONS are faced with demands to be fair and just. Responding to these demands entails considerations of morality and politics that are connected to perceptions of justice. Economic imperatives and competitive pressures may make consideration of political and moral goals beyond the scope of corporate responsibility. Historically, there may be some justification for this reticence, an issue addressed in chapter 3, but the twenty-first century may not replicate the geopolitical conditions of previous centuries. In large part, this may be due to the balances of power that exist among various institutions including nation-states and multinational corporations, and the relationship corporations have with governments and nongovernmental organizations (NGOs). Thus, in order to address the balance of power issues and their relevance to sustainable peace this chapter: (1) describes selected contemporary theories as to how peace can be achieved; (2) examines the debate as to whether democracy is a form of government most suited for creating sustainable peace; (3) articulates a way in which businesses can contribute, if not to democracy, at least to participatory governance models that foster sustainable peace; and (4) concludes with a preliminary set of traits that suggest dimensions of corporate governance relevant to fostering sustainable peace. Corporations cannot be responsible for political dimensions, but they can attend to aspects such as participation and respect for voices of constituents.

I. Contemporary models: balances of power

A. *Corporate notion of balance of power*

Particularly in developed countries, there can be an understandable tendency to think of corporations as private organizations with relatively autonomous authority granted by state chartering. Under this conception, businesses may act to maximize profits provided they do not violate laws enforced by a typically viable government. There is confidence in this model because, at least in First World countries, governments have the capability to enact and enforce regulations. In other words, the power of multinational corporations is balanced by the check of effective legal regulation. If there are strong regulatory structures to keep corporations in check, this model makes intuitive sense. Yet, there are some refinements in this balance-of-power equation that need to be explored and linked to larger considerations of requisite checks-and-balances.

For instance, it is not clear whether governments of developing countries have the same power vis-à-vis corporations as do First World regulatory regimes, particularly when considering the transcendence of multinational corporations beyond geographical borders. The comfortable and traditional characterization of corporations as profit maximizers within the confines of the law may not be sufficient in an environment where there is not an effective regulatory check. In terms of the political array of forces demanding that corporations be just and fair institutions, the profit maximization model is under some duress. This pressure results not so much from the regulatory function of nation-states, but from the multiplicity of organizations that seek to monitor corporate behavior. A key reason the demands are placed on businesses results from the increasing complexity of the world including proliferation of NGOs, the power of multinational corporations themselves, and perhaps most profoundly, the changing nature of the nation-state. Most attention with respect to corporate behavior results from the actions of corporations in particular countries and how those actions affect economic development, labor and human rights issues, and environmental responsibility: the so-called "triple bottom-line."[1]

Peace research shows that mass violence is no longer waged between different states as frequently as it is within borders or about the borders that states claim.[2] According to one study, nearly two-thirds of 1993 conflicts could be defined as identity-based, "constituting a direct challenge to existing state authority as their salient characteristic."[3] Another widely reported study shows that 91 percent of conflicts since the end of the Cold War have occurred within, rather than across, borders.[4] For corporations, these statistics are meaningful because they suggest that violence is more likely to occur within the domestic settings in which the corporation operates. This setting makes the impact corporations may have on a domestic economy, wherever located, more relevant. Corporations are dependent upon the relative stability of the local business environment; simultaneously, they are entities that arouse suspicion, protest, and violence and thus disrupt stability. Self-interest requires that corporations take steps to mitigate the likelihood of violence in the countries in which they operate. More particularly, they may be able to do this by taking steps to improve the atmosphere in the countries in which they operate. As suggested by the correlation between corruption and violence described in chapter 1, one way corporations can do this is by adopting policies that discourage corruption. In addition, corporations can adopt structural policies designed to mitigate the outbreak of identity-based violence that their actions may trigger.

Thus, there remains a belief underlying contemporary business strategy that as long as the corporation operates within the bounds of the law, it is free to engage in any business practice that does not harm its self-interest.[5] Implicit in the understanding of operating a business with the constraints of legal regulation and market viability is the notion that legal and market institutions are in place to protect interests so that it is not the responsibility of a corporation to be concerned with issues of justice.[6] In addition, the argument goes, if stakeholders wish corporations to behave otherwise, the market will send the appropriate signals so that corporations change their behavior.[7] Even a prominent business ethicist and corporate governance scholar such as Thomas Dunfee, has expressed sympathy for this viewpoint, arguing that embedded within markets are moral preferences which if expressed, provide incentives for corporations to take into account the impact of actions on corporate stakeholders.[8]

This approach might be denoted as a traditional balance of power approach. There is an inherent balancing mechanism in this approach that prevents corporations from unduly exerting their influence to the detriment of others who participate in that market. Corporations are thus able to pursue their self-interest attentive only to the market demands and legal constraints, each of which has the capability of sending them the appropriate information regarding whether consumers value their actions.[9] There is much to be said for corporations focusing on economic issues. In becoming profitable, corporations cross borders and establish relationships that might not otherwise exist and, in doing so, provide opportunities and frequently raise standards of living for the societies in which they are located.[10] Yet, there are at least three reasons to be skeptical of the sufficiency of the balance of power analogy.

First, while markets provide information regarding the views of various economic actors, it is unclear whether markets convey adequate breadth of information. Material goods and services are easily quantifiable, whereas intangible goods are less susceptible to arithmetic quantification. For example, the value of a just peace is not quantifiable. This is one response – provided by religious leaders, for instance – in critique of balance of power conceptions of national security. The National Conference of Catholic Bishops, for instance, argues that peace is not the result of the balance of power,[11] but rather contains an inherent aspect of justice that is different from the equilibrium produced by a set of competing interests.[12] In this light, a traditional balance of power model falls short because the contests among governments, markets, and even civil society results in justice mainly as a hoped-for afterthought.

Second, and perhaps surprisingly, the work of a balance of power scholar, Henry Kissinger, reveals an even more pragmatic rationale for the dangers inherent in such an approach. Kissinger describes the balance of power of the Concert of Europe, which successfully maintained almost uninterrupted peace from 1848 until 1914, as one based not only on an equilibrium of national power within Europe, but also based on a "moral element of moderation," particularly linking the three Eastern powers of Prussia, Austria, and Russia.[13] This moderation muted the contests for geopolitical and ethnic dominance for many decades, so much so that Austria subdued its claims to its next-door Balkan nations while Russia soft-pedaled its identification with the same countries that shared ethnic identity.[14] Eventually, however, the moderation among these countries was jettisoned in exchange for a rawer form of pursuit of power for national self-interest.[15] The resulting *realpolitik* eventually produced an insecurity and desperation for power that led to polarization of interests, and alliances that led to World War I.[16]

The import of this analogy is that reliance upon a balance of power, shorn of moral moderation, risks polarization of interests. A company insistent upon profitability, for instance, may be willing to substantially contribute to the corruption of a given country in order to obtain market share and profitability. Yet, for a corporation to do this, it engages in the social milieu that is correlated with violent resolution of conflicts.

A third reason for being skeptical about the persuasiveness of a balance of power model for corporate behavior is simply that it may well be unsustainable for business purposes. If corporations contribute to the corruption of a given country in order to produce short-term profitability, it may well also sow the seeds for opposition to that company's actions within that country.[17] In other words, if the market is an attempt to produce utilitarian benefit – that is, the greatest happiness for the greatest number of people – then E.F. Schumacher's warning is telling. Schumacher argues that a person "driven by greed or envy loses the power of seeing things as they really are, of seeing things in their roundness and wholeness, and his very successes become failures."[18] The foundations of peace, according to Schumacher, cannot be attained by cultivating drives such as greed and envy, because those drives "destroy intelligence, happiness, serenity, and therefore the peacefulness of man."[19] Although the rhetoric and political philosophy are diametrically opposed, the arguments of free market theorist F.A. Hayek would seem to be in agreement, because he too argues that virtues must be taught by religious and other institutions in order for individuals to value moral notions such as truth-telling, honesty, and promise-keeping necessary to sustain the market.[20]

B. Balances of power and sustainable peace

Former US State Department Official and former Yale Law Dean, Walt Rostow addressed the question of a friend who asked, "Why can't we concentrate on what we do best – business and industry, and the development of our country – what we did so well before the First World War?"[21] His answer, in part, was that a weakness of democratic alliances is that they do not have a shared vision of what they want to achieve in world politics.[22] An example can be seen in the searing debate that occurred in 2003 over how the United Nations should deal with Iraq, a debate that highlighted the differences among many long-standing, democratic allies.[23] For Rostow, a defining feature of peace is in obedience to the law.[24] The connection between law and peace is one that will be built upon later in this chapter, but it is worth noting that obedience to the law could occur, according to Rostow, under either a *Pax Romana*, connected to military dominion and a highly developed system of law providing large degrees of autonomy to local tribunals, or under a *Pax Britannica*, involving a balancing of powers of individual sovereign nation-states with legal norms enforced by courts of individual states and some international tribunals.[25] Yet, each of these systems involves relatively clear understandings of jurisdictional divisions and in a time when ethnic rivalries, nationalistic desires, and borders honeycombed by electronic and economic tunnels create unsettled borders, the more relevant questions for sustaining peace revolve around how to establish justice through the available governing institutions. Those institutions include nation-states, but they also include nongovernmental actors working in civil society and in economic markets. Lee Tavis also captures the need for a broader consideration of the institutions affecting peace when he writes:

There is a serious and growing gap in the quality of life between industrialized and developing countries, which is exacerbated by a growing disparity within developing countries themselves. This gap can be described as a bifurcation of society, an increasing separation between people functioning well in the global economic/financial system and those who are not. This separation is associated with massive differences in access – access to markets, services, technology, information, material resources, and other factors that allow people to improve their standard of living. While readily apparent in all countries, this separation is of staggering proportions in the developing countries of Africa, Asia, and Latin America and is rapidly increasing in Central and Eastern Europe.[26]

1. Borders for peace and quality of peace

Arie Kacowicz addresses the question of how to define sustainable peace. A sound-byte answer is that sustainable peace is a peace that endures because it is just. A more detailed assessment would be to differentiate between "negative peace" and "positive peace." Negative peace is more quantifiable as the absence of war.[27] Positive peace, on the other hand, includes ideas of social and economic justice.[28] Gandhi, for instance, thought that poverty was the worst form of violence.[29] Like Kacowicz, the concern addressed in this book is more along the lines of negative peace in the absence of bloodshed. Yet, even in this limited conception, what makes the absence of bloodshed sustainable will be either a hegemonic force so powerful as to prevent all violence or a set of arrangements that promotes a sense of justice sufficient for people to believe that it is better to resolve differences through socially accepted dispute resolution mechanisms rather than to resort to violence. An example of the former is the famous description of Tacitus, who described Rome's utter flattening of Carthage as an act of creating a desert and calling it peace.[30] The latter is akin to Rostow's emphasis on the legal resolution of disputes.[31]

Even under Rostow's definition, however, there is a blend of both *realpolitik* notions of balance of power and nobler notions of justice. This mix is prevalent in Kacowicz's study in which he tries to explain why some, perhaps unexpected, places in the world – West Africa and South America – have been "zones of peace," in terms of relatively little cross-border violence.[32] As Kacowicz admits, a zone of peace does not account for civil war and other domestic conflicts,[33] yet with battles within countries being mostly about border drawing, his study contains some interesting insights for actions corporations might take to encourage peaceful societies.

Kacowicz describes eight zones of peace, defined by areas where a group of nations have maintained peaceful relations for at least thirty years.[34] Democracy and advanced industrialization mark four of these: North America, Western Europe, Australasia, and East Asia (including Japan). The fifth zone is comprised of Eastern Europe, and the final three zones are in the "Third World" countries of South America, West Africa, and Southeast Asia.[35] Some of these areas, particularly West Africa and some former Soviet republics, may no longer meet Kacowicz's tests, but his point is that these areas endured sustained periods of peace and only half of them were industrially advanced democracies. Thus, although economic advancement and democratic institutions may contribute to peace, they may not entirely explain why nations remain at peace.

Kacowicz's study shows that, even without democracy and economic industrialization, zones of peace can occur when the territorial claims are relatively settled.[36] The sufficient condition for sustained peace then is the relative satisfaction with territorial claims.[37] Democratic, industrialized countries, he argues, are also relatively satisfied with their territorial boundaries, but they add to that satisfaction another dimension.[38] More specifically, Kacowicz claims that the quality of peace in those democratic, industrialized countries tends to be higher because, in those countries, there tend to be higher levels of accountability, rule of law, dispute resolution, and protection of human rights.[39] They are strong states with relatively few internal insecurity issues. Conversely, weak states tend to have international disputes arising from the internal dilemmas of the country.[40]

Nationalistic claims of ethnic groups are partly justified by dissatisfaction in the accommodation of the issues important to them.[41] Such complaints may resonate outside of established borders because of shared ethnic identity in other countries.[42] This tends to weaken borders, also common to globalization, even in democratically advanced countries.[43] This is not to suggest that globalization will result in territorial disputes in North America. If there are forces weakening established borders, then the powers that need to be balanced may be related to deeper, psychological human needs than borders *per se* may fully account for.

2. Needs, security, and moral values

In describing what is necessary for sustainable peace, the ever-present instinct is to revert to notions of justice. Yet, the quest for justice raises the issue regarding whether this moral value is objective and universal or whether it is subjective and particular.

Peace is sometimes the enemy of justice, and conflict can be ended only at the price of objectively fair outcomes. Such peace, so the objections go, is illusory: there is no lasting peace without justice. But justice has many referents and is ultimately subjective. A conflict resolution that perfectly combines peace and justice is as rare as other moments of perfection in human action.[44]

Nevertheless, peace and economic research identify two key theories that are helpful for understanding this issue and that are particularly relevant for corporations – needs theory and security theory. These theories provide a template to identify human interests that must be met to prevent the kind of dissatisfaction that can lead to conflict.

Needs theory is an attempt in peace research literature to determine what needs, when not met, are most likely to produce grievances that lead to conflict. Zartman and Rasmussen, for instance, argue that many, if not most, current conflicts result from "the failure of political, economic, and social institutions to pay sufficient attention to the grievances and perceived needs of significant groups in the population."[45] They acknowledge that identification of the relevant specific needs is difficult because those needs can change according to context and cultural setting.[46] Nevertheless, there are some basic needs than can be identified, such as:

Physical and psychological security; basic survival needs, such as food and shelter; identity needs, such as dignity and respect for distinct cultural and linguistic identity; economic well-being in terms of educational and economic opportunity; the need for political participation; and the freedom to control one's own life (for example, the panoply of democratic rights, such as freedom of speech, movement, religious preference, and association)....

Denial of these needs may result in conflict.[47]

A second framework consistent with needs theory for identifying sources of conflict is provided by security theory. Michael Klare identifies six sources of insecurity: low income level, unclean water, illiteracy, lack of food, lack of housing, and preventable death.[48] The combination of these attributes of needs and security theories, together with Sen's articulation of five kinds of freedoms, provides a set of characteristics necessary to avoid conflict. Sen's freedoms are "instrumental" in that they lead to a *telos* of individual human development. They include: (1) political freedoms, (2) economic facilities, (3) social opportunities, (4) transparency guarantees, and (5) protective security.[49]

With respect to corporate involvement, it may be worthwhile to see how some of the above attributes of needs and security theories interface with contemporary theories about the moral responsibilities of corporations. First, there is a set of very basic needs that are concerned with the sustainability of life, such as water, food, housing, health, and preventable death. In business ethics literature, these are akin to Patricia Werhane's notion of "basic rights," protections without which life would be intolerable.[50] This suggests a possible link between corporate behavior and business ethics: to the extent that corporations are engaged in activities that violate basic rights, they risk sowing the seeds for violence. For example, several years ago, Green Giant moved an agricultural processing plant from Salinas, California to Irapuato, Mexico.[51] The stated reason for the move was to enable production of high-quality vegetables, particularly broccoli and cauliflower, year-round.[52] One of the consequences of the relocation, however, was that the water level in Irapuato dropped to an impossible level given the resources of the local population.[53] Prior to the introduction of the plant, water could be found at a depth of 60 feet. After introduction of the plant, it was necessary to drill 450 feet to find water. Although the company brought economic development to the area, the water issue nonetheless caused resentment.[54]

Second, there are psychological as well as physical interests at stake. These theories go further than considering income as a need requiring some degree of stakeholder satisfaction; they also take into account the level of income. They do not simply identify protection from physical harm, but also protection from psychological harm. They do not simply identify the absence of corruption, but also the guarantees of transparency. In short, there is an important component of the perception of fairness that is more elusive than what might be measurably and arithmetically counted that serve important interests, and require satisfaction. If these perceptions are not addressed, the perceived unfairness could be as real as actual deprivation. The relative levels of these interests and the psychological importance attached to them require both clear communication of how the needs and interests are being addressed, and a mechanism for providing those affected with a voice in these decisions.

Needs theory and security theory are thus congruent with the stakeholder and social contract theories of business ethics. Stakeholder theory, most prominently championed by Evan and Freeman,[55] argues that corporations should take into account anyone who is affected by a corporate action.[56] Although it is unlikely that corporations can pragmatically take into account all stakeholder interests in making business decisions,[57] stakeholder theory provides an important insight. The individual best able to identify the significance of an action to a particular stakeholder group is the stakeholder group in question rather than a manager attempting to hypothesize what the impact might be.[58] Consistent with the psychological component of needs theory and security theory, it is important for stakeholders to perceive that interests important to them will be voiced and that their complaints about deprivations will be taken seriously.

Similarly, the notion of contract theory in business ethics is based on the validity of consent of the negotiating parties. This is true in the shareholder version of contract theory, as articulated by Easterbrook and Fischel,[59] who argue that a corporation is a "nexus of contracts" for various individuals to negotiate the fulfillment of needs and desires,[60] as well as in the social contract theory, as articulated by Michael Keeley,[61] Steven Salbu,[62] and Thomas Donaldson and Thomas Dunfee.[63] In the social contract version, consent to a norm is "the justificatory linchpin."[64] To the extent, then, that stakeholders believe that they have not freely negotiated a contract, the more likely they are to perceive an action as unfair.

Finally, there is a communal aspect to conflict. Corporations do business within particular countries, and in doing so will be working with individuals who, as residents of those countries, are subject to existing internal rivalries. The hiring of employees[65] and the relocation of people in order to construct pipelines[66] are examples of ways in which otherwise productive business enterprises can become embroiled in ethnic controversies. Moreover, to the extent that corporate behavior undermines traditions of local communities, resentment may build.[67]

This communal aspect connects with the virtue theory of business ethics because virtues are always connected to a particular community.[68] Yet, virtues appropriate for a particular community may favor one group over another and may be perceived as imposing a set of Western values, displacing traditional values, making virtue theory difficult to apply.[69]

Thus, by focusing on basic needs, it can be seen how corporations may play a role in enhancing or depriving needs. In addition, the perception of how corporations address these needs can be characterized as fair or unfair even within contemporary business ethics theories. For corporations to cope with these perceptions, they must adopt governance practices that institutionalize ethical frameworks. This will enable them directly to address needs as they arise and as they are perceived by the affected individuals. Otherwise, these individuals may feel the need to violently undermine corporate activities to the ultimate detriment of both the corporation and society.

C. *Participatory dimensions*

With free markets, powerful and inexpensive communication, and no world government, people, capital, and ideas float across borders. It is tempting to think that, in this environment, government and governance matter less. In fact, the opposite is true. As Friedman puts it:

In the era of globalization it is the quality of the state that matters. You need a smaller state, because you want the free market to allocate capital, not the slow bloated government, but you need a better state, a smarter state and a faster state, with bureaucrats that can regulate a free market, without either choking it or letting it get out of control.[70]

Governments of nation-states that are able to provide this kind of balanced regulatory environment generally provide transparency, so that decisions can be made where to invest capital, labor, and ideas.[71] This has been the story of the successful emerging economies, such as Poland, that have not simply opened their doors to free markets, but have also undergirded free markets with legal structures that protect capital and contracts.[72]

Not only do nation-states require good governance practices to blend transparency with institutions that protect property and contract, but as Connie Peck argues, many levels of governance structures are necessary to support sustainable peace.[73] It is not just any kind of governance that contributes to sustainable peace, but what Peck calls "good governance," with a linchpin of a participatory structure.[74] A participatory structure has benefits of fairness which reduce the likelihood that grievances will grow into major flashpoints of conflict.[75] Fairness is evidenced in these structures by the capability of people to determine their own priorities; to safeguard and promote their civil, political, economic, social, and cultural rights; and to provide a pluralist environment within which they can live together in peace with the freedom to develop in all ways.[76] Thus, the underlying premise is that democratic systems contribute to sustainable peace. This premise is not promoted simply because democracy is the dominant governance system of the West, however.[77] Rather, it is promoted because inherent within democratic systems are inevitable checks, which limit the possibility of an obsession with single points of ideological differences that cannot be compromised and, as a result, lead to war.

As R.J. Rummel writes, "democratically free people are spontaneous, diverse, and pluralistic."[78] Because they are truly pluralistic, people will belong to different interest groups, pulling them in different directions.[79] This creates "cross-pressure" so that:

The very strong interests that drive people in one direction to the exclusion of all others, even at the risk of violence, do not develop easily. And if such interests do develop, they are usually shared by relatively few persons. That is the normal working of a democratically free society in all its diversity is to restrain the growth across the community of that consuming singleness of view and purpose that leads, if not frustrated, to wide-scale social and political violence.[80]

On the other hand, a totalitarian structure is not spontaneous, but commanded.[81] In Rummel's words, this creates a "management-worker, command-obey division" with the kind of bureaucratic organizational system that incorporates "coercive planning, plethora of rules, lines of authority from top to bottom" that ultimately polarizes major interests.[82] In short, a command-control, hierarchically oriented society fosters the milieu for polarized interests, which are more difficult to compromise. This is a finding validated by anthropologists, who have concluded that "strong respect for authority and the tendency to obey authorities is another predisposing characteristic for group violence. Given this characteristic, in the face of difficult life conditions or an external threat members of the group will be more dependent on guidance by authorities."[83]

A key preventative mechanism from developing the hostility that leads to violence, then, is the prevalence of at least participatory institutions, so that individuals have the legal infrastructure that permits them to develop their capabilities as they see fit. This is the case on the national level. Peck argues, however, "good governance must be instituted at all levels of society – local, national, regional, and international."[84]

In at least one sense the need for participatory structures also applies to corporations. Friedman, for instance, argues that in order to obtain better governance even without a global government to fix issues such as the environment, human rights, and worker conditions, it is necessary for activists "to compel companies to behave better by mobilizing global consumers through the Internet."[85] This "network solution for human rights" depends on "bottom-up regulation" that empowers the bottom, "instead of waiting for the top, by shaping a coalition that produces better governance without global government."[86]

Thus, although it may be true that Kacowicz finds that democratic institutions are related more to the quality of sustained peace than to its existence, the pressures that globalization put on territorial boundaries – what Kacowicz describes as being more central to the maintenance of intergovernmental peace – suggests that the qualitative difference may be even more salient in the future. With that in mind, the next section considers issues of democracy and sustainable peace along with the role of corporations in fostering the good, while mitigating the bad and the ugly.

II. The democratic impulse: the good, the bad, and the ugly

A. *The benefits of democracy*

Immanuel Kant thought that free peoples were inherently peaceful.[87] The historical record, however, is mixed: democracies can be warlike.[88] Yet, the fact remains that democratic countries do not fight each other. Spencer Weart reviews historical data and establishes the claim that "well-established democracies have never made war on one another."[89] Corroborating that claim, Baps studied wars fought since 1500 and found no wars (involving at least 50,000 troops or fought to cause territorial transfer, a change in government, or eradication of a state) had occurred between freely elected, independent governments.[90] Three reasons have been offered for why this is true.

First, democratic republics are more pluralistic than authoritarian regimes.[91] The mediating institutions that proliferate in civil society cut across various social ties so that no one group's anger can automatically lead to belligerence.[92] The multiple ties any one person might feel toward a particular neighborhood, church, or political party create an internal check on political processes and make it more difficult for a central authority to claim the need to go to war to vindicate the interests of a particular group.[93]

Second, Weart writes that the theory "that republicans generally behave more peacefully toward other nations than do autocrats has been confirmed about as reliably as anything can be in statistical studies of human communities."[94] In a democracy, a leader has little choice but to compromise and this leadership style tends to extend to those outside of one's borders assuming that a preference for negotiation also exists on the other side.[95]

For Weart to make his argument about the benefits of democracy vis-à-vis peace, he creates a few basic definitions. These definitions help in beginning the process of transferring democratic principles over to a corporate context. Weart argues that what makes a culture republican are equal rights among citizens and tolerance of dissent.[96] Moreover, a culture does not become an established republic simply by a declaration; instead, to meet this classification, tolerance of dissent must have persisted for at least three years.[97]

Thus, one way businesses might be able to contribute to peace is to support the establishment of democratic regimes wherever they do business. This would require more than rhetoric, it would also require support of equal rights and tolerance of dissent. Even if a corporation cannot nudge a political regime toward democracy, it can implement some of the practices that define a democracy in its governance structure. By doing so, it may well provide a model for democratic-like attributes that could spill over into the political culture and nourish experiments in democratic decision-making.[98]

Benjamin Barber argues that democracy is under attack from two very different sources. One source is Jihad, which typically is thought of in terms of Islamic extremism, but which Barber argues is a metaphor for all parochial groups reacting against globalization.[99] The other source is McWorld, which transcends traditional borders and boundaries to link people together in a quest for consuming goods and achieving profitability. As different as they are:

Jihad and McWorld have this in common: they both make war on the sovereign nation-state and thus undermine the nation-state's democratic institutions. Each eschews civil society and belittles democratic citizenship, neither seeks alternative democratic institutions. Their common thread is indifference to civil liberty.[100]

Barber argues that Jihad is committed to bloody politics of identity whereas McWorld is a bloodless pursuit of profitability.[101] Jihad reacts against the homogenization of culture by fighting global business and, as Barber makes clear, Jihad's disdain is more with capitalism than it is with democracy.[102] McWorld has little argument with democratic institutions, but undermines the community ties necessary for individuals to understand their connection to the common good as opposed to a market where self-interest is the necessary consideration.[103] Moreover, the "twin assault on democratic citizenship from the fractious forces of Jihad and the spreading markets of McWorld in effect undercuts democratic institutions."[104] The paradox is that corporations thrive on democratic virtues, but simultaneously undercut them.[105]

In response to this paradox, Barber claims that civil society, including the traditional mediating institutions that bridge commonly made distinctions between public and private life, must be rebuilt. Barber argues that a "two-celled" distinction between government versus private sector is too often relied on, but the middle ground of civil society is where individuals voluntarily come together to talk about what is necessary for the common good, be it the softball league, religious outreach, or neighborhood crossing guards.[106] Unlike governmental affairs, there is no coercion present – actions are voluntary – but unlike the private sector, there is concern for the common good.[107] It is in this realm, a realm Barber argues that is populated by schools, churches, public interest groups, and other civic organizations, that citizenship is developed.[108] That space, however, has been squeezed, he argues, as corporations encroach on the space of civil society, as governments react to check the rise of corporate power, and as individuals begin to think of themselves as consumers rather than citizens.[109]

Barber's analysis presents the question of whether business is part of civil society. Barber suggests that the answer is no, noting that it may be unfair to ask a corporation to be committed to a vision of justice or democracy.[110] He argues, however, that businesses wade into political issues if only to create a middle class that can purchase their goods. Businesses, according to Barber, are not designed to do what democratic polities do – they are contractual rather than communitarian.[111] Yet, this account misses two important points.

First, although markets may not be designed to create democratic polities, businesses draw people to work for them and invest in them, usually on a voluntary basis. In doing so, they require people to work together for a common good, even if that good is simply profitability. Profitability does not occur without significant practices of human cooperation within the organization. Thus, businesses have the essential features Barber recognizes as emblematic of civil associations.

Second, Barber follows Edmund Burke in arguing that human solidarity is formed by "resemblances, by conformities, by sympathies" rather than by contracts.[112] Yet, experimental psychological testing shows that association can be as arbitrary as whether a person has a dot on his or her nose.[113] In other words, human solidarity is not trapped by ethnic, religious, or genetic characteristics, but by any kind of affiliation, which could include people of differing ethnic origins working together. The so-called private sector is not as private as one might think and within a business organization lies the potential, even the necessity, for working together for some common good. Thus, although Barber argues that the reinvigorization of a variety of mediating institutions in society would be worthwhile, it should also be emphasized that business institutions themselves possess resources for encouraging individuals to exercise voice in working for a common good. The freedom to exercise voice entails a need to tolerate dissent; otherwise only a narrow range of voices will be heard. Within this exercise of voice and tolerance of dissent lay the seeds for a business organization to foster a sense of democracy within its own borders. This does not mean that businesses always or even frequently actualize this potential. Yet, the potential is there, governance regimes are not far from supporting that actualization, and the steps necessary to create that potential lie in a commitment of business to peace. That commitment not only breeds the stability on which business thrives, but also lays the groundwork for democratic republics to rise. If multinational corporations in democratic countries do this, they may have provided a way to overcome challenges raised against them by appealing directly to the source of democratic liberal tradition.

B. The irrelevance of democracy?

Samuel Huntington, like Bobbitt, argues that the end of the Cold War has triggered a new balance of power among state actors.[114] The Cold War was able to submerge the ambitions for nationhood desired by a variety of ethnic groups but without the bipolarity of Soviet–US competition, so that these groups now have a freer reign to pursue goals of creating their own nation-states.[115] These desires are not new, but the desire to bring all ethnic cousins under one state may spark terrible conflicts including, at the extreme, ethnic cleansing.[116] Huntington further argues that the world will increasingly organize itself along these lines of identity rather than nation-state status.[117] Thus, the world will tend to be grouped in terms of North American, South American, European, Russian, Muslim, Indian, African, Chinese, and Japanese peoples.[118] As the 1990s Balkans conflicts demonstrate, however, this means that not only might nation-states be in conflict with each other, but because regions contain differing ethnic groups, there is also the potential for internal conflict.[119] Because Muslims in Egypt might identify with Muslims in Bosnia and Russians might identify with Slavs in Serbia, internal conflict can also exacerbate severe external tensions.[120]

The location of ethnic linkages around the world is nothing new. The Balkan nations have long struggled with this problem and the presence of Germans outside of Nazi Germany was one of Hitler's pretexts for triggering World War II. More benignly, China considers someone of Chinese heritage (such as an adopted child) as Chinese with an assumed identification with the Middle Kingdom[121] and the Czech Republic allows its president to be someone of Czech origin, even if he or she is not a "citizen."[122] Globalization, however, fosters additional immigration and immigration may further engender domestic conflicts in the countries to which the immigrants locate. It may also spark conflicts between the immigrants' home and new countries, if it is perceived either that the emigrees are not being treated well or, alternatively, that the emigrees are undermining the new country's identity. Thus, democracy may not be as important as identity-related organizing principles. Huntington quotes the starkness of this approach in quoting one novelist who wrote "[t]here can be no true friends without true enemies. Unless we hate what we are not, we cannot love what we are."[123]

Huntington is profoundly skeptical of anything like a universal civilization emerging, instead insisting that peoples around the world are defining themselves according to their traditions, language, and religions.[124] Religion, which Huntington names as "a central defining characteristic of civilizations,"[125] has grown in the last part of the twentieth century, but it has done so primarily in fundamentalist terms and those terms tend to focus on differentiating faiths from others rather than finding common ground.[126] Language is another central element, but Huntington reports that there has not been dramatic changes in the past forty years.[127] Nor do free market economics gain universal acceptance: "The Davos Culture," according to Huntington, with emphasis on individualism, market economies, and political democracy, claims the allegiance of fewer than 1 percent of people outside of the West.[128] In particular, the combination of liberal democracy and free markets is less likely to be imposed on the world because of the relative decline of Western power.[129] Even where free markets have spawned economic advances, as in East Asia, the rationale given is often that the Asian culture benefits development precisely because it is not Western.[130] "The revolt against the West was originally legitimated by asserting the universality of Western values; it is now legitimated by asserting the superiority of non-Western, often hierarchical values."[131] Moreover, Huntington notes a paradox of democracy in that the adoption of Western democratic institutions gives rise to native groups and anti-Western movements to oppose the West.[132] In such scenarios, democracy is "a parochializing not a cosmopolitanizing process."[133]

C. The dangers of democracy: Amy Chua

If Huntington's concerns are bad, the picture portrayed by Amy Chua is ugly.[134] Chua's thesis is that global markets and democracy aggravate ethnic hatreds and unleash violent reprisals by majorities against a minority in the country with great wealth perceived to be unfair.[135] Markets, she argues, allow for the accumulation of great amounts of wealth, which is often held by an outside ethnic group or one that is not indigenous.[136] Examples of this phenomena are Chinese minorities in several countries of Southeast Asia.[137] This includes Burma,[138] the Philippines,[139] and Vietnam.[140] Thailand, Laos, and Cambodia also have strong influences of Chinese economic domination.[141] In the Philippines, for instance, Filipino Chinese make up fewer than 2 percent of the population, but they control all of the largest department stores, supermarkets, and fast-food restaurants.[142] A key reason for this dominance, Chua argues, is that already successful ethnic groups have ethnic networks from which to access capital and business know-how.[143] Other examples of "market-dominated minorities" include Sri Lanka,[144] Bolivia,[145] Brazil,[146] Russia,[147] Zimbabwe,[148] Ethiopia,[149] and Rwanda.[150]

The success of an outside minority in each of these countries raised resentments against them.[151] At the time markets arrive, so does democracy with universal suffrage.[152] But universal suffrage does not necessarily unleash thoughtful citizen decisions; too often demagogues use democracy to drum up resentment against a market-dominant minority.[153] Thus, in Zimbabwe, Robert Mugabe's party featured campaign slogans such as "Down with the whites."[154] In Russia, it has led to a resurgence of anti-Semitism.[155] At its worst, the forces of democracy, according to Chua, led to the genocide in Rwanda as Hutus took revenge against the market-dominant Tutsi.[156]

Chua applies her argument to explain how majorities in individual countries have committed indiscriminate murder against market-dominant minorities. She also extends the argument geographically. She argues, for instance, that Israel stands as a regional market-dominant minority and triggers hatred of it as a result.[157] She also applies it globally with respect to the USA, in particular in an attempt to explain the attacks of September 11, 2001.[158] In each case, a tremendous disparity between the economic success of a relatively small minority is bitterly resented by a majority, who eventually take matters into their own hands.

Chua's argument is provocative, but needs to be considered in context. For example, unlike Weart,[159] Chua includes within her definition of democracy regimes that do not tolerate minority dissent. This seems to miss an essential characteristic of democracy. Similarly, the crony-capitalism of the Philippines or of the hegemonic Ethiopian People's Revolutionary Democratic Front, also defined as democracies, seem far removed from the democratic free-market system of the West. Yet, Chua provides a valuable perspective by cautioning that systems allowing for minority wealth in a newly formed, majority-rule democracy may have potential for disaster.

Moreover, Chua is correct to note that Western attempts to export democracy and markets engender difficulty by the failure of the West to understand the evolution of other liberal systems.[160] As further discussed in chapter 3, democratic governance came slowly in the West. Universal suffrage resulted only hundreds of years after the Magna Carta restrained royal prerogatives.[161] Although universal suffrage should serve as an ideal, Chua's concern that its development may be too much too fast is worthy of consideration.[162]

Chua's arguments regarding leveling the economic playing field are also worth noting. She argues in favor of finding a way for the poor in countries to obtain ownership stakes in companies and capital.[163] She also advocates for redistribution programs and for reform of property ownership along the lines of the work of Hernando de Soto.[164] Perhaps most interestingly, she advocates a stakeholder approach and encourages market-dominant minorities to treat stakeholders justly[165] and for multinational corporations to be philanthropically inclined.[166]

III. Constitutional republicanism: democracy in the form of participation and voice

Constitutional law scholar Philip Bobbitt has examined the changes in the nation-state and balances of power throughout history. Bobbitt argues that construction of legal constitutions has resulted historically from the necessities of war.[167] Implicit in this argument is that basic legal frameworks rest on balances of power to assure competitive advantage and sustainable peace. As creations of law, and as factors in the balance of power, corporations are thus inevitably affected by factors of war and peace. This section thus outlines Bobbitt's thesis as it is applicable to the ability of corporations to contribute to sustainable peace.

A. *Law and war (and peace)*

Bobbitt traces primarily European history to describe transitions from princely states to kingly states, territorial states, state-nations, and finally, to nation-states.[168] The key determinant accounting for each transition was a need to organize society effectively to compete with military advances and challenges. For example, Bobbitt notes that prior to Napoleon, most armies were relatively small consisting of fewer than 25,000 men.[169] Armies were professional and therefore expensive, so warfare was largely about avoiding their destruction.[170] Napoleon was an exception in his desire to create clashes in opposing countries to break morale and ultimately induce surrender of extant economic resources.[171] The French Revolution, however, gave rise to popular involvement in politics and Napoleon, by 1794, took advantage of popular passion to create massive armies of almost 1.2 million men which, although untrained, were able to overwhelm smaller, professional armies.[172]

Warfare required popular sacrifice, and therefore required a different kind of political apparatus as well as more detailed laws to describe the basis for government, taxation, and conscription.[173] Thus, although Napoleon is known for his military characteristics of ambitious and strategic innovation, he is also famous for his ability:

to obligate the mass of persons to the French state. Among this vast people various groups from the bourgeoisie were employed in the service of the state; for their members there were lower taxes extracted by France from her conquered neighbors; working men found in the state an employer of last resort – the army (whose mass employment would not have been possible under the strategic and tactical constraints of the armies of the territorial state); and for every class a new meritocracy arose that measured status according to services rendered to the State.[174]

According to Bobbitt's thesis, this example is one of law relating to military strategy and military strategy relating to law, because they both mutually reinforce the state's capacity for warfare.[175]

In the twentieth century this relationship manifested itself in the nation-state, which Bobbitt argues, drew its legitimacy from its ability to satisfy the welfare of its constituents.[176] Coming out of World War I, there were three contenders for the nation-state system that would best accomplish constituent welfare: fascism, communism, and parliamentary democracy.[177] Bobbitt views the era of 1914–1990 as "The Long War," fought to settle the question of which of these alternatives most benefited the welfare of citizens, with parliamentary democracy successively defeating fascism (in World War II) and communism (in the Cold War).[178] Yet, the conclusion of each "epochal war" also brought with it a new set of challenges. Out of the Long War, Bobbitt argues that a new kind of state is emerging – the market state – the legitimacy of which is not based on providing welfare for its citizens (particularly in the form of welfare entitlements, pensions, etc.) but with a *raison d'être* to provide opportunities for its citizens through market opportunities and education.[179] These opportunities allow individuals to participate and to compete effectively in a global economy. This environment recognizes the proliferation of nongovernmental powers, which although they may undermine the traditional nation-state, insist on respect for human rights. They further recognize the increasing power of multinational corporations to provide economic opportunity regardless of the nation-state's traditional economic regulations.[180]

Bobbitt focuses on three models to describe the way these market states are taking shape. They are they US model, the German model, and the Japanese model. If Bobbitt is correct, the question becomes whether there is a way for these market-state systems to evolve so that they may confront violent threats to them collectively (as through challenges from terrorism or from non-democratic regimes) and provide economic innovation to make key border-crossing institutions, such as multinational corporations, instruments of sustainable peace.

B. *The parliamentary models: Germany, Japan, and the USA*

In general, democracies operate according to the wishes of a body of citizens who elect representatives to govern them. In Spencer Weart's historical analysis, a democracy is defined first in terms of a republic.[181] A republic's defining feature is that "political decisions [are] made by a body of citizens who have equal rights."[182] Decisions are made in light of "public contestation" of choices with political officials, who are accountable to the citizens for their actions.[183] Public contestations require free political expression, a rule of law, and toleration of politically dissenting minorities.[184] The implementation of these features can vary significantly. Weart also differentiates between oligarchic republics and democratic republics. An oligarchic republic features voting by only one-third of its citizens whereas democratic republics feature voting by two-thirds of their citizens.[185] Interestingly, oligarchic republics rarely make war on other oligarchic republics and, according to Weart's analysis, democratic republics never make war on other democratic republics.[186]

The specific characteristics of equal rights, tolerance of dissent, voting, and free expression suggest that there is a different character of political solidarity in a democracy than might exist in other kinds of political regimes. Indeed, at the heart of Weart's analysis of republicanism is the idea of political culture.[187] A republican political culture, and particularly a democratic political culture, not only embraces ideas of equal rights, public contestation, and tolerance of political dissent, but also values the political process and resolves disputes among citizens by negotiation and mutual accommodation rather than by coercion.[188]

Benjamin Barber builds upon similar notions when he argues that democracy requires the foundation of civil society.[189] This foundation is not built quickly, as demonstrated by the evolution of democracy in Britain and the USA – nearly three-quarters of a millennium passed between Magna Carta and the Declaration of Independence.[190] As Barber argues, civil society is about an environment "where we talk with neighbors about a crossing guard, plan a benefit for our community school, discuss how our church or synagogue can shelter the homeless, or organize a summer softball league for our children."[191] Civil society, therefore, provides a foundation for democracy because it trains people to organize themselves to solve public issues on the basis of respect, persuasion, and negotiation – the hallmarks of a republic. These activities are not about political organizing as much as they are about being part of a small group within which individuals are empowered to affect the norms of the community.[192] These activities and institutions are public just as the government is public, but they "make no claim to exercise a monopoly on legitimate coercion."[193] That is, these institutions do not seek merely their own self-advancement as a for-profit corporation might, but are instead concerned with issues concerning the common good.[194]

There is a direct link to peace resulting from these societies because leaders who work with equals at home by non-coercive negotiation and

compromise are likely to work the same way with other similarly inclined leaders.[195] This does not mean that democratic (or oligarchic
republican) cultures are incapable of warfare; but rather that they do
not generally engage in warfare with countries espousing similar political cultures.[196] Thus, democratic societies can be defined by public
contestation, equal rights, free expression, negotiation, compromise,
the election of representatives and accountability of those representatives to voters. Underlying democratic societies is civil society where
people voluntarily engage in quests for public goods that define their
mediating institutions, but which also reach beyond special interests
to embrace the common good.

   This kind of political system has, according to Bobbitt, defeated
fascism and communism in the epochal war he calls "The Long War"
lasting from 1914 to 1990.[197] Yet, with the end of the Long War, came
the creation of market-states and new kinds of variations for optimal
organization. It is particularly significant that all three variations – the
German, Japanese, and US models – provide for a system where economic transactions of multinational corporations have a central role.

   As noted above, Bobbitt has coined the term "market-state" to describe a newly emerging state. Bobbitt argues that the maximization of
opportunities for citizens is the basis of legitimacy for market-states.[198]
But each differs according to how it creates those opportunities. In the
USA, it means:

> providing infrastructure (including intangible infrastructure like education
> and the means of enforcing agreements) and relying on private enterprise
> to maximize the abundance of consumer choice and minimize the costs to
> the consumer of exercising choice. In Tokyo, by contrast, maximizing op-
> portunity means protecting domestic industries so that future generations
> will have a full array of employment opportunities, subsidizing research and
> development so that future opportunities for innovation will be practicably
> exploitable, and restricting the import of capital so that the government re-
> mains in control of its capital allocation. In Berlin, maximizing opportunity
> means social and economic equality among citizens so that opportunities
> available to communities, workers and future generations are maximized
> rather than maximizing the short-term profits of shareholders.[199]

Bobbitt characterizes the differing models used by democracies as:
(1) the Entrepreneurial Model; (2) the Mercantile Model; and (3) the
Managerial Model.

The "Entrepreneurial Model," which Bobbitt characterizes as the US approach, but which is not used exclusively by the USA, is a model that stresses autonomy, individual achievement and consumption that "citizens of these states 'invent' their citizenships, identifying themselves with those subgroups within the state with whom they share a consumption pattern."[200] Labor relations in this model tend to be confrontational and immigration is generally welcomed.[201] Thus, the Entrepreneurial Model is a more libertarian, less socially cohesive model, with protections of citizens coming more from media exposure of wrongdoing than from government.[202] This model further stresses guarantees for human rights, free press, and political dissent, which tend to support individualism. The Entrepreneurial Model also has proponents outside of the English-speaking world, including, for example, Thailand and Peru.[203]

In the "Mercantile Model," characterizing the Japanese approach, but not exclusively used by the Japanese, immigration is discouraged in favor of maintaining cultural homogeneity, and labor relations tend to be familial.[204] This model also "retain[s] conscription for military service (though with force levels vastly reduced from those of the twentieth century), affirmative action for certain social groups, and varying degrees of state control of the media."[205] The Mercantile Model provides that human rights are more communitarian than individualistic and that "harmony rather than division" and "respect and reverence are a truer expression of its cultural values."[206] These states, therefore, "attempt to minimize the public expression of opposition."[207]

Finally, Bobbitt's third model, the "Managerial Model," characterizes the German approach, although not exclusively German. This model also retains conscription for military service, affirmative action, and some control of the state media.[208] With regard to labor relations, the Managerial Model "is ambivalent: open to 'guest workers' but hostile to new citizens."[209]

From the snapshots of these models, predictions can be made about some of the salient features of corporate governance systems these models might promote. For example, the Entrepreneurial Model would stress agility subject to free choices. Thus, an underpinning legal infrastructure of this model would stress transparency, fluid labor movement, and a predominant emphasis on protecting investment capital. Indeed, these are features of the US model. Yet, the 2002 corporate scandals in the USA demonstrate that this model also runs great risks of insufficiently accomplishing its goals.[210] In 2002, the country found that corporate executives and boards could be opaque rather than transparent with devastating effects for investors as well as employees.[211]

The Mercantile market-state would typically have a strong central government partnering with business concerns to enhance national industries and subsidize crucial research and development while de-emphasizing consumption.[212] Social cohesion is maintained by suppressing income disparities and subsidizing public housing and access to education with the important proviso, according to Bobbitt, that these benefits are available only for those who are eager to work.[213] Mercantile market-states, such as Singapore, Hong Kong, Taiwan, and South Korea, have had impressive growth although their efficiency and productivity levels are more in the range of Egypt, Greece, Syria, and Cameroon.[214] Thus, the Mercantile Model faces the challenges of:

opening up domestic markets to foreign competition; reforming the banking sector to bring greater scrutiny to credit transactions; allowing access to cheaper credit for smaller firms that are usually restricted to relatively high priced domestic finance and letting the cost of capital to dominant firms rise....The Korean Model is characterized by the concentration of power in four great companies (Samsung, Hyndai, Lucky-Goldstar, and Daewoo)....In Japan, the largest six companies account for over half the total assets of all listed enterprises. Furthermore, some three-quarters of all shares are mutually held between companies and their financial institutions.[215]

From this, it can be predicted that the Mercantile Model would encourage a corporate governance system that is less concerned with transparency and its concomitant fluidity and more focused on social cohesion. In such a system, tight, opaque control of capital with an offsetting corporate culture stressing loyalty to a corporate community would be expected. Indeed, these are features of this model. Yet, the 1990s show that this model also brings with it significant limitations on creativity and growth, which may undermine the corporate goals.[216] Lifetime employment may not be achievable under this system and capital investment returns may be dampened.[217]

The Managerial market-state, according to Bobbitt, "consists of three basic elements: free and open markets within a regional trading framework, a government that provides a social safety net and manages a stringent monetary policy, and a socially cohesive society."[218] Protections are provided for ownership of private property but ownership must also contribute to the public good.[219] Labor and management are required to share power on corporate boards.[220] This system creates the "stakeholder company," that attempts to balance all of the actors affected by a corporate action, although corporate ownership is typically closely held through a centralized commercial bank.[221] Bobbitt describes the goal of the Managerial Model as that of social equality whereas the goal of the Mercantile Model is social stability. Governmental intervention tends to be more aligned with labor in the Managerial Model as opposed to capital in the Mercantile Model.[222] Although cohesion is also as important for the Managerial Model as it is for the Mercantile Model, the states following the Managerial Model, according to Bobbitt, tend to pay productive workers well and provide generous welfare benefits for those who do not have a job.[223] Beyond Germany, practitioners of the Managerial Model include India, Turkey, and Egypt.[224]

It follows that corporate governance regimes under a Managerial Model would encourage the long-term goals of justice and consensually endorsed notions of the affected stakeholders. This system would be fortified by equipping stakeholders, particularly employees, with power to influence decisions. Yet, this approach also limits creativity and, paradoxically, limits the influence of actors that could be affected because the number of actors is so large that a delegation of responsibility is inevitable. Thus, it is questionable whether this model would achieve its goals.

Admittedly, there is not a perfect system – any organizational and political theory will carry with it contradictory elements. Yet, there are at least three reasons why each model should be open to influences from the others.

First, each model is potentially a target of terrorism. For example, Japan suffered from attacks via sarin gas and the USA suffered via the attacks of September 11, 2001. If a sense of justice mitigates some of the passions that might trigger such attacks, then each system needs to consider how to mitigate its weaknesses. This is not to argue that mitigating weaknesses will prevent terrorism or that the weaknesses cause terrorism. Yet, improving the perception of the justness of capitalism and democracy may help moderate social frustration.

Second, each model contains concerns for its own constituents. As Bobbitt argues:

each model must contend with its own sort of alienation: the lowest paid workers in the United States are vastly worse off than high wage earners, while the unemployed in Europe can get by on welfare benefits alone but have little prospect of a job. By contrast, the Mercantile Model maintains artificially high employment rates, at wages that reflect far less disparity between the highest and lowest paid. The unavoidable cost is in productivity and efficiency, which sets the stage for a new kind of alienation, that of the young from the old.[225]

Finally, the framework implicit in this tripartite delineation is that to prevent the models from becoming too ideological and competitive, "it is to be hoped that informal private networks that cross international lines – for example, the large multinational corporations developed in the twentieth century, or the extensive social networks developed by overseas Chinese in East Asia and the USA, or global nongovernmental organizations – will supply the links necessary to prevent the growing divergence of the three models of the market-state."[226]

The next question concerns how this will be accomplished. Given the realities that the major governing paradigms are variations of democracy, it seems appropriate to examine the benefits democracy may offer.

IV. Participation and voice: corporate contributions to balances of power

A starting point for the role corporations may be able to play in working toward peace lies, surprisingly, in the realist and neo-realist notion of foreign relations. As Donald Kagan assesses, realists believe that states and nations seek as much power as they can, whereas neo-realists understand the behavior of states in terms of security.[227] The notion of security connects with governance, in that "the evidence suggests that the most secure are those that provide the greatest human security to their populations. Weak states are those that either do not, or cannot, provide human security."[228] Moreover, this very weakness may lead political elites into a vicious cycle that further weakens their security and that of their people. Securing the interests of the people requires responding to human needs, and thus:

involves the institutionalization of participatory processes in order to provide civil and political rights to all peoples. It requires adequate legal enforcement and judicial protection to ensure that all citizens are treated equally and fairly and that their human rights are safeguarded. It involves equitable economic development and opportunities so that economic and social rights can be provided. Finally, it entails the development of pluralistic norms and practices that respect the unique cultures and identities of all. Sustainable peace also requires education of dominant groups to convince them that their own long-term security interests lie in the development of a just society.[229]

In this light, corporations may have a self-interest in undertaking action to alleviate the pressures that cause conflict, if for no other reason than to limit the likelihood of the angry empowered person of which Friedman writes.[230] More generally, if the arguments made to support these correlations are true and understood, there may be a genuine interest among corporate leaders to aspire to orient policies to mitigate the likelihood of bloodshed.

This does not require, however, enactment of an international law that would mandate corporations to alter their governance practices. As Myles McDougal claims:

In pluralistic and rapidly changing communities, rules are always complementary, ambiguous, and incomplete.... The conception of "international law" as a body of rules regulating the interrelations of nation-states is doubly myopic. Beyond the infirmities of its over-estimating of the potentialities of rules, it has infirmities in the scope of the activities it seeks to make subject to law.[231]

Rather, a model is proposed that would encourage corporate boards to work toward a goal of peace in addition to shareholder profit. There are at least five reasons for this approach.

First, clear aims are important for establishing ethical governance mechanisms designed to foster peace. As David Messick notes, psychological studies demonstrate the unsurprising finding that human beings tend to value self-interest over that of others.[232] Because of this tendency, Messick argues that clearly identified ethical principles provide a check against individuals simply acting in self-interest.[233] Ethical principles create a distance that make individuals consider additional consequences of their actions.[234]

This would seem to hold true in corporations. If the only criterion for success is increasing shareholder value, then it is more difficult for other considerations, which may have an impact on profitability in the long term, to enter into a decision-maker's calculus.[235] It has been argued that the corporate constituency statutes effective in many US states, which generally allow managers to take into account the impact of actions on non-shareholder constituents, are superfluous because a well-run company always takes these stakeholder interests into account.[236] The difficulty, however, is that not all companies are well run.[237] A clearly identified responsibility to stakeholders increases the likelihood that such interests will be considered.

Indeed, a clearly identified goal has also been called an "aim" by another business ethicist, Joshua Margolis.[238] Margolis argues that according to psychological studies, a clearly defined "aim" acts to discipline the mind to hold it accountable.[239] This Aristotelian notion suggests that corporations must do more than be aware of the possibility that their actions could contribute to a social milieu that fosters violence. To the extent that they wish to avoid contributing to bloodshed, they must establish a goal, an aim, or a *telos* that commits the corporation to practices that lead to the achievement of that goal. In doing so, corporations may be aspiring to more than one goal. To some, this is dangerous because it requires the corporation to serve too many masters.[240] Yet, well-run corporations already serve shareholders, public opinion, bondholders, and other stakeholders; serving multiple masters is part of the job.[241] For example, shareholder value proponents Daniel Fischel and Frank Easterbrook note that the *New York Times* is free to pursue goals of profitability, as well as journalistic excellence.[242]

Second, this raises the question of the role of law. Advocating an international law requiring corporations to adopt this kind of *telos* is not the solution. Rather, there is an opportunity for corporations to include peace as a goal and, perhaps, corporations could be encouraged to do so through various domestic and international incentives. Domestically, this could be in the form of tax incentives. Internationally, it could be in the form of trade benefits. The difficulty with a law that mandates specific rules, however, is the diversity of communities. Even natural law, which "did achieve conceptions of a larger community of humankind and of a common human nature and, hence, made immense contribution to the development of transcommunity perceptions of law"[243] also tends to apply ethnocentric interpretations as universal principles, although there can be diversity of beliefs. It is important to identify overarching aspects of human nature and human events, but it is also important to do so in a way that does not disempower individuals in particular communities. The characteristics of good governance stress the importance of giving individuals within a community an opportunity to voice their concerns. Thus, the overarching governance structure should allow for this type of contribution from those affected by a corporate action.

There is also a question regarding just how much law individuals need. For instance, Gandhi, a British-trained lawyer, thought that 90 percent of people did not need to be governed.[244] The only people who required governance were the top 5 percent, comprised of the avaricious, the hoarders, and the black marketers, and the bottom 5 percent, comprised of common thieves, murderers, and gangsters.[245] Rather than attempt to provide specific rules for all individuals, a corporate governance regime could provide a forum through which individuals may have a voice in their own affairs while protecting against the mere few who may cause problems.

The third reason for corporations to consider pursuing peace as part of their business identity relates to the power of corporations generally. Although, it is important not to confuse economics and politics, nevertheless, it is difficult to dispute the proposition that multinational corporations are powerful. A central premise of democratic institutions is that power requires checking; otherwise that power can do evil as well as good.[246] In an advanced nation-state, an effective government may check corporate power,[247] but when a large multinational corporation does business in an emerging market, the relative power of the corporation vis-à-vis the government suggests that governmental regulation of business may be insufficient to prevent corporate misconduct.[248]

Fourth, peace literature and psychological research emphasize the importance of taking action. In corporations, people work side by side with others with whom they may not otherwise have an association. Sociologist Ronald Takaki, for instance, argues that it is at work that Americans encounter diversity that they may not find in neighborhoods, churches, families, and voluntary associations.[249] If countries are more prone to ethnic violence and civil strife than they are to cross-border warfare, then a business can serve as a place where individuals can make connections with those of other identities that they might not otherwise have made. This can have an important psychological and consequential effect. Ervin Staub reports that:

Psychological research shows that people learn by doing. As people help or harm others, they become increasingly helpful or capable of inflicting increasing harm.... The evolution of helping and harming is also apparent in real life. Many heroic rescuers of Jews in Nazi Europe started out intending to help an acquaintance for a short time, but then became increasingly helpful and committed. Helpful actions create psychological change in the actor.[250]

Business organizations provide a place where individuals can develop face-to-face relationships with others. They can form a sense of community with those whom they previously did not know. This kind of learning-by-doing has roots in other kinds of peace-related projects. For instance, the "Seeds of Peace" program annually brings approximately four hundred Arab and Israeli teenagers to Maine.[251] One of the first steps is simply to give the enemy a face.[252] Creating personal relationships breaks through stereotypes,[253] and thus creates a sense of community with individuals who have a stake in the preservation of that community.[254] Further, giving the young a voice – that is, the opportunity to speak – empowers them.[255]

The fifth reason that corporations should include peace as a corporate goal is that it creates a sense of community. Aristotle long ago emphasized the connection between individual virtue and the role of the community in forming the moral character of someone who possessed excellent virtue.[256] A community is held together by a common goal or set of goals.[257] If people learn by action, as described above, then the action taken within an organization will impact how people behave generally.[258] If a corporate community is held together by a pursuit of profit that may inadvertently rationalize corruption and abuse, that culture may have deleterious effects on individual behavior. The nature of the corporate community is the critical link between ethics and governance because it is in the governance of a community where certain kinds of behaviors are produced, both positive and negative. Thus, it is important to specify more clearly the attributes a corporation would possess if it were to link governance, ethics, and sustainable peace.

Conclusion

Anthropologists have studied the attributes of peaceful societies. These studies may provide insights applicable to corporate communities. Leslie Sponsel, for instance, in studying ethnographies of the Semai,

Chewong, Buid, and Piaroa peoples concludes that there is a positive correlation between gender equality and peace.[259] David Fabbro provides a comprehensive list of the attributes absent as well as those present in peaceful communities.

Peaceful communities, according to Fabbro, do not have inter-group violence or feuding, internal or external warfare, a threat from an external enemy group or nation, social stratification, a full-time political leader or centralized authority, or police or military organizations.[260] Peaceful societies, he argues, tend to be small and open communities with face-to-face, interpersonal interactions. They possess an egalitarian social structure, maintain a generalized notion of reciprocity, reach decision-making through group consensus, and encourage nonviolent values throughout the community.[261] This list seems to argue against a hierarchical community structure and, given the size and bureaucracy of multinational corporations,[262] the likelihood of the other attributes related to interpersonal interaction and equality seem remote. Indeed, Nicholas Carr notes that globalization works directly against these tendencies even though it pays lip service to a diluted dimension of cooperation in terms of teams. Carr states that:

> To be flexible is to lack attachments . . . but forming connections and communities, holding on to one's olive trees – just being able to decorate your own desk and call it your home away from home – is one of the most defining characteristics of human beings. Globalization, by creating a world in which we are constantly being asked to break such connections, reinvent ourselves, think in the short term and stay flexible, sets us all adrift and leaves everyone feeling like a temporary worker . . . we don't bond with others; we "team" with them. We don't have friends; we have contacts. We're not members of enduring nurturing communities; we're nodes in ever-shifting, coldly utilitarian networks.[263]

In contrast, globalization connects people so that they cannot be aloof to the rest of the world. Nevertheless, the efficacy of face-to-face interaction in open communities has been demonstrated in school mediation situations in which:

> Disputants are few in number, know each other well through daily interaction, and expect to have an ongoing relationship after the dispute is resolved. Close to 90 percent of those involved in school peer mediating, for example, report satisfaction with the agreement and are willing to honor their agreements over time. In contrast, peer mediation with large groups is often less effective.[264]

The anthropologists are onto a conception of mediating institutions. Mediating institutions are relatively small organizations where moral identity and behavior is formed. The size of the organizations is critical because "people can be themselves only in small comprehensible groups."[265] Large business organizations, like any large organization,[266] may contain economic efficiencies, but "most of the sociologists and psychologists insistently warn us of... dangers to the integrity of the individual when he feels as nothing more than a small cog in a vast machine and when the human relationships of his daily working life become increasingly dehumanized."[267]

A central difficulty of modernity is its emphasis on large organizations. As Michael Nagler writes, the shift from *oikos* networks to that of *poleis* in ancient times and further codified by the nation-state system "led in similar ways to less peace in their respective systems... because they swept aside valuable modes of association that had evolved in their respective cultures while creating a framework for even larger polarizations."[268] Yet, small-scale organizations do not necessarily have the perspective by which they can adopt policies for a common good, such as the environment. Homer-Dixon, for instance, argues that small groups in developing countries may already have wealth, power, and status because of their extant social position.[269] As such, they frequently have narrow interests that can impede efforts to establish social institutions, laws, and other broader interests of society.[270] In critiquing Robert Putnam, whose civic association reliance would challenge the above argument, Homer-Dixon finds that "social segmentation can tear apart the civic networks essential to building and maintaining social trust and good will; in turn, loss of trust and good will removes a critical restraint on the severity and harmfulness of the social competition that arises from greater environmental scarcity."[271]

The central task of a governance system that fosters peace, then, will be to develop a sense of community by empowering individuals and providing them with a voice in the institutions that govern them. It will also be necessary for the governance system to provide transparency so that actions of any one group or multiples of groups can be evaluated and called to account.[272] It is therefore proposed that corporate governance systems that incorporate the attributes of peaceful societies as the criteria by which they are evaluated can help achieve both economic progress and social harmony.[273] The idea is one desired by Gandhi, who saw "individuals would voluntarily serve the family, the family would serve the state, the state the nation, and the nation the entire world."[274] More specifically, Gandhi hoped that:

In this structure composed of innumerable villages there will be ever-widening, ever-ascending circles. Life will not be a pyramid with the apex sustained by the bottom. But it will be an oceanic circle whose center will be the individual always ready to perish for the village, the latter ready to perish for the circle of villages, till at last the whole becomes one life composed of individuals ... sharing the majesty of the oceanic circle of which they are integral units. Therefore, the outermost circumference will not wield power to crush the inner circle, but will give strength to all within and derive its own strength from it.[275]

It is plausible to conclude that there are reasons why corporations may be able to contribute to stable societies that foster nonviolent resolution of disputes. They can do so by incorporating aspirations of justice in addition to relying on competitive forces to keep them in check. But how do these notions of corporations correspond to normative constructs for business action? That is, do contemporary notions of corporate governance and ethical business behavior offer room for the goal of corporations being governed with an eye toward sustainable peace?

Business is part of an emerging balance of power equation. Part Two pushes this issue further by addressing the attributes of peaceful societies in this equation and considers whether these attributes, in ways consistent with contemporary business ethics scholarship, could be incorporated into current business frameworks. Building on chapter 2's comparative analysis of the models presented by the USA, Germany, and Japan, chapter 3 delves deeper into these models to determine whether the objective of sustainable peace is more compatible with the governance practices of one regime over another.

Notes

1. See JOHN ELKINGTON, CANNIBALS WITH FORKS: THE TRIPLE BOTTOM LINE OF 21ST CENTURY COMMERCE (1998). See also the work of the United Nations and its Global Compact, which seeks to have corporations address nine principles of good business behavior categorized in terms of human rights, labor issues, and environment. George Kell and David Levin, *The Global Compact Network: An*

Historic Experiment in Learning and Action, 108 Bus. & Soc. Rev. 151 (Summer 2003).

2. J. Lewis Rasmussen, *Peacemaking in the Twenty-First Century, New Rules, New Roles, New Actors*, in International Conflict, Methods and Techniques 23, 30 (William Zartman and J. Lewis Rasmussen eds., 1997).

3. Ibid., at 30.

4. Connie Peck, Sustainable Peace, The Role of the UN and Regional Organizations in Preventing Conflict 9 (1988).

5. Timothy L. Fort and Cindy A. Schipani, *Corporate Governance in a Global Environment: The Search for the Best of All Worlds*, 33 Vand. J. Transn'l L. 824, 842–45 (2000).

6. Ibid., at 844 n. 65.

7. See e.g. ibid., at 836 (discussing the basic tenets of contractarianism).

8. Thomas W. Dunfee, *Corporate Governance in a Market with Morality*, 62 Law & Contemp. Probs. 129, 139–43 (1999).

9. See e.g. Milton Friedman, Capitalism and Freedom 15 (1962).

10. Martin Crutsinger, *Greenspan Warns of Protectionism*, Wash. Post, April 5, 2001, at E3.

11. National Conference of Catholic Bishops, The Challenge of Peace: God's Promise and Our Response 21 (1983).

12. Ibid.

13. Henry Kissinger, Diplomacy 102 (1994).

14. Ibid., at 94.

15. Ibid., at 94.

16. Ibid., at 103.

17. See Jonathan Berman, *Boardrooms and Bombs: Strategies of Multinational Corporations in Conflict Areas*, Harv. Int'l Rev., Fall 2000, at 28.

18. E.F. Schumacher, Small is Beautiful: Economics as if People Mattered 21 (1973).

19. Ibid.

20. F.A. Hayek, The Fatal Conceit: Errors of Socialism (1988).

21. Eugene V. Rostow, Toward Managed Peace: The National Security Interests of the United States, 1759 to the Present 3 (1993).

22. Ibid., at 4.

23. *How Deep is the Rift? Not a Shot Fired, But the Iraq War Has Already Inflicted Needless Collateral Damage on the Western Alliance*, The Economist, February 15, 2003, at 11–13.

24. Rostow, above n. 21, at 35.

25. Ibid., at 36–37.
26. Lee A. Tavis, Power and Responsibility: Multinational Managers and Developing Country Concerns 3 (1997).
27. Arie M. Kacowicz, The Zones of Peace in the Third World, South America and West Africa: A Comparative Perspective 7 (1998).
28. Ibid., at 7.
29. Ved Mehta, Mahatma Gandhi and His Apostles (1977).
30. Charles Glass, *Chronicle of a War Foretold: On the Move With Ahmad Chalalsi, The Man Who Would be King*, Harper's Magazine, July 1, 2003, at 57.
31. See Rostow, above n. 21.
32. See generally Kacowicz, above n. 27.
33. Ibid., at 9.
34. Ibid., at 9.
35. Ibid., at 25.
36. Ibid., at 31.
37. Ibid., at 31.
38. Ibid., at 51–52.
39. See ibid., at 99.
40. Ibid., at 14.
41. Thomas L. Friedman, The Lexus and the Olive Tree 248 (2003).
42. Samuel Huntington, The Clash of Civilizations (1996).
43. Philip Bobbitt, The Shield of Achilles: War, Peace and the Course of History 8 (2002).
44. I. William Zartman, *Introduction: Toward the Resolution of International Conflicts*, in Peacemaking in International Conflict: Methods & Techniques 15–16 (I. William Zartman and J. Lewis Rasmussen eds., 1999).
45. See Rasmussen, above n. 2, at 23.
46. Ibid., at 23.
47. Ibid., at 33.
48. Michael T. Klare, *Redefining Security: The New Global Systems*, in Approaches to Peace: A Reader in Peace Studies 54 (David P. Barash ed., 2000).
49. Amartya Sen, Development as Freedom 10 (1999).
50. Patricia Werhane, Persons, Rights, and Corporations (1985).
51. Videotape: "Your Job or Mine: Green Giant's Decision to Move to Mexico" (University of Michigan Business School documentary, 1991) (on file with authors).
52. Ibid.

53. Ibid.
54. Ibid.
55. William M. Evan and R. Edward Freeman, *A Stakeholder Theory of the Modern Corporation: Kantian Capitalism*, in *Ethical Theory and Business* 97, 101–05 (Tom L. Beauchamp and Norman E. Bowie eds., 7th ed., 2002).
56. Ibid.
57. See e.g. Fort and Schipani, above n. 5, at 824, 842–45; Timothy L. Fort, *The Corporation as Mediating Institution: An Efficacious Synthesis of Stakeholder Theory and Corporate Constituency Statutes*, 73 NOTRE DAME L. REV. 173 (1997).
58. Steven Cohen, *Stakeholders and Consent*, 14 BUS. & PROF. ETHICS J. 3, 13 (1996).
59. See FRANK H. EASTERBROOK AND DANIEL R. FISCHEL, THE ECONOMIC STRUCTURE OF CORPORATE LAW (1991).
60. See ibid.
61. See MICHAEL KEELEY, SOCIAL CONTRACT THEORY OF ORGANIZATIONS (1988).
62. See Steven R. Salbu, *Insider Trading and the Social Contract*, 5 BUS. ETHICS Q. 313 (1995).
63. See THOMAS DONALDSON AND THOMAS W. DUNFEE, TIES THAT BIND (2002).
64. Thomas Donaldson and Thomas W. Dunfee, *Toward a Unified Conception of Business Ethics: Integrative Social Contracts Theory*, 19 ACAD. MGMT. REV. 252 (1994).
65. Allen Cowell, *Belfast Shipyard Loses Bid to Build Queen Mary 2 and Many Jobs*, N.Y. TIMES, March 11, 2000, at C1.
66. See *Texaco in the Ecuadorian Amazon*, in ETHICAL THEORY AND BUSINESS 637 (Tom L. Beauchamp and Norman E. Bowie eds., 7th ed., 2002).
67. Donald O. Mayer, *Community, Business Ethics, and Global Capitalism*, 38 AM. BUS. L.J. 215 (2001).
68. ROBERT SOLOMON, ETHICS AND EXCELLENCE 105 (1993).
69. Mayer, above n. 67, at 253.
70. See FRIEDMAN, above n. 41, at 158.
71. Timothy L. Fort and James J. Noone, *Gifts, Bribes and Exchanges in Pre-Market Economies: Lessons for Pay E-Commercia*, 33 CORNELL INT'L L.J. 515, at 521–22 (2000).
72. Peter Finn, *For This President Bush, A Newly Booming Warsaw*, WASH. POST, June 16, 2001, at A17.
73. See generally Peck, above n. 4.
74. Ibid., at 17.

75. Ibid.
76. Ibid.
77. See generally FUKAYMA, THE END OF HISTORY AND THE LAST MAN (1992) (arguing that with the fall of communism, there is an "end of history" in which ideological battles have now been won by liberal democracies).
78. R.J. RUMMEL, POLITICAL SYSTEMS, VIOLENCE, AND WAR, in APPROACHES TO PEACE, AN INTELLECTUAL MAP 354 (W. Scott Thompson and Kenneth M. Jensen eds., 1991).
79. Ibid., at 354.
80. Ibid., at 354–55.
81. Ibid.
82. Ibid.
83. Ervin Staub, *The Psychological and Cultural Roots of Group Violence and the Creation of Caring Societies and Peaceful Group Relations*, in APPROACHES TO PEACE: A READER IN PEACE STUDIES (David P. Barash ed., 1999).
84. Peck, above n. 4, at 17.
85. FRIEDMAN, above n. 41, at 207.
86. Ibid.
87. See SPENCER R. WEART, NEVER AT WAR, WHY DEMOCRACIES WILL NOT FIGHT EACH OTHER 3 (1988).
88. Ibid., at 3.
89. Ibid., at 13.
90. Dean V. Baps, *A Force for Peace*, 55 INDUSTRIAL RESEARCH (April, 1972).
91. WEART, above n. 87, at 44.
92. Ibid., at 44.
93. Ibid.
94. Ibid., at 89.
95. Ibid., at 90. Although the first two reasons why democratic governments do not engage in conflict with each other characterize democratic countries in terms of pluralism and compromise, the third reason is not so flattering. Weart argues that a country that is not republican can be characterized by a democratic republic as an outgroup that is "inherently treacherous and aggressive." Ibid. There is an extensive literature demonstrating that violence often accompanies the characterization of another group of people as an outgroup. Thus, it is important to recognize that democratic republics are not themselves more peaceful, but they may be more peaceful toward like-minded political regimes. See ibid., at 90.
96. Ibid., at 15.

 97. Ibid., at 20.
 98. Timothy L. Fort and Cindy A. Schipani, *The Role of the Corporation in Fostering Sustainable Peace*, 35 VAND. J. TRANSN'L L. 389, 434 (2002) (noting anthropological studies of peaceful societies which have characteristics of face-to-face interaction, non-hierarchical decision-making, gender equity, being relatively small in population, and the practicing of nonviolent dispute resolution).
 99. BENJAMIN R. BARBER, JIHAD VS. MCWORLD, HOW GLOBALISM AND TRIBALISM ARE RESHAPING THE WORLD (1995).
100. Ibid., at 6.
101. Ibid., at 8.
102. Ibid., at 20.
103. Ibid., at 243.
104. Ibid., at 219.
105. WEART, above n. 87, at 228. Economist Jane Jacobs, for instance argued that she could divide political beliefs into two categories in which one focused on hierarchy, discipline, obedience, and vengeance and the other focused on collaboration, negotiation, avoiding force, and respecting contracts. These commercial virtues seem similar to republican virtues, but present a series of issues. Can commerce thrive without stability? More deeply, if respect for contracts and property is a central requirement for capitalism to flourish, is not the market dependent upon things like the rule of law, which arises in a manner more complex than via economic rationality? And if stability and the rule of law are nourished by democratic virtues, then what does one do if markets undermine notions of citizenship? See BARBER, above n. 99, at 14.
106. BARBER, above n. 99, at 281.
107. Ibid.
108. Ibid.
109. Ibid., at 282–83.
110. Ibid., at 282.
111. Ibid., at 242.
112. Ibid.
113. See David M. Messick, *Social Categories & Business Ethics*, 1 BUS. ETHICS Q. (Special Issue: Ruffin Series) 149 (1998) (explaining that the arbitrary selection of who belongs in an in or an out group is such that the division could be contractual rather than one based on Burke's sense).
114. HUNTINGTON, above n. 42.
115. Ibid., at 20–29.
116. Ibid., at 21.

117. Ibid., at 32–33.
118. Ibid., at 36.
119. Ibid., at 272–91.
120. Ibid., at 126–27.
121. Ibid., at 129 (noting the differences with which Chinese treat Chinese foreigners and non-Chinese foreigners).
122. This is why former Secretary of State, Madeleine Albright, was offered the presidency of the Czech Republic.
123. HUNTINGTON, above n. 42, at 20 (quoting Michael Dibdin). See also Robert W. Merry, *The Great Friedman-Huntington Debate: The Coming Clash Between Two Fundamentally Opposed Post-9/11 Global News,* 17 THE INTERN'L ECON. 12 (February 22, 2003).
124. HUNTINGTON, above n. 42, at 21.
125. Ibid., at 47.
126. Ibid., at 64.
127. Ibid., at 61.
128. Ibid., at 58.
129. Ibid., at 92.
130. Ibid., at 93.
131. Ibid., at 92–93.
132. Ibid., at 94.
133. Ibid., at 94.
134. See generally AMY CHUA, WORLD ON FIRE: HOW EXPORTING FREE MARKET DEMOCRACY BREEDS ETHNIC HATRED AND GLOBAL INSTABILITY (2003).
135. Ibid., at 9.
136. Ibid., at 19.
137. Ibid., at 31.
138. Ibid., at 23–30.
139. Ibid., at 32.
140. Ibid., at 33–34.
141. Ibid., at 35–37.
142. Ibid., at 36–38.
143. Ibid., at 42.
144. Ibid., at 46.
145. Ibid., at 54.
146. Ibid., at 66.
147. Ibid., at 78.
148. Ibid., at 97.
149. Ibid., at 111.
150. Ibid., at 112.
151. Ibid., at 16.

152. Ibid., at 14.
153. Ibid., at 123.
154. Ibid., at 129.
155. Ibid., at 138.
156. Ibid., at 170.
157. Ibid., at 211.
158. Ibid., at 230–31.
159. Weart, above n. 87, at 15.
160. Chua, above n. 134, at 193–94.
161. Richard A. Gonce, *John R. Lommon's "Five Big Years"*, 61 The Amer. J. Econ. & Soc. 755 (2002).
162. Chua, above n. 134, at 194. We do not take the position that a rollout of free market democracy should take the form it did in the USA with deprivations of voting to African-Americans and to women.
163. Ibid., at 268.
164. Hernando de Soto, The Mystery of Capital: Why Capitalism Triumphs in the West and Fails Everywhere Else (2000). See ch. 1 for a discussion of DeSoto's arguments.
165. Chua, above n. 134, at 279–81. For example, Chua argues for the elimination of child labor.
166. Ibid., at 285.
167. Bobbitt, above n. 43.
168. Ibid., at 215–16. Bobbitt describes the differentiation as follows:

> The princely state promised external security, the freedom from domination and interference by foreign powers. The kingly state inherited this responsibility and added the promise of internal stability. The territorial state added the promise of expanding material wealth, to which the state-nation further added the civil and political rights of popular sovereignty. To all these responsibilities the nation-state added the promise of providing economic security and public goods to its people. The failure of the Soviet Union to live up to this expectation, as much as any other cause, contributed to its delegitimation in the eyes of its nation. Very simply, the strategic innovations of the Long War will make it increasingly difficult for the nation-state to fulfill its responsibilities. That will account for its delegitimation. The new constitutional order that will supercede the nation-state will be one that copes better with these new demands of legitimization, by redefining the fundamental compact on which the assumption of legitimate power is based.

169. Ibid., at 162.
170. Ibid., at 187.
171. Ibid., at 187.

172. Ibid., at 175.
173. Ibid., at 175.
174. Ibid., at 539.
175. Ibid., at 5–17.
176. Ibid., at 5–6.
177. Ibid., at 24–25.
178. Ibid., at 24–64.
179. Ibid., at 222 (citing in particular the UK policies of Tony Blair as well as the US policies).
180. Ibid., at 222.
181. WEART, above n. 87, at 11.
182. Ibid.
183. Ibid.
184. Ibid. This designation of democracy has been applied to situations where two-thirds of men vote. Although there are historical reasons to accept and normative reasons to support this as good, it may be desirable to think more broadly of citizenship as democracies developed in the twentieth century with increased universality of suffrage.
185. Ibid., at 12.
186. Ibid., at 14. Weart provides a caveat that these republics must be "well-established." By this, he means that toleration of dissent has persisted for at least three years. Ibid., at 21. He indicates that the differentiation feature between oligarchic and democratic republics is that oligarchic republics suppress a "crucial domestic enemy" whereas democracies are more embracing of them. Ibid., at 18.
187. Ibid., at 15.
188. See ibid. (the designation of these features being particularly prevalent in democracies is the authors' addition to Weart's argument).
189. BARBER, above n. 99, at 276.
190. See ibid., at 278.
191. Ibid., at 281.
192. See PETER BERGER AND RICHARD JOHN NEUHAUS, TO EMPOWER PEOPLE (1977) (noting that in small, mediating structures, human beings find their public face).
193. BARBER, above n. 99, at 281.
194. Ibid.
195. WEART, above n. 87, at 16.
196. Ibid., at 16–17.
197. BOBBITT, above n. 43, at 24.
198. Ibid., at 669.
199. Ibid.
200. Ibid., at 670.

201. Ibid., at 671.
202. Ibid., at 670–71.
203. Ibid., at 675.
204. Ibid., at 671.
205. Ibid., at 670.
206. Ibid., at 675.
207. Ibid.
208. Ibid., at 674
209. Ibid., at 671.
210. See e.g. Timothy McCormally, *Responding to the New Age of Transparency*, INTERN'L TAX REV., June 1, 2003, at 1.
211. See generally Depree Grant and Gerry Grant, *Earnings Management and the Abuse of Materiality*, J. OF ACCOUNTANCY, http:www.fin.ntu.edu.tw/~mingshen/Earnings%20Management%20and%20Earnings%20Quality.pdf; Andy Server, *Dirty Rotten Numbers*, FORTUNE 74, February 11, 2002.
212. BOBBITT, above n. 43, at 675.
213. Ibid.
214. Ibid., at 672.
215. Ibid.
216. See Michael Bradley, et al., *The Purposes and Accountability of the Corporation in Contemporary Society: Corporate Governance at a Crossroads*, 62 LAW & CONTEMP. PROBS. 9, 65–67 (1999).
217. Ibid.
218. BOBBITT, above n. 43, at 672–73.
219. Ibid.
220. Ibid.
221. Ibid.
222. Ibid.
223. Ibid., at 674.
224. Ibid.
225. Ibid., at 675.
226. Ibid.
227. DONALD KAGAN, ON THE ORIGIN OF WAR AND ONE PRESERVATION OF PEACE 6–7 (1995).
228. PECK, above n. 4, at 16.
229. Ibid., at 16.
230. See generally FRIEDMAN above n. 41.
231. Myres S. McDougal, *Law and Peace*, in APPROACHES TO PEACE: A READER IN PEACE STUDIES 134 (David P. Barash ed., 1999).
232. David M. Messick and Max Bazerman, *Ethical Leadership and the Psychology of Decision Making*, 37 SLOAN MGMT. REV. 9 (no. 2, 1996).

233. Ibid.
234. Ibid.
235. LaRue Tone Hosmer, *Why Be Moral? A Different Rationale for Managers*, 4 Bus. Ethics Q. 191 (1994).
236. See e.g. Joseph Biancalana, *Defining the Proper Corporate Constituency: Asking the Wrong Question*, 59 U. Cin. L. Rev. 425 (1990); William J. Carney, *Does Defining Constituencies Matter?*, 59 U. Cin. L. Rev. 385 (1990).
237. See generally Timothy L. Fort, Ethics and Governance: Business As a Mediating Institution (2000).
238. Joshua Margolis, *Psychological Pragmatism And the Imperative of Aims: A New Approach for Business Ethics*, 8 Bus. Ethics Q. 409 (1998).
239. Ibid.
240. Fort, above n. 237, at 180.
241. Ibid., at 180.
242. Easterbrook and Fischel, above n. 59, at 36.
243. McDougal, above n. 231, at 138–39.
244. Ved Mehta, Mahatma Gandhi and His Apostles 214 (1977).
245. Ibid.
246. Friedman, above n. 9, at 3.
247. Cf., Cass Sunstein, Republic.com (2001) (warning about the influence of corporate power even in places like the USA as demonstrated through debates over campaign finance reform).
248. See e.g. William E. Newberry and Thomas N. Gladwin, *Shell and Nigerian Oil*, in Ethical Issues in Business: A Philosophical Approach 522 (Thomas Donaldson and Patricia H. Werhane eds., 7th ed., 2002) (noting the influence of Shell on the government of Nigeria).
249. Ronald Takaki, A Different Mirror: A History of Multicultural America 426 (1993).
250. Staub, above n. 83, at 140.
251. John Wallach, The Enemy Has a Face: The Seeds of Peace Experience 3 (2000).
252. Ibid., at 7.
253. Ibid., at 39.
254. Ibid., at 7.
255. Ibid., at 52–53.

Empowering, even if you don't change another person's opinion, is literally giving somebody a voice. A voice doesn't mean that you always get heard. In the adult world, we don't always get heard. But sometimes we simply need to speak. This sense of empowerment is an important step for the youngsters. They are able to move beyond self-pity and come closer to acknowledging their own role in the conflict. They are forcing the people around them to understand their pain, even to experience it. Yet if the youngsters themselves don't re-experience the pain as well, if they simply force it onto other people, they are not able to make a connection between their suffering; they only reaffirm the righteousness of their cause. As long as they continue to pursue that argument, they remain closed to the other side. The youngsters are not accepting or acknowledging what those around them have to share.

256. See Aristotle, Nichomachean Ethics (Martin Ostward trans., 1962); Alasdair MacIntyre, After Virtue (1981); Robert Solomon, Ethics and Excellence: Cooperation and Integrity in Business (1993); Jeffrey Nesteruk, *Law and the Virtues: Developing a Legal Theory for Business Ethics*, 5 Bus. Ethics Q. 361 (1995); Bill Shaw and John Corvino, *Hosmer and the "Why Be Moral" Question*, 6 Bus. Ethics Q. 373 (1996).
257. See Amitai Etzioni, The New Golden Rule (1996).
258. See Sandra L. Robinson and Anne M. O'Leary-Kelly, *Monkey See, Monkey Do: The Influence of Work Groups on the Antisocial Behavior of Employees*, 41 Acad. Mgmt. J. 658 (1998) (concluding that individuals tend to follow the prevailing norms of the organization in which they work).
259. Leslie E. Sponsel, *The Natural History of Peace: The Positive View of Human Nature and its Potential in* A Natural History of Peace 95, 103 (Thomas Gregor ed., 1996).
260. David Fabbro, *Peaceful Societies: An Introduction*, 15 J. Peace Res. 67 (1978).
261. Sponsel, above n. 259, at 108.
262. See e.g. Robert Jackall, Moral Mazes: The World of Corporate Managers (1988).
263. Friedman, above n. 41, at 424–25.
264. David Steele, et al., Use Cooperative Conflict Resolution in Just Peacemaking: Ten Practices for Abolishing War 59 (Glen Stassen ed., 1998).
265. Schumacher, above n. 18, at 80.
266. Vaclav Havel compares the attributes of socialist organizations and large corporations because of the diminution of the importance of the individual in each. Fort and Schipani, above n. 5, at 831 (citing Vaclav Havel, Disturbing the Peace: A Conversation with Karel Hvizdala 14 (Paul Wilson ed., 1990)).
267. Schumacher, above n. 18, at 257.

268. Michael N. Nagler, *Ideas of World Order and the Map of Peace*, in Approaches to Peace: A Reader in Peace Studies 378 (David P. Barash ed., 1999).

269. Thomas F. Homer-Dixon, Environment, Scarcity and Violence 118 (1999).

270. Ibid.

271. Ibid., at 122.

272. Schumacher explains the dilemma this way: "[W]e must learn to think in terms of an articulated structure that can cope with a multiplicity of small-scale units." Schumacher, above n. 18, at 80.

273. Ibid., at 80.

274. Nagler, above n. 268, at 380–81.

275. See Nagler, above n. 268, at 380–81 (quoting Gandhi).

II | *Current standards and their amenability to peace*

3 | Corporate governance and sustainable peace

T HIS chapter examines three models of corporate governance and considers whether it is feasible for these models to add peace to their objectives. Corporate governance has been defined generally as a top management process, that when operating correctly, should manage value creation and value transference among various corporate claimants in a way that ensures accountability toward those claimants.[1] Claimants can be broadly defined to include all of those with a stake in corporate operations, including shareholders, customers, employees, suppliers, creditors, and the local community.[2] This definition emphasizes both efficiency and fairness.

There are several different ways to approach issues of corporate governance. In the USA, dating at least back to 1919, when the famous case of *Dodge v. Ford*[3] was decided, the approach has been a model that has focused primarily on the shareholder, the residual claimant of the corporate form. In *Dodge v. Ford*, the court specifically stated that a "business corporation is organized and carried on primarily for the profit of the stockholders."[4] In other regimes, such as Germany and Japan, the interest of society and employees have historically been the first focal point. All three regimes have had both prosperous as well as trying times.

Although these models, in some way or another, consider interests of various constituencies, including society at large, these models do not focus on the goal of peace as a general aspiration. Yet consideration of peace as a goal is not a far stretch from what the regimes are already doing, and has the potential for far-reaching effects not only for society at large, but also for business.

I. Corporate-governance regimes of competing market-state models

Chapter 2 outlined three models by which Philip Bobbitt describes emerging market-state democracies.[5] This section considers those models in the context of their corporate governance regimes.

A. *The US model*

Consistent with Bobbitt's characterization of the Entrepreneurial Model to describe the US model of democracy,[6] corporate governance in the USA has focused on the rights of shareholders. The concern in the USA has been that separation of ownership from control may allow management to act in its self-interest to the detriment of the firms' owners. To protect against this possibility, the law has imposed fiduciary duties on corporate officers and directors, including the fiduciary duties of care and loyalty.[7] Fiduciary duties are owed to the corporation and its shareholders.[8] These duties require corporate officers and directors to exercise the degree of care in the conduct of corporate affairs of the reasonably prudent person acting in similar circumstances. This includes the duty to act in good faith and in the "honest belief that the action taken is in the best interests of the corporation."[9] The law of fiduciary duty also mandates that officers and directors put corporate interests ahead of personal interests, in other words, avoid conflicts of interest.[10] The emphasis on fiduciary duties and relationships indicates that shareholder protection is a paramount objective expressed in the legal realm of corporate governance.[11]

The US model is, however, multi-faceted. According to the American Law Institute (ALI) Principles of Corporate Governance, even if corporate profit is not enhanced, corporations may also take into account "ethical considerations that are reasonably regarded as appropriate to the responsible conduct of business."[12] A corporation may attain this objective by "devot[ing] a reasonable amount of resources to public welfare, humanitarian, educational, and philanthropic purposes."[13] Most states endorse this position by statutorily permitting corporations to take into account the interests of stakeholders, other than shareholders, when making corporate decisions. The New York statute, for example, expressly provides that interests of other constituencies, including current employees, retired employees, customers, and suppliers, may be considered when making corporate decisions.[14] Connecticut goes further to require the interests of other constituencies be taken into account in decision-making.[15] Connecticut appears to be somewhat of an aberration though, because most states simply permit rather than require these considerations.

Yet, stakeholder constituency statutes are not without controversy. On their face, they appear to promote goals of corporate social responsibility, even if the goal of shareholder gain might not be served. As such, they have come under fire. Some commentators prefer a more direct anchor to shareholder interests. Nicholas Wolfson,[16] Oliver Williamson,[17] James W. Walker, Jr.[18] and James D. Cox[19] have expressed this view, criticizing the ALI approach. According to Wolfson, there is no empirical support for the ideas in the ALI model, and inclusion of these other objectives compromises efficiency and invites various trade-offs.[20] Perhaps even more troubling is M.J. Pritchett, III's argument that the ALI's optional approach might give management a free reign to promote its self-interest under the guise of promoting social responsibility.[21]

The debate surrounding alternate constituency statutes in the USA indicates that the US approach to corporate governance is an approach based in shareholder primacy, but includes a fair amount of flexibility. That is, although shareholders still appear to be the most important constituent, the interests of other constituencies are significantly recognized.

Irrespective of the arguments surrounding the weight US corporate boards and management can place on the interests of stakeholders who are not shareholders, the US shareholder primacy model has created a corporate governance system that values transparency and disclosure. These values are evident in both the federal and state securities laws and federal insider trading rules.

Federal and state securities laws are based on the premise that shareholders are entitled to full and fair disclosure regarding the nature of their investments. To effectuate full and fair disclosure, the federal securities regime, regulated by the Securities Act of 1933[22] and the Securities Exchange Act of 1934,[23] requires corporations to disclose all significant aspects of their business before they can issue securities to the public. The Securities Act of 1933 mandates this disclosure by requiring any corporation wishing to sell its securities to the public to register its securities with the Securities and Exchange Commission.[24]

As part of the registration process, the corporation must prepare a prospectus, disclosing the material aspects of the corporation's business to potential investors.[25] The prospectus must include not only the price of the securities to be sold but also detailed financial information about the corporation,[26] as well as information concerning its management and key shareholders.[27] After a corporation's securities have been registered, the duty to disclose information continues both on an annual basis[28] and in the event of a major change in corporate affairs.[29] If the corporation sells its securities in private transactions rather than in a public offering, registration is not necessary, but in certain circumstances the corporation must still make similar disclosures to the purchasers of its securities.[30] To supplement the federal rules, each state has its own disclosure rules concerning the sale of a corporation's securities within the boundaries of its state.

Strict penalties for noncompliance with the securities laws attempt to ensure US corporations take these disclosure and transparency rules seriously. A corporation that issues securities under a registration statement containing omissions or material misstatements exposes its officers, directors, underwriters, and certain experts to civil liability.[31] In addition, a corporation can be held liable for damages for any loss sustained by a purchaser of securities issued under a registration statement with omissions or material misstatements. In certain circumstances, a corporation may also be subject to criminal fines and penalties.

The ban on insider trading also highlights the importance US corporate governance regimes place on transparency and disclosure. The purpose of insider trading rules is to prevent trading of securities on the basis of material, nonpublic, confidential information.[32] The classic case of insider trading arises when a corporate insider buys or sells shares of the corporation using confidential information obtained through the insider's corporation position and, as a result, earns a profit. Federal common law has expanded the notion of insider trading to include "outsider trading." Outsider trading occurs when a corporate insider learns that his or her firm (or a related firm) will do something that affects the value of another corporation's stock and trades using this information.[33] Thus, insider trading emphasizes the US notion of disclosure by imposing on corporate insiders the duty to "abstain or disclose."[34] This duty to abstain or disclose requires a corporate insider with confidential information to either abstain from trading or disclose the information to the investing public. Failure to adhere to federal insider trading rules subjects the trader to liability under the Securities and Exchange Act Rule 10b-5. The US emphasis on transparency and disclosure has been reaffirmed in light of the corporate accounting scandals of 2002[35] and the passage of the Sarbanes-Oxley legislation,[36] with implications for corporate governance yet to be determined.

B. *The German model*

Bobbitt characterizes the German form of democracy as a Managerial Market State.[37] This system creates a "stakeholder company."[38] It is therefore not surprising to find that the corporate governance model in Germany emanated from very different roots than the US model. German corporate law, as originally enacted in 1935, did not mention the shareholder as a constituency to be served by the corporation. Instead, it provided that "[t]he managing board is, on its own responsibility, to manage the corporation for the good of the enterprise and its retinue (*Gefolgschaft*), the common weal of the folk (*Volk*) and realm demand (*Reich*)."[39] It was not until 1965 that shareholders were mentioned.[40] In contrast to the USA, shareholders are only one of many constituencies served by the German corporate form.

Unlike the US model, one constituency that appears to have some prominence in the German corporate governance model is the employee. Firms with more than 500 employees are required to utilize a two-tier board structure, with a supervisory board providing oversight and general corporate strategy and a management board providing more of a day-to-day management oversight function.[41] If the firm has more than 2,000 employees, 50 percent of the supervisory board must consist of employee representatives.[42] The remaining 50 percent consists of shareholder representatives.[43] The management board consists almost entirely of the senior management of the company.[44] Board members tend to possess technical skills related to the product, in addition to considerable firm- and industry-specific knowledge. This is because careers are often built up from the ground level and are focused on building asset-specific skills through extensive apprenticeship systems. The result of the two-tiered board structure is explicit representation of stakeholder interests other than interests of shareholders – no major decisions are made without the input of employee representatives.[45] This is in stark contrast to the structure of corporate boards in the USA where the board structure is single-tier and labor has no right of representation. In fact, board members in the USA are required to act in the best interest of the corporation and its shareholders and may not specifically represent any particular constituency.

Banks play a larger role in German corporate governance than they do in the USA. Approximately 14 percent of corporate shares are owned by banks.[46] More importantly, a substantial portion of equity is in the form of bearer, rather than registered stock,[47] and these shares are left on deposit with the *Hausbank* of the corporation, which handles dividend payments and record keeping.[48] Relatively little stock is publicly traded.[49] German law allows banks to vote such equity by proxy, unless depositors explicitly instruct banks to do otherwise.[50] It appears inertia "work[s] in favor of banks having proxy votes."[51] The power banks hold in German corporations is compounded by many company charters disallowing non-bank shareholders from exercising more than 5 to 10 percent of the total votes, regardless of the proportion of shares they own.[52]

The role of the bank in German corporate governance is also strengthened by financing patterns. German companies, taken as a whole, are more leveraged than their US counterparts.[53] Moreover, instead of relying on public debt financing, German companies finance their debt through bank or intermediated loans.[54] Bank financing of long-term debt has averaged around 50 percent, and this percentage has remained fairly stable throughout the past two decades.[55]

Creditor interests are also protected through corporate governance regimes.[56] Dividend payout rules are designed to protect creditor interests.[57] German law stipulates that dividends may not be paid out from paid-in capital, even if such paid-in capital includes a premium over the face value of equity.[58] This provision makes it difficult for German corporations to undertake share repurchases,[59] and consequently, also makes it difficult for German shareholders to cash out of the corporation.[60]

The incorporation of other stakeholder interests in corporate decision-making affects governance issues. Consider, for example, management compensation. Unlike in the USA, the compensation of German board members must be approved by the shareholders, and this approval affects the amount and structure of compensation. In 1997, CEOs of listed German companies earned about half of what their US counterparts earned,[61] and their compensation usually took the form of fixed salaries and bonuses.[62] In 2001, the average pay of the CEOs of US corporations with sales of over $500 million was $1.9 million, while the average salary of their German counterparts was $455,000.[63] Providing stocks or stock options as part of top management's compensation packages is still fairly rare.[64] German blue chip stocks have recently started offering stock options, and these stock option plans require shareholder approval.[65]

Although corporate governance in Germany explicitly takes into account stakeholder interests other than shareholders, compared to US firms, the quality of disclosure in German firms is poor.[66] The legal and regulatory framework for disclosure is considered relatively lax, compared to that in the USA.[67] An OECD survey of disclosure quality states that, as of 1989, none of the German firms in their sample had complied fully with OECD disclosure guidelines.[68] Similarly, until recently, Germany had no insider trading laws; if insider trading was discovered, the penalty was simply to turn over the profits.[69]

C. Japanese model

The traditional corporate governance model in Japan has, like the German model, emphasized protection of employee interests, as well as creditor interests. Bobbitt describes the model of the Japanese market-state as a Mercantile Model.[70] Accordingly, company growth is the ultimate goal of the Japanese corporation; there has been little incentive to be concerned with shareholder value, *per se*.[71] This may be due in large part to Japan's corporate ownership structure. Historically, firms in Japan have been networked in the form of *keiretsus*, groups of firms that own reciprocal, minority interests in each other.[72] Although the firms in *keiretsus* are usually independent, they tend to have relational and implicit contracts with each other on matters such as ownership, governance, and commercial contracts.[73]

Like Germany, banks also play a significant role in Japanese corporate governance structures. For example, a large main bank that conducts business with all of the member firms and holds minority equity positions in each will be a member of a horizontal *keiretsu*. Although a single bank is not permitted to hold more than 5 percent of a single firm's stock, a group of four or five banks typically may control between 20 and 25 percent of the company's stock.[74] More importantly, the corporation's largest bank shareholder is often the largest creditor. Thus, the interest of the shareholder is in effect the same as the interest of the creditor. Banks, as creditors and shareholders, are more concerned about credit risk than return on stock investment, and thus are more interested in long-term growth than short-term profits. This proportion has remained fairly stable over the past fifteen years, and these closely held shares rarely, if ever, make it into the financial marketplace.[75] Japanese corporations are also typically more leveraged than corporations in the USA. The largest bank shareholder is usually also the largest debtholder in the company.[76]

Quite apart from the lending and the direct intervention roles they play, banks also may facilitate the governance process. They are likely to have a great deal of access to inside information and hence may perform a very effective monitoring role.[77] Given the governance role of the banks, resolution of financial distress is a more informal process in Japan as compared to the USA. This is also true in Germany.

In addition to protection of creditor interests, Japanese corporate governance is concerned with employee interests. Japan has been known for the practice of "lifetime employment."[78] Employees have remained at their firms due to the grant of responsibility and benefits this has provided.[79] The early retirement age in Japan, at age fifty-five, may also contribute to this practice of "lifetime employment."[80]

The structure of boards in Japan is similar to that in the Anglo-American system with single-tier boards.[81] However, in terms of membership, the Japanese board is similar to the German board. A substantial majority of board members consist of current or former senior and middle management of the company.[82] The board in theory is elected by the shareholders, but typically it is chosen by an operating committee, which usually only consults with the largest shareholders.[83] Fukao notes that nearly 78 percent of Japanese directors are promoted from among employees.[84] Thus, unlike in the USA, outside directorships are rare. The one exception to outside directorships is the main banks. Their representatives usually sit on the boards of the *keiretsu* firms with whom they do business.[85] However, unlike in Germany where employees and sometimes suppliers tend to have explicit board representation, the interest of stakeholders other than management or banks are not directly represented on Japanese boards.[86]

Management compensation is not a matter for shareholder approval in Japan. Compensation, including that of top management, relies on salaries and bonuses.[87] Stocks or stock options are rarely used as a basis for remuneration. Total compensation of top managers, including bonuses, is about six to eight times the compensation of the most highly paid blue-collar worker and about seventeen times that of the average worker.[88] A managerial labor market along US lines, especially for mid-career workers, is thin.[89]

Share ownership in Japan is concentrated and stable. Individual share ownership in Japan, like in Germany, has steadily declined from about 50 percent in the 1950s to about 20 percent at present. Thus, in a typical Japanese firm, approximately two-thirds of the equity is owned by banks, insurance companies, and other corporations.[90] Internal management styles and control systems in Japanese firms rely on building long-term, consensus-based relationships and are characterized by a great deal of informal interactions, personal relations, and information-sharing among relatively culturally homogeneous individuals.[91] There is an apparent reliance on trust, reputation-building, and face-saving considerations as the basis for contracting,[92] in part because the corporation is seen by its employees as much as a social entity as an economic entity.[93] Companies thus rely on face-to-face contacts to resolve issues.[94] Japanese firms in the larger, organized sector of the economy emphasize lifetime employment and building human capital by maximizing asset-specific and relation-specific skills. Lateral inter-functional transfers of managers and horizontal information flows among functions and departments, both within the firm and across firms within the network, are common.[95] Upward mobility within Japanese organizations is carried out through a process of moving up through a cross-functional spiral rather than through a series of promotions within a particular functional area.[96]

Disclosure quality, although considered superior to that of German companies, is poor relative to that of US firms. Although there are rules against insider trading and monopolistic practices, the application of these laws is, at best, uneven and inconsistent.[97]

II. A comparative assessment

To analyze the possibility of adding the goal of sustainable peace as a consideration in corporate governance regimes, the US, German and Japanese alternatives are compared on the basis of the corporation's sense of citizenship and the extent to which corporations equip citizens with voice in the affairs that affect them. In doing so, a model emerges that suggests that corporations of each parliamentary democracy might wish to consider the creation of authentic communities that encourage peace rather than a solipsistic notion of community.

A. Citizenship

For several years, corporate governance scholarship has focused on a debate between contractarian and communitarian approaches.[98] In a nutshell, the contractarian approach argues that the corporation is a nexus of contracts and that transactions therefore should focus on the best interest of the shareholders, the residual claimants of corporate activity.[99] Communitarianism, on the other hand, argues for consideration of a wide range of constituencies, with shareholders being one in a group of many stakeholders to be affected by corporate actions.[100] In an important sense, this debate is related to Barber's concern, addressed in chapter 2, regarding whether corporations create a McWorld that undermines democratic values by undermining a sense of citizenship.[101] In a contractarian paradigm, which underscores the US version of Bobbitt's Entrepreneurial Model, notions of citizenship are likely to revolve around legally enforceable duties, such as obeying laws generally and, more particularly, those laws that protect investors through fiduciary duty, securities, and other regulation.[102] Thus, according to Bobbitt and Barber, the notion of citizenship in this model is thinner than in other models. Yet, the US variant on this model has been flexible enough to accommodate various notions of citizenship, as evidenced by adoption of statutes in a majority of states that explicitly permit management to consider the interests of constituencies other than shareholders when making decisions.

The notions of citizenship may be more pronounced in the German (Managerial) and Japanese (Mercantile) models, however.[103] In both models, there is an expectation that corporations will serve a societal good. In Germany, this is explicit in a stakeholder model that directs the company to be concerned with society generally as well as employees and creditors.[104] In Japan, this is tied to cultural notions of solidarity and employee enmeshment with work.[105] In both regimes, there is a clear understanding that corporations are part of a greater social fabric and corporate duties require maintenance of that fabric. It would seem that these models could adapt to the introduction of an additional goal, such as a commitment to the public good of sustainable peace.

B. Voice

As important as the societal purposes of corporations is the extent to which the key democratic virtue of voice varies according to each model. Although citizenship notions seem to be more akin to the German and Japanese models, the US model may have greater sensitivity to voice. As discussed above, the US model emphasizes transparency and disclosure.[106] Both transparency and disclosure equip a recipient with the capability to exercise voice. Transparency and disclosure have other significant beneficial effects with respect to sustainable peace. They give other stakeholders information by which they can more powerfully exercise their own voice, even if it is simply in criticism of the corporation. The 2002 corporate scandals demonstrate, however, that the Entrepreneurial Model is not perfect in its accurate disclosure of information. But the scandals demonstrate the need for even better transparency and disclosure, and they also demonstrate another powerful constituent voice, that of management.

Management's voice is also heard strongly in the Mercantile and Managerial Models. In the Mercantile Model, the voice of management, together with that of other corporate leadership represented through cross-ownership mediated through creditors, dominates corporate affairs.[107] Similarly, the Managerial Model emphasizes the voice of creditors and senior management.[108] In addition, the Managerial Model features the institutionally empowered voice of employees through board representation and society in general.[109] Yet, given the diminished degree of transparency and disclosure in both models, the capability of dissent is minimized. Only a few individuals have access to the information necessary to exercise voice meaningfully. Thus, although the Managerial and Mercantile Models are both more communitarian and thus theoretically more conducive to a goal of peaceful stability, they lack a central attribute essential to stability, that of meaningful voice.

C. Mediating institutions

A common problem for each of the regimes, regardless of whether they are more communitarian or more contractarian, is the potential diminishment of the individual in a large society. As noted by Vaclev Havel, both capitalist corporations and socialist plants share the common problem of being so large as to dwarf the individual working for them.[110] This can be true of a large US company, but it can also be true of an organization that is devoted to the entire nation-state of Germany or Japan.[111]

An alternative model of a corporation as a megastructure, is a model of business as a mediating institution, where businesses enable individuals to interact with others in their organization on an interpersonal basis, experience the consequences of their actions, and develop their moral identity.[112] This does not suggest that corporations need to be limited in size, but instead suggests that corporations consciously attempt to structure themselves to have communities within their overall corporate structure.[113] This model could preserve and enhance an authentic community identity of the corporation while at the same time require transparency and disclosure supportive of voice.[114] Moreover, anthropologists have found that the traits of mediating institutions – relatively small, face-to-face interactions, reduced hierarchy, and consensual decision-making – are all attributes of peaceful societies.[115] Thus, a model of communities within corporations is a potential model for peaceful societies.

D. Lessons to counteract cynicism

Dana Muir has addressed the history of employee benefit programs as related to issues surrounding peace.[116] Muir notes that employee benefit programs have been championed as a way to mitigate some of the harshness of capitalism so that employees believe that they were participants in the system rather than being exploited.[117] Muir traces this hope in the USA and in other countries and suggests that these programs offer some degree of participation fostering harmony over competition.[118] Yet, she also warns, that superficial programs, like those that promise employee involvement, participation, and voice, but do not deliver, can sow the seeds of cynicism.[119] This potential problem exists, for instance, in employee programs where putative employee stock owners do not have the right to vote their shares of stock.[120] Thus, if the promise of voice, participation, ownership, transparency, disclosure or other attributes that appear to be beneficial to harmonious relationships is not fulfilled, there is a risk of increasing cynicism and distrust. At the same time, Muir's analysis shows that there are models for such extensions that could prove to be beneficial for connecting business and peace.

Conclusion

It does not appear that there is anything inherently problematic about connecting corporate governance and sustainable peace in the US, German, or Japanese corporate governance systems. In each country, there is openness to values in addition to profitability. Although maximizing shareholder value is an important, overriding goal for a corporation and for the nation-states establishing the legal governance rules for the society, Anglo-American law allows for consideration of non-shareholder constituents, Japanese law provides room for concern for the social aspect of work, and German law is concerned for employee and social welfare in business management. Although questing for sustainable peace may sound idealistic, it is also a goal that may benefit corporations by contributing to more stable societies.

This quest will require some adaptations of corporate governance, but in a world where access to powerful technologies of violence is relatively easy, it becomes incumbent on corporations, as well as other citizens, to consider what contributions they might be able to make for reasons of survival. With this in mind, chapter 4 will address four proposed contributions corporations can make toward sustainable peace. These involve: (1) fostering economic development; (2) exercising track two diplomacy; (3) adopting external evaluation principles; and (4) nourishing a sense of community.

These contributions provide direction to the goals corporations might pursue in a way that seems compatible with current practices. Moreover, they are very much in line with the practices offered by contemporary normative scholarship in the field of business ethics. Chapter 4 thus provides a way for corporate leaders to think specifically about a structure that is aligned with the currently prevailing legal rules, yet focuses more directly on a goal of sustainable peace.

Notes

1. Timothy L. Fort and Cindy A. Schipani, *Corporate Governance in a Global Environment: The Search for the Best of All Worlds*, 33 VAND. J. TRANSN'L L. 829, 832 (2000); Michael Bradley, et al., *The Purposes and Accountability of the Corporation in Contemporary Society: Corporate Governance at a Crossroads*, 62 LAW & CONTEMP. PROBS. 9, 61 (1999).

2. See e.g. Fort and Schipani, above n. 1, at 833; Bradley, et al., above n. 1, at 11.
3. *Dodge v. Ford*, 170 N.W. 668, 684 (Mich. 1919).
4. Ibid., at 684.
5. See ch. 2. See also PHILIP BOBBITT, THE SHIELD OF ACHILLES: WAR, PEACE, AND THE COURSE OF HISTORY 2002.
6. Ibid.
7. See e.g. Michael Bradley and Cindy A. Schipani, *The Relevance of the Duty of Care Standard in Corporate Governance*, 75 IOWA L. REV. 1 (1989).
8. Ibid.
9. Franklin Balotti and Mark J. Gentile, *Commentary from the Bar, Elimination or Limitation of Director Liability for Delaware Corporations*, 12 DEL. J. CORP. L. 5, 14 (1987); Bradley and Schipani, above n. 7, at 25.
10. Bradley and Schipani, above n. 7, at 25.
11. AMERICAN LAW INSTITUTE, PRINCIPLES OF CORPORATE GOVERNANCE: ANALYSIS AND RECOMMENDATIONS, Section 2.01 (1994).
12. Ibid., at Section 2.01 (b) (2).
13. Ibid., at Section 2.01 (b) (3).
14. N.Y. BUS. CORP. LAW § 717(b)(1) (2002).
15. CONN. GEN. STAT. § 33-756 (2002).
16. Nicholas Wolfson, *A Critique of the American Institute Draft Proposals*, 9 DEL. J. CORP. L. 629, 631 (1984).
17. Oliver E. Williamson, *Corporate Governance*, 93 YALE L.J. 1197, 1219 (1984).
18. James W. Walker, Jr., *Comments on the ALI Corporate Governance Project*, 9 DEL. J. CORP. L. 580 (1984).
19. James D. Cox, *The ALI, Institutionalization, and Disclosure: The Quest for the Outside Director's Spine*, 61 GEO. WASH. L. Rev. 1212, 1212–13 (1993).
20. Wolfson, above n. 16.
21. M.J. Pritchett, III, Comment, *Corporate Ethics and Corporate Governance: A Critique of the ALI Statement on Corporate Governance Section 2.01(b)*, 71 CAL. L. Rev. 994, 1001, 1007 (1983). Others have criticized the ALI Project for opposite reasons. These detractors contend that the ALI approach simply articulates current business practice and is thus unnecessary. See e.g. Donald E. Schwartz, *Defining the Corporate Objective: Section 2.01 of the ALI's Principles*, 52 GEO. WASH. L. REV. 511, 514 (1984).
22. The Securities Act of 1933, 15 U.S.C. § 77a et seq. (2002).
23. The Securities Exchange Act of 1934, 15 U.S.C. § 78a et seq. (2002).

24. See the Securities Act of 1933 § 5(a).
25. See ibid., Regulation S-K, 17 C.F.R. 229 et. seq. (2002).
26. 17 C.F.R. 229.200, 229.300.
27. Ibid.
28. The Securities Exchange Act of 1934 § 12(g)(1) (requiring the annual filing of Form 10-K which discloses much the same information as required in the Securities Act registration).
29. Ibid. (requiring the filing of Form 8-K disclosing specified events such as bankruptcy, merger, or a director's controversial resignation).
30. See Rule 502(b)(2) (an issuer selling to any non-accredited investors in 505 or 506 exempt transactions must furnish its most recent annual report and any subsequent Exchange Act filings, along with a brief description of the particular offering, otherwise the disclosure requirements vary with the size of the offering).
31. See SEC. EXCH. ACT R. 10b-5.
32. This is should be compared with the absence of a duty of candor by corporate insiders to shareholders in anonymous trading markets as explained in *Goodwin v. Agassiz*, 186 N.E. 659 (Mass., 1933) (rejecting a duty of insiders to shareholder except in face-to-face dealings).
33. See *O'Hagan v. United States*, 521 U.S. 642 (1997).
34. See *SEC v. Texas Gulf Sulphur*, 401 F.2d 833 (1968).
35. See Timothy McCormally, *Responding to the New Age of Transparency*, INTERNATIONAL TAX REV., June 1, 2003, at 1.
36. Sarbanes-Oxley Act of 2002, Pub. L. No. 107-204, 116 Stat. 745.
37. BOBBITT, above n. 5.
38. Ibid.
39. Bradley, et al., above n. 1, at 52; Detlev F. Vagts, *Reforming the "Modern" Corporation: Perspectives from the German*, 80 HARV. L. REV. 23, 40 (1966).
40. Vagts, above n. 39, at 40–41.
41. Bradley, et al., above n. 1, at 52.
42. Ibid., at 53 (indicating that the other 50 percent of the supervisory board consists of shareholder representatives).
43. Ibid.
44. Stephen Prowse, *Corporate Governance in an International Perspective: A Survey of Corporate Control Mechanisms Among Large Firms in the United States, the United Kingdom, Japan, and Germany*, BANK FOR INTERNATIONAL SETTLEMENTS ECONOMIC PAPERS NO. 41, 43 (July, 1994).
45. Ibid.
46. ORGANIZATION FOR ECON. COOPERATION AND DEV., ECONOMIC SURVEYS: GERMANY 87 (1995) (hereinafter OECD GERMANY).

47. Mitsuhiro Fukao, Financial Integration, Corporate Governance and the Performance of Multinational Corporations 27 (1999).
48. See OECD Germany, above n. 46, at 89.
49. Edward S. Adams, *Corporate Governance After Enron and Global Crossing: Comparative Lessons for Cross National Improvement*, 78 Ind. L. J. 723 (2003).
50. Fukao, above n. 47, at 27.
51. Bradley, et al., above n. 1, at 54.
52. Fukao, above n. 47, at 27.
53. Bradley, et al., above n. 1, at 54.
54. Prowse, above n. 44, at 93.
55. See OECD Germany, above n. 46, at 93.
56. German bankruptcy law is also skewed toward protecting creditor interest. See Fukao, above n. 47, at 123.
57. Bradley, et al., above n. 1, at 55.
58. Fukao, above n. 47, at 120.
59. Ibid.
60. See e.g. Bradley, et al., above n. 1, at 54.
61. Kevin J. Murphy, 3 Handbook of Labor Economics tbl. 4 (1999).
62. Bradley, et al., above n. 1, at 53.
63. Eric Pfanner, *Anger Stirs in Britain Over CEO's High Salary*, Int'l Herald Trib., April 18, 2003, at 11.
64. Ibid.
65. Bertrand Benoit, *German Groups Face Investor Confrontations*, Financial Times, May 22, 2003, at 29.
66. Ibid., at 55.
67. Ibid.
68. See Prowse, above n. 44, at 29.
69. Bradley, et al., above n. 1, at 56.
70. Bobbitt, above n. 5.
71. Adams, above n. 49, at 749.
72. Fukao, above n. 47, at 2. Fukao translates *keiretsus* as "a series of things organized to perform a function." For more details on the Japanese *keiretsu*, see generally W. Carl Kester, Japanese Takeovers: The Global Contest for Corporate Control 54–55 (1991); Erik Berglof and Enrico Perotti, *The Governance Structure of the Japanese Financial* Keiretsu, 36 J. Fin. Econ. 259 (1994); David Flath, *Shareholdings in the* Keiretsu, *Japan's Financial Groups*, Econ. Persp., January–February, 1991, at 20.
73. See Bradley, et al., above n. 1, at 57.

74. FUKAO, above n. 47, at 15.
75. Ibid.
76. Ibid.
77. Ibid.
78. Masahiko Aoki, *Toward an Economic Model of The Japanese Firm*, 28 J. ECON. LITERATURE 1, 11–12 (1990); Ronald J. Gilson and Mark J. Roe, Essay, *Lifetime Employment: Labor and Peace and the Evolution of Japanese Corporate Governance*, 99 COLUM. L. REV. 508, 529 (1999).
79. Wai Shun Wilson Leung, *The Inadequacy of Shareholder Primacy: A Proposed Corporate Regime that Recognizes Non-Shareholder Interests*, 30 COLUM. J. L. & SOC. PROBS. 587, 630 n. 223 (1997).
80. Gilson and Roe, above n. 78, at 530.
81. Prowse, above n. 44, at 42.
82. FUKAO, above n. 47, at 14.
83. See Adams, above n. 49, at 748.
84. FUKAO, above n. 47, at 14.
85. Ibid., at 25.
86. Bradley, et al., above n. 1, at 58.
87. OECD GERMANY, above n. 46, at 107, fig. 10.
88. See FUKAO, above n. 47, at 17.
89. Ibid., at 57.
90. Bradley, et al., above n. 1, at 60.
91. Ibid., at 60.
92. Ibid.
93. Ibid.
94. Ibid.
95. Ibid., at 61.
96. Ibid.
97. Ibid.
98. See Bradley, et al., above n. 1 (providing a comprehensive analysis of the various arguments for competing styles of contemporary corporate governance).
99. Ibid., at 9. Contractarianism views the corporation as the collection of contracts that ties stakeholders groups. It is a theory that says the objective of corporate managers is to maximize the residual claims, which is usually evidenced by the firm's common stock.
100. See ibid. Communitarianism views the firm as a more organic entity that has ties to objectives other than profit, such as how the corporation can serve society.
101. BENJAMIN R. BARBER, JIHAD VS. McWORLD, HOW GLOBALISM AND TRIBALISM ARE RESHAPING THE WORLD (1995); see also ch. 2.

102. See Bobbitt, above n. 5; see also ch. 2.
103. See above nn. 38–97 and accompanying text.
104. See above nn. 37–69 and accompanying text.
105. See above nn. 70–97 and accompanying text.
106. See Bradley, et al., above n. 1.
107. See ch. 2 for a discussion of the Japanese version of the Mercantile Model.
108. See ch. 2 for a discussion of the German version of the Managerial Model.
109. See ch. 2 for a discussion of the German approach.
110. See Fort and Schipani, above n. 1 (citing Vaclev Havel).
111. Ibid. (arguing that large communities can inhibit the capacity of an individual to feel that he or she makes an authentic contribution to the welfare of that community).
112. Ibid.
113. See ibid. (arguing for the need of relatively small groupings within the corporation to address the human need for relatively small groups).
114. See generally ibid. (arguing that such a corporate structure might serve as the best of all possible worlds).
115. See David Fabbro, *Peaceful Societies: An Introduction*, 15 J. Peace Stud. 67 (1978).
116. Dana M. Muir, *Groundings of Voice in Employee Rights*, 36 Vand. J. Transnat'l L. 427 (2003).
117. Ibid.
118. Ibid.
119. Ibid.
120. Ibid.

4 | *Ethical business behavior and sustainable peace*

THE gist of the argument that there is a plausible, conceptual relationship among the roles of business, business ethics, and sustainable peace is that multinational corporations can contribute to reduction of violence.[1] Given the challenges confronting the process of globalization, particularly as they apply to business, corporations have the potential to play an important role in contributing to the conditions of sustainable peace. As previously mentioned in chapter 1, business can do this by:

(1) fostering economic development, particularly for the marginalized;
(2) exercising track two diplomacy;
(3) adopting external evaluation principles, such as transparency and supporting a legal system that enforces those principles, i.e. a "rule of law;" and
(4) nourishing a sense of community both within the company and in the areas in which the company is located.

The purpose of this chapter is to sketch this model conceptually and illustrate the themes by the actions of specific companies.

Corporate governance regimes, attentive to the comparative concerns already raised, can integrate these characteristics in culturally appropriate ways. Because the issues involved in this book and particularly in this chapter revolve around assessments of the moral responsibilities of business, Section I assesses the concept of businesses contributing to sustainable peace from the perspective of leading theories from the field of business ethics. Section II discusses the four contributions companies can and already do make toward sustainable peace.

I. Business ethics and sustainable peace

The past ten or so years have seen a flurry of activity as corporations adopt various mechanisms to make their affairs more transparent and undertake various activities that extend beyond the short-term interests of shareholders. A growing number of companies in Organization for Economic Cooperation and Development (OECD) countries have already adopted corporate codes of conduct.[2] A KPMG survey of Canadian firms showed that over 86 percent of firms have already done so.[3] A series of nongovernmental organizations, such as Business for Social Responsibility, The Prince of Wales Business Leaders Forum, the United Nations Global Compact, the Ethics Officers Association, and the Global Reporting Initiative operate programs that broaden ways corporations work with a variety of constituents affected by their actions.[4] In addition, the US Alien Tort Act provides a legal weapon to hold global companies accountable for human rights violations.[5]

Haufler states that concern for avoiding violence is one reason corporations undertake such actions. For instance, she notes that in Nigeria, opponents to the government have sabotaged oil pipelines and held platform workers hostage; similar problems have also occurred in Columbia.[6] Concern for a company's reputation has been linked, at least in part, to statistics that show more than 50 percent of US Fortune 500 companies issue environmental reports.[7] Given this activity, it seems that corporations are at least desirous of portraying an image of being interested in issues of social responsibility.

Critics charge that these efforts do not necessarily help those they purport to help and that the pressures placed by nongovernmental organizations (NGOs) can be problematic because of the nature of NGOs. Professor Ethan Kapstein, argues that "the corporate ethics crusade" has forced executives to take into account human rights, labor, and environmental issues, and that this may be counterproductive.[8] He further argues that this crusade amounts to an attempt to impose one group's values on others, potentially creating conditions for greater conflict rather than more harmony.[9] Moreover, according to Kapstein, when there are differences between visions of corporate responsibility, there should be clear considerations of the advantages and disadvantages of adopting higher business standards; otherwise, all that is left is "ethics by intimidation."[10]

It is difficult, however, to see how challenges to corporate behavior intimidate. NGOs use media publicity, protests, and boycotts to influence behavior, but this seems in line with the interchange of liberal polities. Robust arguments about proper ethical standards are too often marginalized by claims of imposition of values.

Corporations can consider how to improve their governance structures in conjunction with relevant, extant, and applicable regulatory environments, so that corporate contributions to sustainable peace are regularized rather than episodic. Development of corporate communities that regularly practice certain kinds of activities is likely to have a long-term inspirational impact on sustainable peace.

A. Peace as a hypergoal of business

Is it possible to identify a set of specifiable goals applicable to all publicly owned, for-profit corporations independent of their purpose, type, business or legal governance? The term "hypergoals," can reflect the extensive authority and reach of such principles.[11] If corporate hypergoals can be identified, the implications are far reaching.

The extraordinary diversity of types and forms of corporations seems to constrain the search for hypergoals. National approaches to corporate governance vary widely and allow a veritable garden of corporate forms to bloom. In spite of recent tendencies toward greater commonality, the unique attributes of German, Japanese, and US corporations demonstrate the considerable range of extant variations.[12] These national differences have a major impact on the goals of the corporations formed under their regimes. On their face, the diversity of forms of corporate law would seem to counter any claim that a set of hypergoals independent of any legal regime can be identified. Yet this diversity has not prevented scholars from attempting to articulate universal norms applicable to all corporations.

Research on universality in the field of business ethics has focused on the question of identifying the moral responsibilities of all corporations. This topic has attracted considerable interest resulting in commentators developing concepts of "moral minimums,"[13] "hypernorms,"[14] and "guidelines"[15] that establish moral obligations considered binding for global corporations.

In general, those searching for universal moral obligations ground their principles in established moral and ethical theory. Donaldson bases his moral minimums in social contract theory[16] while DeGeorge employs a pluralistic, ecumenical approach reflecting multiple ethical theories.[17] In their search for moral universals, commentators have often found it necessary to limit their analysis to only certain types of corporations and contexts. Thus, DeGeorge makes it clear that his guidelines apply only to US and European corporations doing business in less developed countries.[18] Donaldson limits his analysis to global or multinational corporations.[19] That these thoughtful commentators find it necessary to limit their analysis to certain types of corporations implies that it may be impossible to develop more generalized standards that would, for example, also apply with equal force to corporations from less developed or communist countries.

Yet, the pragmatic limitations recognized by Donaldson and De-George are not based on facts or assumptions that exclude the possibility of identifying hypergoals. Instead they are explicitly offering guidance to a designated set of decision-makers.[20] The next section considers whether there are rational and moral arguments supporting the existence or identification of manifest, universal hypergoals, followed by consideration of whether hypergoals may be compatible with existing legal and economic regimes.

1. The rational, instrumental argument

Business activity requires an environment conducive to sustainability. It cannot reach its full potential in repressive circumstances, such as those that existed for black-market entrepreneurial activities in the USSR.[21] In order to thrive, business demands more than a merely neutral environment. Efficient background institutions must enforce contracts and minimal property rights while policing fraud and theft.[22] In addition, a nurturing business environment requires that its practitioners hold compatible values, particularly those associated with fundamental honesty and promise-keeping.[23] Fukuyama recognizes the importance of societal social capital and extends that recognition to the claim that economic "[c]ommunities depend on mutual trust and will not arise spontaneously without it."[24]

Fukayama and others argue further that in order to thrive, an economy requires the structures of liberal democracy.[25] Many of the most successful economies have been found in democratic, capitalist countries. Yet, counterexamples exist in both directions. China is a non-democratic nation that has had economic success,[26] while India, a practicing democracy, is a mediocre economic performer.[27] Thus, the case has not been made that a particular form of government is an essential prerequisite for a successful business environment. According to Fukuyama, Hayek and others, the keys for a nurturing business environment include: (1) sufficient social capital in the form of individual values conducive to exchange; and (2) efficient background institutions necessary to develop and maintain sufficient levels of essential social capital. Business firms may act in ways that either support or weaken these pillars. The Enron case is instructive. The company aggressively lobbied to exempt itself from regulation by the Commodities Futures Trading Commission and from certain energy regulation oversight.[28] Thus given the opportunity to act in an unrestrained, opaque way, the firm engaged in self-serving opportunism that ultimately contributed to an undermining of business credibility in the USA. These and similar abuses at Tyco, Worldcom, Xerox, RiteAide, and many others, caused a severe negative reaction both in capital markets and among regulators.[29] It is likely that some of the reactions to the loss of credibility will be overbroad and will ultimately constrain business efficiency. Ultimately, though, the blame for any reduction in efficiency must rest not with regulators or investors, but rather with those managers who so aggressively abused the system.[30]

More broadly and systemically, the pervasive corruption that exists today harms background institutions, particularly in developing countries, and often in very significant ways. Transparency International, the corruption-fighting NGO located in Berlin, emphasizes that there is both a demand side and a supply side to corruption.[31] The demand side is reflected in corrupt government officials who request or accept bribes.[32] Corporate managers who willingly pay or even initially offer payments are the complementary supply side.[33] Corruption distorts the decisions of background political institutions, reducing their efficiency. It also weakens public trust in those organizations while at the same time destroying social capital.[34] Corruption is particularly pernicious in its damaging effects on the overall environment for business activity.[35]

Although business has the power to harm the pillars of a nurturing environment, it also has the power to strengthen them. The efficient functioning of background institutions is highly dependent upon honest, fair dealing business firms.[36] Respect for the jurisdiction and authority of the institutions regulating business is also critical, as attested by the experience in many developing countries.[37] Implementation of non-adversarial compliance systems whereby corporations act fairly and openly in host environments is a significant way to support background institutions in developing countries.

2. The social contract

Thomas Donaldson and Thomas Dunfee elaborate a social contracts-based analysis of business ethics introducing the idea of hypernorms.[38] Hypernorms are manifest, universal principles that stand at the top of the pyramid of all ethical and moral norms.[39] They are based upon principles so fundamental that they establish standards by which all other norms are to be judged.[40] Donaldson and Dunfee identify a series of indicators available to help managers determine the existence of hypernorms in the context of a given ethical decision.[41]

Donaldson and Dunfee describe a hypernorm of necessary social efficiency.[42] This hypernorm identifies duties to maintain the efficiency of societal systems, including economic institutions, at a level essential to provide critical social goods necessary to meet minimal needs for health, food, housing and education.[43] These duties apply to business organizations. The basis of the obligation to act in conformity with this hypernorm is similar to the case made above that business organizations need to support the background institutions securing the pillars of a nurturing environment. The obligation to act consistently with the hypernorm of necessary social efficiency would indicate the existence of a hypergoal that businesses need to aspire to reduce the supply side of corruption. Similarly, it would require that a firm act to reduce violence and conflict.

A plausible case can be made for a hypernorm relating to respecting human well-being.[44] An example of an action inconsistent with this hypernorm would be diversion of potentially unsafe tires to developing countries on the assumption that the weaker regulatory framework of the developing countries would be unlikely to identify or effectively sanction the sale of dangerous products. Not all hypernorms translate into hypergoals for business. Only those that pertain to the basic nature and objectives of business firms would qualify.

The implication of mandatory hypernorms is that firms must act consistently with their guidance.[45] Firms have a moral obligation to internalize applicable hypernorms into organizational hypergoals. Dunfee connects the two by arguing that firms should act consistently with three basic principles in response to moral pressures arising from the business environment.[46] According to Dunfee:

(1) The starting presumption is that all corporate actions must be undertaken to maximize shareholder wealth;

(2) In order to maximize shareholder wealth, managers must anticipate and respond to existing and changing moral pressures in their relevant markets that may pose threats to firm strategies, or that may provide competitive opportunities;

(3) Organizations must act consistently with manifest universal moral norms and principles (hypernorms).[47]

Donaldson further considers the implications of a social contracts-based approach for global firms conducting international operations.[48] Donaldson envisions a global social contract setting a minimal floor of responsibility for all business firms.[49] Specifically, global firms have an obligation to enhance the long-term welfare of employees and consumers, minimize the drawbacks of large productive organizations and refrain from violating minimal standards of justice and human rights.[50] These obligations are defined in terms of ten fundamental rights: (1) freedom of physical movement; (2) property ownership; (3) freedom from torture; (4) fair trial; (5) nondiscriminatory treatment; (6) physical security; (7) freedom of speech and association; (8) minimal education; (9) political participation; and (10) subsistence. Global firms should avoid deprivation of any of these rights.[51] In some limited circumstances, Donaldson argues that global firms have an obligation to protect potential victims against deprivation of these fundamental rights by others.[52] Recognizing limits derived from the nature and role of business, Donaldson is unwilling to extend a duty to global corporations to aid those deprived of any of the ten fundamental rights.[53] Donaldson also recognizes that sometimes there are variances in standards among nations due to differing levels of economic development, and is thus willing to accept some lowering of ethical standards so long as core human rights are not violated.[54] Thus, the basic assumptions and concepts of Donaldson's approach are consistent with the identification of specific hypergoals applicable to corporations wherever situated.

3. Normative considerations
There appear to be strong moral reasons for the recognition of hypergoals. Whether following a duty-based approach or an aspirational approach, there appear to be several overarching objectives common

to everyone. By identifying the objectives, they become more concrete for decision-makers. To the extent they are positive, these hypergoals counteract an assumption that human beings are only motivated by a narrowly defined sense of self-interest. Moreover, in identifying hypergoals, a two-tiered analysis can be utilized by corporate decision-makers. The first level is for corporate actions to be made consistent with hypergoals and the norms that have been demonstrably linked to that goal. The second level is to attend to the emotions, sentiments, and interests of those stakeholders immediately affected by corporate action.

A concept of corporate hypergoals is not useful if it is inconsistent with extant legal rules or political expectations. Milton Friedman, the best-known proponent of wealth maximization for shareholders, is equally famous among business ethicists for his important qualification requiring corporations to conform "to the basic rules of the society, both those embodied in law and those embodied in ethical custom."[55] Hypergoals which reflect manifest, documentable universal moral principles are likely to be compatible with law. The most appropriate solution is to note that hypergoals must, of necessity, be generally compatible with the legal regimes in which corporations operate. Therefore it is sensible when identifying hypergoals to consider the constraints likely to result from the legal and political environment. As argued in chapter 3, integrating a hypergoal of peace is consistent with extant corporate governance regimes either implicitly or explicitly.[56]

To understand how corporations approach decisions with implications for sustainable peace, it is useful to begin with a brief discussion of how firms generally manage their ethics strategies. Ethics programs are now ubiquitous in corporate USA and provide an opportunity for developed statements of corporate goals, including those supporting the hypergoal of sustainable peace. Currently, few firms formally state their overall orientation for ethical decision-making, so it is necessary to imply their strategic orientation from their policies and the manner in which their corporate ethics programs are organized. Ultimately, the type of ethics programs and policies a firm employs signals how the firm is, or is not, implementing strategies consistent with sustainable peace.[57]

The overall philosophy underpinning an organization's ethics program may be signaled by language in a parental or unified code. One key difference is the important distinction between ethics programs that are compliance based and those that are integrity based.[58] The former are essentially internal social control systems based upon external standards, typically home-nation laws. They are more likely to involve lawyers in their design and operation. Their principles are often more specific, sometimes supplemented by references to legal restrictions. In contrast, integrity-based approaches are focused on values internal to the firm. The principles may be very general, sometimes expressed as a credo. The values underlying the principles expressed derive from the firm's history and culture. Non-lawyer executives, including senior management, are more likely to be involved in the formulation of the code. These descriptions represent the extremes. Many firms have programs that reflect elements of both types.[59]

B. A descriptive typology of corporate strategy

How then may firms manage specific decisions relevant to the hyper-goal of sustainable peace? Thomas Dunfee has proposed a framework that can help with understanding alternative strategies available to firms in dealing with the difficult cases resulting from cultural conflicts in global transactions.[60] The framework is designed to allow classification of the basic or most fundamental options. There are other options and some firms may combine strategies in a wide variety of ways. The purpose here is limited to discussion of the implications of the alternatives and to showing how they fit into a two-tiered approach to business ethics. The framework classifies corporations as Corporate Imperialists, Corporate Chameleons, Corporate Nationalists, or Corporate Opportunists.[61] A comparison of the four categories is provided in table 4.1.

1. Corporate Imperialists
The Corporate Imperialist tends to be admired by business ethicists. Corporate Imperialists operate on the basis of a strong and clear set of organizational values. Their values are internally derived and focused and will often be developed with primary reference to the history and culture of the firm. Most importantly, the employees will ordinarily buy into these organizational values so that they become widely accepted norms included in global subsidiaries. For US and leading European firms, these values are likely to be reflected in a unified or single code.[62]

Table 4.1 *The Adapted Firm as a Corporate Decision Type*

Type	Decision rule	Source of values	Code	Ethics program	Flag	Ethical orientation
Imperialist Citicorp, Nike	apply own ethical values everywhere	internal, from company culture and history	corporate level, unified specific	integrity oriented, centralized, strong ethics officer	company	ethical absolutist
Chameleon Shell, United Technologies	adopt ethical values from host environments	norms and customs of host environment	decentralized code, separate subsidiary	business practice officers at each subsidiary	host country for each subsidiary	ethical relativist
Nationalist Honda, AT&T, Renault	adopt values of home country for decisions everywhere	laws and customs of home country	references to home country laws	compliance oriented	home country	ethical absolutist
Opportunist Texaco, Northrup, Huntingdon Life Sciences	maximize firm's profits, strategic use of ethics to enhance profits	any source enhancing profits	general, focused on performance goals	if any, results oriented goals	many flags (including pirate) depends on context	ethical egoist
Adapted Levi Strauss	profit-making consistent with relevant marketplace morality and universal norms	firm, local communities and manifest universals	local norms and manifest universals integrated into overall corporate code	integrity oriented, strong ethics officer, role for subsidiaries	UN, national, host, corporate	contractarian

In US firms there is an ever-increasing likelihood that there will be a formal ethics program headed by a senior executive with the title of ethics officer.[63] However, a formal code or ethics program is not an absolute requirement for qualifying as a Corporate Imperialist. There are other means through which organizational values can be established and supported throughout an organization, such as one embedded in a homogenous culture with strong cultural or religious values. Non-code, non-program based approaches would presumably be more likely for global firms with headquarters in Europe and South America, and even more so for global firms based in Asia because of frequent deference to cultural activities.

The fundamental decision principle employed by the Corporate Imperialist is to apply its own values and principles wherever the company does business. It might be imagined as always flying the corporate flag wherever it does business. The company's values dominate and trump all conflicting customs and norms. For example, a strong Corporate Imperialist would rely on its own policies in deciding whether to respond to bribe solicitations and would follow its own rules about gender discrimination to the letter. This decision principle is also stressed in employee training.

The ethics program of the Corporate Imperialist would be integrity based and would likely be managed outside of the legal department. The program would be highly centralized and the foreign operating units would be under the overall jurisdiction of the parent corporation's ethics managers.[64]

2. Corporate chameleons

The second alternative is denoted the Corporate Chameleon. The tendency of these firms is to follow local norms and customs. They do not merely respect local customs and traditions; they fully adopt and internalize them in their foreign operations. If they operate subsidiaries, they tend to see them as local firms within the host environment. Thus, a European Corporate Chameleon would view its Japanese subsidiary as a Japanese firm. The Corporate Chameleons can be recognized by their sub-codes for regional or national subsidiaries. They may also have corporate practice officers assigned to each subsidiary with full responsibility for matters involving ethical standards and practices. Thus, across the Corporate Chameleon organization, there may be substantial variances in norms and in attitudes toward certain types of ethical issues. The norms of the local environments in which the firm operates would become part of the overall value system of the firm. For instance, a strong Corporate Chameleon would accede to local norms in deciding whether to make requested payments and would follow local practice in its treatment of women.[65]

3. Corporate Nationalists

The third category of firm is the Corporate Nationalist. This approach may be thought of as a global version of a compliance-oriented firm.[66] Professor Lynn Paine makes an important distinction between firms that follow a compliance approach to business ethics and firms that emphasize integrity by instilling a "sense of shared accountability among employees" keyed to the organization's values.[67] Firms following a compliance strategy focus on externally imposed standards found in laws, industry codes, and outside sources.[68] In contrast, an integrity strategy is based upon standards reflecting the company's values and aspirations and is typically led by senior management.[69] Corporate Nationalists would tend to be global versions of Paine's compliance-oriented firms that look to the laws and customs of their home country as the primary reference point for resolving cross-cultural issues. Wherever possible, they seek to mold the local environment where they operate to be consistent with the home culture. Certain US and Japanese firms have been perceived as taking this approach. The ethical philosophy would be absolutism, with its absolutist standards derived from the home country's laws and customs.

4. Corporate Opportunists

The final alternative is the Corporate Opportunist. These firms are the business equivalent of the pragmatic politician. All decisions are focused toward achieving a particular immediate or short-term goal. There is no anchor or core set of values designed to be a first point of reference in any given circumstance. Instead of an *a priori* approach to ethics, its managers pick and choose among local customs and practices, organizational norms and home-country values, depending on the circumstances and strategies most likely to enhance the firm's goals. Although some of these firms may have a consistent decision-making matrix for deciding which flag to hoist, it seems plausible that many firms basically approach these issues on an *ad hoc* basis. Thus, a US-based global drug company with research operations in the UK and Singapore may take a vastly different approach to its policies regarding use of animals in research in each country. That is, the strong and vociferous animal rights movement in the UK may require it to be more restrictive in its use of animals for research purposes than in Singapore where the animal rights movement is relatively mute. On the other hand, if the management of that same Corporate Opportunist believes they will have a more productive workforce by applying the same human resources policies concerning leaves and benefits across all subsidiaries, they will do so even in the face of greatly differing local practices. If they find that not following US law concerning gender discrimination will lower wage costs in South American operations, they will ignore the US policies.

Yet, the Corporate Opportunist should not necessarily be painted in a negative light.[70] One explanation for Corporate Opportunist behavior is that the managers of those firms might be seeking a sensible middle ground between the extreme absolutist and extreme relativist positions reflected in the other alternatives. Although they are picking and choosing their policies to fit specific situations, they may be doing so as a means to avoid the criticisms of extreme relativist or absolutist positions.

II. Four contributions to sustainable peace

The typology presented aims to sketch the ways in which corporations act and are thus descriptive. This section proceeds with a normative assessment of ways in which corporations could or should act in order to foster sustainable peace. They involve: (1) fostering economic development; (2) exercising track two diplomacy; (3) adopting external evaluation principles; and (4) nourishing a sense of community.

A. *Fostering economic development*

As discussed earlier in chapter 1, the first thing companies can do to help work toward the goal of peace is what they do best: foster economic development. A World Bank report showed a highly positive correlation between underdevelopment and violence.[71] Intuitively, this correlation makes sense: in an environment of extremely scarce resources, competition for the necessities of life could lead to conflict that could turn violent.[72] Although critics of globalization often downplay the economic advantages corporations bring with them to a country, there are a number of ways in which corporations contribute to more stable societies.

Corporations can make a number of contributions toward stability. First, stability is promoted by providing jobs to residents of the country. For instance, Frigorifico Canelones, a division of Land O'Frost and recognized by the US Secretary of State as a winner of the Award for Corporate Excellence,[73] turned a bankrupt meat processing plant into a profitable Uruguayan operation.[74] The resulting 800 jobs, in a town with no other major employer, provided economic development to an impoverished area.[75] The same kind of experiences holds true in Malaysia, where Motorola, also an award winner, invested $1.1 billion and employed more than eight thousand people,[76] as well as in Ethiopia, through the work of F.C. Schaffer & Associates, a small Louisiana sugar company employing 7,000 people.[77]

George Lodge reports a similar example where corporations have partnered with governments to provide jobs.[78] In 1992, Daimler-Benz (now DaimlerChrysler) found itself in the midst of competing governmental pressures. In Germany, the Green Party pressured the company to be more ecologically responsible with regard to use of renewable fibers in its automobiles.[79] Meanwhile, the government of Brazil demanded that companies expand the local content in their products.[80] In conjunction with a Brazilian antipoverty program, Daimler-Benz constructed a new high-tech factory that made headrests and seats out of coconut fibers from locally grown trees.[81] Ten years later, more than 5,000 people were employed in the project.[82] Not surprisingly, the spillover effects of the project have resulted in higher retention rates for school children because their families could afford to have them study rather than work, people became more active politically, and health care facilities improved.[83]

The second dimension of economic development results from the benefits it provides to the local population.[84] Michael Santoro, studying the effects of business operations in China, found this to be true.[85] Santoro differentiates between companies that establish factories with a commitment to being in the country for the long term as opposed to those who intend to reap the benefits of inexpensive labor for a short period of time before moving onto other locales.[86] Santoro argues that those companies who build for the long term typically provide good working conditions because it is in their financial interest to attract the best possible employees.[87] For example, Frigorifico Canelones supports training and educational programs for homeless and abused youth as well as recreational programs for children.[88] Ford Motor Co., also a winner of the Award for Corporate Excellence, sponsors AIDS-related programs in Africa, working with local healthcare authorities.[89] Xerox, which won an Award in 1999, not only contributes to programs for children, but also addresses another stakeholder group – employees – by providing counseling programs designed to help lift people out of poverty in Brazil.[90] In addition, it offers space in its facilities for local cultural activities.[91] These companies are investing for the long term.

The third aspect of economic development relates to resource transfer. This transfer could be in technological development or development of human managerial capabilities, or both. Motorola's work in Malaysia exemplifies both of these features. By building a high-tech manufacturing plant, it provided technological know-how to the Malay people,[92] providing the foundation for additional economic development. Moreover, the managers of Motorola's facilities are not US expatriates, but citizens of Malaysia,[93] thereby managerial skills in addition to technological know-how, are transferred to the country. F.C. Schaffer & Associates exhibits these characteristics with a bit of a novel twist. After devastating floods racked Ethiopia, the company shared its expertise in running sugar refineries with competitors.[94] It continues to provide consulting services for the design of co-generation, environmentally safe power plants.[95]

A fourth dimension of economic development relates to the simple task of paying taxes. The benefit to society provided by tax revenues, however, is dependent on the quality of the government collecting the taxes and the use made of them. Assuming just governmental regimes, tax revenues may be quite beneficial in helping to provide a much-needed infrastructure.

B. Exercising track two diplomacy

Nation-states compete for power. Corporations can play a role in mediating some of the contests for power through what has become known as "track two" diplomacy. This can happen in three different ways.

In general, due to diplomatic protocol, governmental leaders talk with other governmental officials. Not only does this practice limit the number of available conversation partners, it limits the flexibility of negotiations between leaders of countries in the midst of a dispute. Utilizing track two diplomacy, an outside party can relay unofficial messages to governmental officials. For instance, *New York Times* columnist Thomas Friedman notes that the 2002 nuclear showdown between India and Pakistan was mitigated, at least in part, by business executives convincing the Indian government of the need to come to a peaceful resolution of the conflict.[96] Although governments with interest in expanding power may still bluster at each other, businesspeople have a perspective on the security and stability that should be factored into political equations. Businesses, in short, can play a role.

Business executives are in a good position to engage in these activities because they are part of a middle-range leadership in a society.[97] Individuals who are leaders in the fields of education, business, agriculture, and health, to name a few, are generally respected and thus have the capability to deal directly with governmental officials as well as society.[98] Because their power is not based on politics or military capability, these leaders can exercise their power from other sources, such as the relationships they have with others.[99] These relationships, including professional associations and other structures of civil society, allow them to interact with a broader range of actors than may governmental leaders.[100]

A second kind of track two diplomacy involves the perception of businesses as unofficial ambassadors for their countries. As already explained, there are many actions corporations can take to be constructive citizens in their communities. These actions range from environmental responsibility to respect for human rights to promoting educational opportunities for employees and others beside.

Finally, a third kind of track two diplomacy might occur in the workplace, due to the opportunity provided for different people, perhaps even ethnically conflicting, to work together toward a common goal. For instance, Futureways, a company in Ireland, purposely hires both Protestants and Catholics, in an approximate fifty-fifty ratio, for its workforce.[101] Not only do these often-warring populations work together for the goal of a profitable company, they also talk about their experiences with each other. Seeds of Peace, a nonbusiness example of the same philosophy, brings together Israeli and Palestinian youths to a summer camp in New England each year in order to demonstrate that "the enemy has a face."[102] People typically walk away from the experience with the view that the outgroup member is a person rather than an enemy.[103] Other examples of this would occur through firms bringing people together from different groups for work even without promoting explicit discussion of their differences.[104] Corporations, particularly those with employees from diverse ethnic groups, therefore, have a significant opportunity, and perhaps a self-interested responsibility, to provide a forum for contributing to more harmonious relationships between groups.

C. Adopting external evaluation principles

With modern communications technology, it is difficult for any company to be immune from the potential glare of publicity and investigative reporting. Yet some companies welcome transparency. Transparency requires willingness to have actions evaluated by others. Although not all transparency is universally good – there are balances that need to be struck between transparency and privacy – accountability to external standards may contribute toward a social environment where violence is less likely to occur. Two aspects of transparency are particularly worth noting: transparency with respect to corruption and support of a rule of law.

Chapter 1 explained a correlation between corruption and violence.[105] John Noonan, an expert in the study of bribery, once noted that bribery is typically hidden unless the leaders are so brazen and secure in their power that they can flaunt their corruption.[106] Keeping corruption hidden denies the opportunity to raise meaningful objections to the practice. As ethicists Thomas Donaldson and Thomas Dunfee have argued, keeping bribery hidden skews the efficient distribution of resources because decisions are not made on the basis of a merit that can be publicly evaluated and justified, but on the basis of a kind of power that is immune from evaluation.[107] Corruption stifles the voice of people evaluating the action.

No one company is going to solve a country's corruption problems. Yet, companies can try to limit the corruption endemic to a country and also work to try to change the enforcement of laws so that anti-bribery laws are effective. Indeed, this is the recommendation of the OECD to promote efficient markets.[108] Moreover, if there is also a correlation between corruption and violence, then the cause of peace could be beneficially supported by corporate efforts to limit or eliminate corruption.

This commitment to support laws that reduce or eliminate bribery lead to the second kind of evaluative commitment: support of the rule of law. One of the lessons from the emerging economies of central and Eastern Europe after 1989 is that those countries that quickly established a commitment to a rule of law, particularly in terms of contract and property protection, flourished more than others. Even the free market is not completely free – it requires a legal and moral infrastructure to work. This has been acknowledged by devout free marketers such as F.A. Hayek[109] and Milton Friedman.[110] Perhaps even more interestingly, economist Jane Jacobs has argued that those countries with strong commercial values, including values of promise-keeping in contracts, respect for property, and nonviolent, negotiated resolution of disputes tend to be more peaceful.[111]

There are at least three ways in which companies can support a rule of law. First, they can comply with legal requirements.[112] Unfortunately, not all laws are just. Nevertheless, compliance with most legal requirements typically yields good results. Second, they can educate people about laws and how they can be useful. Johnson & Johnson currently operates a program in rural China in conjunction with the Chinese government and UNICEF that teaches healthcare workers about regulations pertaining to childbirth.[113] This is done with the hope that by increasing the knowledge of midwives and other health-care providers the quality of medical services may be improved. Thus, by teaching people about law, living conditions may be improved.

A third way is more controversial. As outlined in chapter 1, Hernando de Soto has made a provocative argument claiming that nearly $1.3 trillion lay in the hands of the very poor around the world.[114] The problem is that the poor are unable to access those resources because the most valuable assets are their homes and the legal title requirements in emerging countries often do not allow the marginalized to acquire clear title to their homes.[115] Without title, the poor cannot exercise the most basic entrepreneurial strategy of taking out a home loan to start a business. As a result, there is enormous potential that could be unleashed if certain kinds of property systems – akin to the Homestead Act in the USA in the early part of its history[116] – are developed. This is, admittedly, a legal reform dependent upon governmental action, but corporations have influence, often significant influence in law reform. De Soto's point is that such reforms would improve the plight of the marginalized, which itself would contribute to stability, and also provide more economic opportunity as the creative potential of the poor is unleashed. The market is not a zero-sum game, but grows with increased economic activity.

D. *Nourishing a sense of community*

The neorealist school of foreign policy argues that people are concerned with filling their needs, including their psychological needs of security and identity.[117] The post-Cold War era has made this point painfully on numerous occasions. According to one study, more than 90 percent of post-Cold War conflicts have occurred within the borders of an existing nation-state and the battles have been fought on the basis of ethnic, cultural, and religious identity.[118] Religious historian Scott Appleby analyzed fundamentalist religious movements in all faiths and argues that when a group feels threatened, i.e. their security in their identity is at risk, extremism can take hold.[119] Extremism is not necessarily violent, but it can be.

In a rare cross-cultural study of attributes of peaceful societies, anthropologist David Fabbro notes that those societies that are relatively small, have a great deal of face-to-face interaction, allow for most, if not all, community members to participate in decisions, are relatively egalitarian, including gender equity, practice nonviolent resolution of conflicts, and are geographically separated from others, tend to be more peaceful.[120] There is not much a company can do to influence geographical separation, but there are things companies can do to mirror other attributes of peaceful societies.

First, businesses can become genuine communities. More specifically, companies can become mediating institutions. There are both moral and neurobiological reasons for why human beings develop their values in relatively small groups – mediating institutions – such as family, neighborhood, religious groups, and voluntary associations.[121] Large bureaucratic companies do not necessarily lend themselves to being communities, but creating a connection among members of an organization can provide a sense of security and identity to the people who work there.

As part of this process, the second thing companies can do is to encourage the use of voice by those in the company. Having a voice in the promulgation of rules is a critical, identifying characteristic of a democracy. Although subtle, when a company committed to quality processes insists that its employees speak up when they recognize a product defect, these employees learn something about participatory governance, and this knowledge may spill over into the political realm. This could be significant because, as noted in chapter 2, democratic countries rarely, if ever, go to war with each other.[122]

For instance, after World War II, some Americans went to Japan and helped to redevelop Japanese industry. Several theorists, including W. Edwards Deming, brought with them management techniques that had been rejected in the USA.[123] Their emphasis on quality management became pervasive in Japan and is credited with the resurgence of the Japanese economy during the latter part of the twentieth century.[124] Central to the management technique is an emphasis on clear statistical measurements of manufacturing capabilities, but equally important is the concept that all members of an organization have a responsibility to articulate problems and that management has a responsibility to listen.[125] These two factors create what Deming calls "pride in workmanship,"[126] an antidote to many costs and quality issues.[127] Cultivating pride of workmanship, Deming notes, is more important than company gymnasiums, tennis courts, and recreational areas.[128] This pride of workmanship theme relates to the employees' sense of participation and voice in their work. This suggests that knowing how to exercise voice and how to participate in productive collective decisions is not an exclusively Western value. Fatema Mernissi further emphasizes the cross-cultural importance of notions of participation.[129] Contradicting a popular perception that Islam is inimical to democracy, Mernissi argues that at its roots, Islam is open to expression of personal opinion in religious matters.[130] She concedes that for centuries, Islamic leaders have emphasized *din* (religion), *i'tiqad* (belief), and *ta'a* (obedience) over *ra'y* (personal opinion), *ihdath* (innovation, modernization), and *ibda* (creation), but claims that notions of participation and voice in the workplace may have further resonance in the Islamic world as well.

If concepts of voice and participation resonate in a culture supposedly at significant odds with Western values, then voice and participation may be values embedded deeply in all cultures. Creating workplace structures conducive to their expression, whether in Japan, the USA, or in the Muslim world, seems to be a task that if undertaken with local sensitivity can be linked to the goal of sustainable peace.

Yet another example of the importance of participation and voice and its cross-cultural resonance comes from Africa.[131] Countering contemporary arguments that African tradition lends itself toward authoritarian regimes, George Ayittey argues that African cultures traditionally use highly participatory village councils to reach consensus on problems and to resolve disputes.[132] Some African countries such as South Africa are reviving these traditions.[133] Participation in collective decisions are the norm and history of Africa.[134] The authoritarian dictatorship predominated only in the latter part of the twentieth century. In the West, Germany had no substantial collective national history of democracy in the mid-twentieth century but adapted its corporate law to require employee participation in governance decisions of large companies.[135] Although political regimes may have authoritarian dimensions, the idea of participation and voice is one that can find resonance in a wide variety of cultural examples.

Employee benefits scholar Dana Muir begins a recent article with the following quotation: "Today on the world's horizon are seen the forces of political and economic reaction . . . fomenting revolution against private capitalism and free enterprise until thrown out of equilibrium."[136] This quotation is not a statement from a post-September 11, 2001 commentator nor related to the 2003 war in Iraq, but is instead taken from a 1939 US Senate Report studying whether profit-sharing might be a response to World War I and the economic woes of working men and women resulting from the Great Depression.[137] Muir traces the connection between employee ownership, participation, and sustainable peace in the USA back to 1794 when a glassworks business owner viewed it appropriate to extend democratic principles to industrial operations as well as to political processes.[138] Since then others have argued for profit-sharing plans as an antidote to potential strife.[139] Muir notes that by creating a culture of participation and empowerment, corporations can also contribute to democracy.[140] Muir further surveys legislation around the world and finds profit-sharing programs in France, Egypt, and Russia.[141]

Conclusion

Corporations can foster harmonious relationships by acting as good citizens in the locales where they do business.[142] One example of a prominent corporate involvement creating social change occurred in

South Africa. The Sullivan Principles, signed initially by twelve multi-national companies,[143] were designed generally to challenge the consequences of apartheid through threatened disinvestment and, more specifically, to obtain specific objectives such as paying living wages to lowest-paid workers.[144] As part of its participation in the Sullivan Principles, Eli Lilly focused on improving the healthcare infrastructure and laws.[145] Ford Motor Company created an employee-representation program and when the company left the country, donated the company's assets to an outgrowth of that program.[146]

Lee Tavis reports a program sponsored by Johnson & Johnson in Brazil where the company provides its workers with a nutritious snack.[147] Of course, well-fed employees are likely to be more productive than starving ones, but the company could have taken an approach where people were ordered to eat before coming to work. Instead, it addressed the problem with an admirable act of corporate citizenship and promoted positive, harmonious relationships in Brazil.

In addition, a corporation can contribute to the psychological security and identity of a country by investing in the people of that country. Earlier, the Motorola example of having its Malay plant run by Malay managers was noted. To the extent companies can develop and empower leaders in the countries where their plants are located, the less likely those plants will be seen as threatening of local culture.

Corporations can prioritize these four contributions. They can encourage economic development while being open to evaluations in order to make development less corrupt, more lawful, and more open to the poor. Contemporary management techniques show how companies can successfully integrate values in the corporate culture with tools promoting voice and participation. These values not only build democratic skills conducive to sustainable peace, but they resonate in US, Asian, European, Muslim, and African cultures. Many corporations are already doing good works as evidenced by the awards they have received. Finally, corporations can help to create conditions and act as intermediaries to lessen the likelihood of violence. None of these actions are beyond the scope of practical, contemporary corporate governance. The question of whether corporations will adapt these strategies is a question of corporate will. The contributions could be applied to a wide range of issues and decisions. For example, questions regarding where to locate a business, how to hire, whom to hire, how to train, how to establish policies against corruption, how to evaluate philanthropic issues, and how to guarantee employee voice are all worthy of independent analysis. The four contributions provide a set of criteria and objectives to link corporate behavior to the practices that foster sustainable peace. Further research is required to specify how to accomplish these objectives in particular situations.

Part III provides some illustrative examples of how these criteria apply in two contexts. The first context is internal; the other is external to the corporation. Chapter 5 addresses the important internal dimension of corporate conduct toward gender issues. From an external standpoint, chapter 6 considers ecological issues, and their significance to the corporation.

Notes

1. See generally Timothy L. Fort and Cindy A. Schipani, *The Role of the Corporation in Fostering Sustainable Peace*, 35 VAND. J. TRANSN'L L. 389 (2002).
2. VIRGINIA HAUFLER, A PUBLIC ROLE FOR THE PRIVATE SECTOR: INDUSTRY SELF-REGULATION IN A GLOBAL ECONOMY 12 (2001).
3. Ibid., at 13.
4. Ibid.
5. Ibid., at 23.
6. Ibid., at 13.
7. Ibid., at 39.
8. Ethan B. Kapstein, *The Corporate Ethics Crusade*, 105 FOREIGN AFF. (September–October, 2001).
9. Ibid., at 106.
10. Ibid.
11. This section is drawn from Thomas W. Dunfee and Timothy L. Fort, *Corporate Hypergoals, Sustainable Peace, and the Adapted Firm*, 36 VAND. J. TRANSN'L L. 563 (2003) and is used with permission.
12. See Timothy L. Fort and Cindy A. Schipani, *Corporate Governance in a Global Environment: The Search for the Best of All Worlds*, 33 VAND. J. TRANS. L. 829 (2000); see also Michael Bradley, et al., *The Purposes and Accountability of the Corporation in Contemporary Society: Corporate Governance at a Crossroads*, 62 LAW & CONTEMP. PROBS. 9 (1999).
13. See e.g. JURGEN HABERMAS, MORAL CONSCIOUSNESS AND COMMUNICATIVE ACTION (C. Lenhardt and S.W. Nicholsen trans., 1990) (establishing the argument for basic minimums upon which thicker notions of morality might later be derived).

14. Thomas Donaldson and Thomas W. Dunfee, Ties That Bind: A Social Contracts Approach to Business Ethics 49–82 (1999).
15. Richard T. DeGeorge, Competing with Integrity in International Business (1993).
16. Thomas Donaldson, The Ethics of International Business (1989).
17. DeGeorge, above n. 15, at 23–41.
18. Ibid., at 43–45.
19. Donaldson, above n. 16, at 65–94.
20. Although Donaldson's and DeGeorge's analyses seem applicable to all types of corporations, the emphasis herein is on publicly held, for-profit firms. See Donaldson, above n. 16; DeGeorge, above n. 15.
21. See R.T. Naylor, Wages of Crime: Black Markets, Illegal Finance, and the Underworld Economy 38 (2002) (explaining how the emergence of Russia mafia came from the dysfunctions of communist society).
22. See generally F.A. Hayek, The Fatal Conceit (1988). Background institutions include courts and police forces, regulatory agencies, executive branch bureaus with responsibility for business regulation, NGOs such as the Red Cross and Red Crescent. For a provocative argument connecting property rights and sustainable peace, see O. Lee Reed, *Reduction in Property, Liberty, and Corporate Governance*, 36 Vand. J. Transn'l. L. 673 (2003).
23. See DeGeorge, above n. 15, at 26–27 (discussing the importance of background institutions).
24. Francis Fukayama, Trust: The Social Virtues and the Creation of Prosperity 25 (1995).
25. Ibid.
26. See e.g. Margaret M. Pearson, China's New Business Elite (1997) (analyzing the growing strength of the business class in China that has arisen apart from democratization of the country's politics).
27. See e.g. *We Need This Passion, but for Another Battle*, The Indian Express, May 31, 2002, available at http://www.indianexpress.com/full_story.php?content_id=3564 (arguing that the passion for a war against Pakistan needs to be rechannelled to revive an economy "in shambles").
28. See e.g. *How to Fix Corporate Governance*, Bus. Wk., May 6, 2002, at 69.
29. Ibid.
30. A central premise of Milton Friedman's arguments is that managers have a duty to shareholders, not to themselves. Milton Friedman, *The*

Social Responsibility of Business is to Increase Its Profit, N.Y. TIMES MAGAZINE, September 13, 1970, at 32. The corporate scandals are more about managerial profiting at the expense of the shareholders rather than shareholder abuse of other stakeholders. Michael J. O'Hara makes a similar point with respect to the extent to which businesses managers actually allocate resources to cover risks; frequently, they do not fund even a small amount for what might be seen as minimal risk. Michael J. O'Hara, *Governing for Genuine Profit*, 36 VAND. J. TRANS. L. 765 (2003).

31. See http://www.transparency.org.
32. See ibid.
33. See ibid.
34. See ibid.
35. See ibid.
36. See http://www.unglobalcompact.com (principles and work of the United Nations in offering the Global Compact as a standard for business behavior). There may also be a dimension related to business's responsibility for the individual flourishing of those who work for the corporation. See Caryn L. Beck-Dudley and Steven H. Hanks, *On Virtue and Peace: Creating a Workplace Where People Can Flourish*, 36 VAND. J. TRANS. L. 427 (2003); see also Frances E. Zollers and Elletta Sangrey Callahan, *Workplace Violence and Security: Are There Lessons For Peacemaking?*, 36 VAND. J. TRANS. L. 449 (2003) (discussing how inattention to individual flourishing can result in workplace violence).
37. See http://www.unglobalcompact.com.
38. DONALDSON AND DUNFEE, above n. 14.
39. Ibid., at 49–81.
40. Ibid., at 43–44.
41. Ibid., at 60–61.
42. Ibid., at 117–38.
43. Ibid., at 119.
44. Ibid., at 117.
45. Ibid., at 46–47.
46. See generally Thomas W. Dunfee, *Corporate Governance in a Market with Morality*, 62 LAW & CONTEMP. PROBS. 129 (1999).
47. Ibid., at 149.
48. DONALDSON, above n. 16.
49. Ibid., at 64.
50. Ibid., at 54.
51. Ibid., at 81.
52. Ibid., at 83.

53. Ibid., at 84.
54. Ibid., at 82.
55. Friedman, above n. 30.
56. See generally Timothy L. Fort and Cindy A. Schipani, *Adapting Corporate Governance for Sustainable Peace*, 36 VAND. J. TRANSN'L. L. 377 (2003).
57. Although the rise of NGOs and the pressure they can apply to corporate reputation is significant, perhaps a more compelling reason for corporations to adopt ethics programs is the 1991 Federal Sentencing Guidelines ("the Guidelines"). In general, the Guidelines reduce fines otherwise applicable to violations of federal law if a corporation has adopted an effective compliance program. Elements of an effective program include a clear code of conduct, mission statement, or values statement; the appointment of a high-level executive to oversee the program; education of employees as to the dimensions of the program; a safe place (such as an ombudsperson office) to register complaints about unethical behavior; and self-reporting of violations to government authorities. Policies need to be perceived to apply to top management as well as to rank-and-file employees and companies need to have well-designed training sessions in order for the programs to be part of corporate culture.
58. See Lynn Sharp Paine, *Managing for Organizational Integrity*, HARV. BUS. REV. (March/April, 1994).
59. The design of formal ethics programs can also vary. A growing number of US firms have appointed ethics officers. Ideally an ethics officer is a senior executive who has direct access to the Chief Executive Officer, and if necessary, to the Board of Directors. Some oversee relatively large staffs, run extensive training programs, helplines, and services and may participate in critical decisions. The relative power of the ethics officer signals the approach of the firm to resolving cultural conflicts. For example, does the ethics officer have authority over foreign units of the organization? Or, instead, do the foreign units have separate practice officers responsible for the decisions within that unit? Answers to these and similar questions determine the extent to which the ethics program is centralized and unified.
60. Dunfee, above n. 46.
61. Other commentators have proposed models of ethical approaches for global corporations. For example, Enderle has proposed a framework involving four categories of global firms, denoting them as Foreign Country, Empire, Interconnection, and Global firms. Georges Enderle, *What is International? A Typology of International Spheres and Its Relevance for Business Ethics*, Paper Presented at the Annual Meeting of the International Association of Business and

Society, Vienna, Austria (1995). See also DONALDSON AND DUNFEE, above n. 14, at 217–19.

62. Dunfee and Fort, above n. 11, at 600.
63. Ibid.
64. The ethical philosophy of this approach can be characterized as one of absolutism.
65. The ethical philosophy for this approach would be relativism, i.e. "When in Rome do as the Romans do."
66. Paine, above n. 58.
67. Ibid., at 11.
68. Ibid.
69. Ibid.
70. Note that the Corporate Opportunist is not a utilitarian. A utilitarian would make the best decision from the viewpoint of all affected. The Corporate Opportunist is only acting in its best interest. Further, if the firm were seeking to achieve positive utilitarian outcomes, it should be classified as a Corporate Imperialist, i.e. it would be seeking to apply its preferred values wherever it does business.
71. POST-CONFLICT UNIT OF THE WORLD BANK, SECURITY, POVERTY REDUCTION AND SUSTAINABLE DEVELOPMENT: CHALLENGES FOR THE NEW MILLENNIUM 4–11 (September, 1999) (assessing the links between poverty and violence).
72. These issues are discussed in ch. 6.
73. This award was established by the State Department in 1999 to recognize US businesses that act as good corporate citizens abroad. Recipients include both multinational and small- to medium-sized enterprises. The criteria for the Secretary of State's Award for Corporate Excellence are:

- Maintaining good corporate citizenship by engaging in ethical business practices, maintaining the integrity of the company, and dealing with consumers in accordance with fair business practices.
- Displaying exemplary employment practices and a fair opportunity for trade unions to represent employees as well as avoiding discrimination based on race, gender or ethnicity.
- Creating a healthy workplace environment for all workers. This includes working for the effective abolition of child labor and forced labor practices as well as maintaining a working environment equal to, if not exceeding, comparable local industry standards of health and safety.
- Conducting business with an astute consciousness of local, national, and global environmental concerns. This includes the collection and ongoing monitoring of useful information

regarding the environmental, health, and social impacts of operations. Also, working with local, national, and international officials
to adequately communicate to the public regarding potential environmental and health issues without compromising the businesses's
integrity and ability to operate successfully.

- Contributing to the overall growth and development both economically and socially of the local society. This includes work-specific
skills training, general academic improvement, and opportunities
for personal self-improvement, as well as other programs, services,
and philanthropic endeavors for the local public, all aimed at
providing a base for growing and sustaining an increased quality of
life.

- Endeavoring to ensure that business activities are compatible with
the science and technology policies of the countries and, as appropriate, contribute to the development of local innovative capacity.

- Developing and maintaining a healthy respect for the local, national, and international authority. This includes rejecting the practices of bribery, extortion, illegal tax exemption, and favoritism in
favor of creating a fair and open marketplace beneficial to all.

74. US Department of State, *2000 Award for Corporate Excellence*, Frigorifico Canelones, available at http://www.state.gov/
e/eb/cba/bs/ace.

75. Ibid.

76. US Department of State, *2000 Award for Corporate Excellence*, *Motorola Malaysia*, available at http://www.state.gov/e/eb/cba/bs/ace.
See also Adeline Orgs, *"Corporate News" Skilled Workforce Can
Cushion the Blow*, THE EDGE (Malaysia), February 5, 2001, at
3; Anna Chidambar, *Talent Bank*, MALAYSIAN BUSINESS, April 16,
2000, at 26.

77. US Department of State, *2000 Award for Corporate Excellence*,
F.C. Schaffer & Associates, available at http://www.state.gov/e/eb/
cba/bs/ace.

78. George C. Lodge, *The Corporate Key: Using Big Business to Fight
Global Poverty*, 81 FOREIGN AFF., July/August, 2002, at 13.

79. Ibid., at 15.

80. Ibid.

81. Ibid.

82. Ibid.

83. Ibid.

84. See generally MICHAEL SANTORO, PROFITS AND PRINCIPLES: GLOBAL
CAPITALISM AND HUMAN RIGHTS IN CHINA 46–47 (2000).

85. Ibid., at 46.

86. Ibid., at 44.
87. Ibid., at 45–46.
88. *Frigorífico Canelones,* above n. 74.
89. US Department of State, *2001 Award for Corporate Excellence, Ford,* available at http://www.state.gov/e/eb/cba/bs/ace.
90. US Department of State, *2001 Award for Corporate Excellence, Xerox,* available at http://www.state.gov/e/eb/cba/bs/ace.
91. Ibid.
92. *Motorola,* above n. 76.
93. Ibid.
94. *F.C. Schaffer,* above n. 77.
95. Ibid.
96. Thomas L. Friedman, *India, Pakistan, and G.E.,* N.Y. TIMES, August 11, 2002.
97. JOHN PAUL LEDERACH, BUILDING PEACE: SUSTAINABLE RECONCILIATION IN DIVIDED SOCIETIES 41 (1997).
98. Ibid.
99. Ibid., at 42.
100. Ibid.
101. JANE NELSON, THE BUSINESS OF PEACE: THE PRIVATE SECTOR AS A PARTNER IN CONFLICT PREVENTION AND RESOLUTION 118–19 (2000).
102. JOHN WALLACE, THE ENEMY HAS A FACE: THE SEEDS OF PEACE EXPERIENCE (2000).
103. Ibid.
104. See RONALD TAKAKA, A DIFFERENT MIRROR: A HISTORY OF MULTICULTURAL AMERICA (1993) (arguing that it is at work where Americans of different ethnic origins meet and learn to work together).
105. See Fort and Schipani, above n. 1, at 398.
106. See JOHN T. NOONAN, BRIBES (1984).
107. DONALDSON AND DUNFEE, above n. 14, at 226–30.
108. See Miguel Scholoss, *Luncheon Address at the Symposium on Fighting International Corruption & Bribery in the 21st Century,* 33 CORNELL J. INT'L L. 469, 478 (2000); see also DONALDSON AND DUNFEE, above n. 14.
109. See F.A. HAYEK, THE FATAL CONCEIT (1988) (arguing that the free market depends on legal protection of contracts and property rights).
110. Friedman, above n. 30 (arguing that the free market is dependent upon a functioning legal system that restrains some kinds of behavior).
111. See generally JANE JACOBS, SYSTEMS OF SURVIVAL: A DIALOGUE ON THE MORAL FOUNDATIONS OF COMMERCE AND POLITICS (1992).

112. See sources cited above n. 73 and accompanying text (specifying rule of law as a criteria for the Award of Excellence).
113. Johnson & Johnson Worldwide Contributions Program Annual Report 2000, at 3, available at http:/www.jnj.com/community/contributions/publications/2000_contributions.pdf (last visited October 27, 2003).
114. See generally HERNANDO DESOTO, THE MYSTERY OF CAPITAL: WHY CAPITALISM WORKS IN THE WEST AND FAILS EVERYWHERE ELSE (2000).
115. See ch. 1 for further discussion of DeSoto's insights.
116. De Soto, above n. 114.
117. See CONNIE PECK, SUSTAINABLE PEACE: THE ROLE OF THE UN AND REGIONAL ORGANIZATIONS IN PREVENTING CONFLICT (1998).
118. Ibid.
119. R. SCOTT APPLEBY, THE AMBIVALENCE OF THE SACRED: RELIGION, VIOLENCE, AND RECONCILIATION 17 (2000).
120. David Fabbro, *Peaceful Societies: An Introduction*, 15 J. PEACE STUDIES 67 (1978).
121. TIMOTHY L. FORT, ETHICS AND GOVERNANCE: BUSINESS AS MEDIATING INSTITUTION (2000).
122. See GEORGE ECKES, THE SIX SIGMA REVOLUTION: HOW GENERAL ELECTRIC AND OTHERS TURNED PROCESS INTO PROFITS 1–11 (2000) (particularly with emphasis on quality processes involving management at every level of the organization).
123. Timothy Fort, *The Spirituality of Solidarity and Total Quality Management*, 14 BUS. & PROF'L. ETHICS J. 3, 7–11 (1995).
124. Ibid.
125. Ibid., at 7–8.
126. W. EDWARDS DEMING, OUT OF THE CRISIS 77 (1982).
127. Ibid., at 83.
128. Ibid., at 85.
129. See generally FATEMA MERNISSI, ISLAM AND DEMOCRACY: FEAR OF THE MODERN WORLD (Mary Jo Lakeland trans., 2002).
130. Ibid., at 40.
131. See generally GEORGE B.N. AYITTEY, AFRICA IN CHAOS (1999).
132. Ibid., at 314.
133. Ibid.
134. Ibid.
135. See Mark J. Roe, *German Codetermination and German Securities Markets*, COLUM. BUS. L. REV. 167, 171–173 (1998).
136. SUBCOMM. OF THE COMM. ON FIN., SURVEY OF EXPERIENCES IN PROFIT SHARING AND POSSIBILITIES OF INCENTIVE TAXATION, S. REP.

No. 76-610 (1939), at 17 (hereinafter Vanderburg Report), cited in Dana M. Muir, *Groundings of Voice in Employee Rights*, 36 VAND. J. TRANSN'L L. 485, 487 (2003).

137. Muir above n. 136, at 487.

138. Ibid., at 490.

139. Ibid., at 491 (citing ROBERT S. HARTMAN, FREEDOM TO LIVE, THE ROBERT HARTMAN STORY (Arthur R. Ellis ed., 1994) and Daniel Vaughan-Whitehead, *France: The Driving Force of Comprehensive Legislation*, in WORKERS' FINANCIAL PARTICIPATION: EAST-WEST EX-PERIENCES 55 (Daniel Vaughan-Whitehead, et al. eds., 1995) (noting the views of General Charles DeGaulle in the 1940s)).

140. Ibid., at 516.

141. Ibid., at 501–505.

142. Kapstein, above n. 8.

143. The companies were American Cyanamid, Burroughs, Caltex Petroleum, Citicorp, Ford Motor, General Motors, IBM, International Harvester, Minnesota Mining & Manufacturing, Mobil, Otis Elevator, and Union Carbide. S. PRAKASH SETHI AND OLIVER F. WILLIAMS, C.S.C., ECONOMIC IMPERATIVES AND ETHICAL VALUES IN GLOBAL BUSINESS 3–4 (2001).

144. See ibid., at 133.

145. Ibid., at 127–35.

146. Ibid., at 151–56.

147. Lee A. Tavis, *Corporate Governance and the Global Social Void*, 35 VAND. J. TRANSN'L L. 487 (2002).

III | Two illustrative issues: gender equality and ecology

5 | *Gender, voice, and correlations with peace*

I n developing countries, involving women in the economy as wage earners[1] can "lead to output gains and a reduction in poverty in general."[2] As has been argued elsewhere, a reduction in poverty promotes stability and leads to a more peaceful society.[3] As the locus of production shifts away from the home, an initial decline in employment opportunities may occur. When women are transitioning in society into the workforce, violence may increase.[4] However, when women have attained status through economic empowerment, the violence[5] and decline in employment opportunities disappear and both women and men benefit.[6]

A significant factor affecting the participation rate of women is the dominant religion in the country. Approximately one-third of the variation in participation rates between countries can be explained by religion.[7] Such statistics have led to a call for secularization of the law in some countries such as India because traditional interpretations marginalize the perspective of women.[8] Secularization is justified as a matter of social utility, logic, and modern values.[9] Additionally, traditional interpretation is only one possible interpretation, and "common understanding" is sometimes not the best interpretation.[10] Depending on the interpretation of Islamic Law, for example, girls have a right to education on a par with boys in their family and a right to work and earn before and after marriage,[11] or they do not. This can be seen in the societies of Turkey and Afghanistan in 2000.[12]

The statistics regarding violence in today's society are staggering. A recent study published by the World Health Organization, making headlines in the *Wall Street Journal*, reports that "Violence Took 1.6 Million Lives in 2000."[13] Notably, this report considers only the data obtained from the seventy countries that report statistics to the World Health Organization. It does not include reports from many countries where violence is also high, such as Burundi, Rwanda, Iraq, Liberia, and Afghanistan.[14] There are other studies of violence throughout the world. As noted in chapter 1, the Heidelberg Institute for International Conflict Research studies conflicts and compiles data comparing how various types of conflicts are resolved.[15] Previous research has compared the Heidelberg Institute's data on how conflicts are resolved with an index prepared by Transparency International. Transparency International ranks countries throughout the world based on the perception of corruption in business.[16] This research, described more fully in chapter 1, showed a direct correlation between corruption and violence. That is, countries that were reported by the Heidelberg Institute to have addressed conflict in peaceful or mostly nonviolent means were the same countries that were perceived as least corrupt according to the index prepared by Transparency International.[17] Conversely, those countries that the Heidelberg Institute reported as mostly violent in their conflict resolution were also found by Transparency International to be perceived as the most corrupt.[18]

This chapter seeks to address some of these issues of violence by considering issues of gender. The question posed is whether there may be some correlation between violence and the lack of meaningful involvement of women in the economy. If the countries that appear more violent are also countries where women are systematically excluded from business opportunities, perhaps one way to curb some of the societal violence would be to improve the opportunities for women in the economy.

To address this question, this chapter is organized as follows. Section I examines data compiled by the United Nations and the Heidelberg Institute, and finds that many violent nations do not rate positively on gender-related indices. Conversely, the more peaceful nations tend to have more positive gender-related scores. Pushing the results in Section I a step further, Section II considers how some of these gender imbalances might be corrected. This Section notes that laws are only partially successful and suggests that business might play a role by granting social rights and by adopting policies on nondiscrimination, providing mentoring and training programs, and implementing childcare and other family friendly policies. Concluding remarks follow Section II.

I. Data

As noted in chapter 1, previous research has compared the Heidelberg Institute's work on conflicts throughout the world with

Transparency International's data on the perception of corruption, finding an interesting correlation between violence and corruption.[19] This chapter utilizes the same data from the Heidelberg Institute and compares it to the Gender Development Index published by the United Nations.[20] Here, significant correlations were found between countries that resolve disputes by peaceful, or mostly nonviolent means, and more positive rankings on the Gender Development Index. Similarly, countries that ranked in the violent or mostly violent tiers of the Heidelberg Index, had poorer rankings in gender development.

In undertaking this analysis, 144 countries, for which data was available on gender development from the United Nations, were ranked. Each year, the United Nations publishes a human development index (HDI) as a composite measure of human development.[21] The HDI measures the achievements in a country in three basic dimensions of human development: longevity, knowledge, and a decent standard of living.[22] These categories are measured using life expectancy, adult literacy, combined primary, secondary and tertiary enrollment, and adjusted income per capita in purchasing power parity in US dollars.[23] Because the HDI assesses only average achievements, it disguises gender differences in human development. To reveal these differences, the United Nations extrapolates data from the HDI to compile the gender-related development index (GDI).[24] We use the latter measure, the GDI, in our statistical comparison. The GDI uses the same components as the HDI, but "captures inequalities in achievement between women and men."[25] If a state had achieved gender equality in human development, its GDI and HDI would be the same.[26] However, the United Nations study indicated that for all countries studied, the GDI was lower than the HDI, indicating the presence of gender inequality everywhere.[27] Therefore, as the report describes, the GDI is "simply the HDI adjusted downward for gender inequality."[28]

This analysis begins with each country's GDI ranking. For the 2001 study, the GDI was estimated for 144 countries, measuring: (1) the female and male life expectancy at birth; (2) the female and male adult literacy rates and the female and male combined primary, secondary and tertiary enrollment rates; and (3) the estimated female and male earned income. The last category reflects women's and men's command over resources.[29] Australia, Norway, Belgium, and Canada ranked at the top of the United Nations GDI index, indicating the lowest levels of gender inequality.[30] At the other end of the spectrum, Burkina Faso,

Burundi, and Niger ranked the lowest, indicating the highest levels of gender inequality.[31]

Each country's GDI ranking was compared to its ranking on the Heidelberg Institute's violence index, to the extent data was available.[32] The data used are detailed in table 5.1 below. The Heidelberg Institute's violence index, described in chapter 1 uses a variety of sources[33] to define the types of conflict involved and the methods used by parties to those conflicts to resolve them.[34] The database was used to rank the countries according to the number of conflicts resolved violently and the total number of conflicts between 1975 and 2000.[35]

Next, the countries were divided into six groups, of approximately twenty-five countries, to compare the country's GDI rank to its Kosimo rank. This resulted in a linear progression of the percentage of violent resolution of conflicts ranging from 11 percent in the first group of twenty-five countries, to 71 percent in the last group. These results are reported in table 5.2.

In the first group, the only countries that report violent conflicts are the USA, UK, Ireland and Israel. Israel is the anomaly in the group with three violent conflicts of five total conflicts while the other three countries report only one violent conflict each. The total percentage of violent resolution of in this group was is 10.7 percent.

When the second group is considered, the percentage of conflicts being resolved violently increases to 35.4 percent. Eleven of the seventeen violent conflicts in this group involve Latin American countries. Middle Eastern countries accounted for the remaining six conflicts.

In the third group, violent resolution of conflict goes up to 38 percent; increasing to 58 percent in the fourth group, remaining at 58 percent in the fifth group and increasing again to 71 percent in the final and sixth group.

In addition to grouping the data according to GDI rankings, correlation statistics between a country's ranking on the GDI and its Kosimo ranking were computed. The correlation coefficient between these variables is .73, with a Spearman rank correlation of 767.8. These numbers indicate a correlative relationship between a country's ranking on the GDI and the level of violence involved in resolution of disputes. Of course, this does not indicate causation. For example, it may be that in countries with weak, corrupt, or ineffective legal systems, people will tend to resolve disputes outside of the courtroom, often violently. These same countries may also not have laws or practices promoting gender development. Nevertheless, these figures seem to run in tandem.

Table 5.1 *Gender Development and Conflict Resolution Rankings*

Country	GDI Rank	Heidelberg Rank	Conflicts resolved violently	Total number of conflicts between 1975–2000
Australia	1	13	0	1
Belgium	2	25	0	1
Norway	3	6	0	2
Sweden	4	3	0	2
Canada	5	5	0	3
USA	6	14	1	8
Iceland	7	6	0	1
Finland	8	1	0	2
Netherlands	9	9	0	1
United Kingdom	10	10	1	7
Japan	11	23	0	1
France	12	21	0	9
Denmark	13	2	0	3
Switzerland	14	11	–	–
Austria	15	15	–	–
Germany	16	17	0	3
Ireland	17	19	1	1
New Zealand	18	3	0	1
Luxembourg	19	11	–	–
Italy	20	39	0	1
Spain	21	20	0	1
Israel	22	22	3	5
Hong Kong	23	15	–	–
Singapore	24	6	0	0
Greece	25	35	0	3
Cyprus	26	–	0	1
Slovenia	27	28	–	–
Portugal	28	23	0	1
South Korea	29	48	0	1
Malta	30	–	0	1
Brunei Darussalam	31	–	–	–
Czech Republic	32	42	0	1
Argentina	33	52	2	6
Slovakia	34	52	0	0
Hungary	35	32	0	2
Poland	36	43	0	2

(*cont.*)

Table 5.1 (*cont.*)

Country	GDI Rank	Heidelberg Rank	Conflicts resolved violently	Total number of conflicts between 1975–2000
Uruguay	37	–	3	6
Bahamas	38	–	–	–
Chile	39	18	0	3
Bahrain	40	–	1	3
Costa Rica	41	30	3	4
Lithuania	42	43	0	1
Croatia	43	51	2	2
Kuwait	44	–	4	6
Trinidad and Tobago	45	–	–	–
Latvia	46	57	0	1
United Arab Emirates	47	–	0	1
Qatar	48	–	1	4
Mexico	49	59	1	1
Belarus	50	43	0	1
Panama	51	–	1	2
Russian Federation	52	82	2	9
Bulgaria	53	52	–	–
Malaysia	54	36	0	2
Romania	55	68	–	–
Colombia	56	60	–	–
Venezuela	57	71	0	2
Belize	58	–	1	3
Mauritius	59	37	0	2
Thailand	60	60	0	2
Libya	61	–	0	1
Armenia	62	76	1	2
Philippines	63	69	2	2
Brazil	64	49	0	2
Fiji	65	–	–	–
Ukraine	66	87	0	2
Jamaica	67	–	–	–
Maldives	68	–	–	–
Lebanon	69	–	9	10
Sri Lanka	70	–	3	3
Turkey	71	50	1	6
Saudi Arabia	72	–	1	3
Peru	73	–	5	11

Table 5.1 (*cont.*)

Country	GDI Rank	Heidelberg Rank	Conflicts resolved violently	Total number of conflicts between 1975–2000
Albania	74	–	0	2
Paraguay	75	–	0	1
Uzbekistan	76	79	2	2
China	77	63	5	6
Oman	78	–	0	2
Dominican Republic	79	–	–	–
Ecuador	80	74	3	5
Tunisia	81	32	2	3
Cape Verde	82	–	–	–
Iran	83	–	7	18
Jordan	84	39	0	1
Guyana	85	–	0	1
Moldova	86	74	–	–
El Salvador	87	43	1	2
South Africa	88	34	2	4
Vietnam	89	76	1	4
Algeria	90	–	3	3
Indonesia	91	85	4	5
Syria	92	–	–	–
Equatorial New Guinea	93	–	–	–
Tajikistan	94	–	3	3
Mongolia	95	–	–	–
Bolivia	96	71	0	1
Nicaragua	97	–	3	4
Honduras	98	–	3	3
Egypt	99	63	3	3
Guatemala	100	–	2	4
Namibia	101	–	0	1
Morocco	102	37	2	4
Swaziland	103	–	–	–
Botswana	104	26	0	1
India	105	69	5	7
Myanmar	106	–	1	2
Zimbabwe	107	65	1	2
Ghana	108	52	1	2
Cambodia	109	–	1	2

(*cont.*)

Table 5.1 (*cont.*)

Country	GDI Rank	Heidelberg Rank	Conflicts resolved violently	Total number of conflicts between 1975–2000
Papua New Guinea	110	–	1	3
Lesotho	111	–	1	2
Kenya	112	82	2	4
Congo	113	–	3	3
Comoros	114	–	1	2
Cameroon	115	84	–	–
Sudan	116	–	6	7
Togo	117	–	2	2
Laos	118	–	0	2
Nepal	119	–	0	1
Pakistan	120	–	5	6
Bangladesh	121	–	1	3
Haiti	122	–	1	1
Madagascar	123	–	–	–
Nigeria	124	90	1	4
Uganda	125	80	4	6
Tanzania	126	76	1	1
Mauritania	127	–	1	1
Yemen	128	–	5	9
Zambia	129	57	1	3
Senegal	130	52	2	2
Congo, Dem Repub	131	–	–	–
Côte d'Ivoire	132	71	–	–
Eritrea	133	–	2	4
Benin	134	–	–	–
Rwanda	135	–	2	2
Gambia	136	–	–	–
Malawi	137	43	0	1
Mali	138	–	2	2
Central African Republic	139	–	0	1
Chad	140	–	7	9
Guinea Bissau	141	–	1	1
Ethiopia	142	60	5	7
Burkina Faso	143	65	2	2
Mozambique	144	81	3	3

Table 5.2 *Gender Development and Conflict Resolution Comparison*

Country's Gender Development Index Rank	Composite percentage of violent resolutions of conflict
1–25	10.7
26–50	35.4
51–75	38.0
76–100	58.0
101–125	58.0
126–144	71.0

II. Implementation

A. Laws

Discrimination against women in the workforce is economically inefficient. As the proportion of women in the workforce rises, the effects of the inefficiency rise.[36] Thus, it makes economic sense for countries to pass nondiscrimination laws. There is also broad global support for nondiscrimination. Many international treaties and conventions call for the elimination of discrimination against women.[37] As countries become signatories, they begin to change their laws. Ratification of the ILO Convention 156 on workers with family responsibilities, the United Nations Convention on the Elimination of All Forms of Discrimination Against Women,[38] and the OECD Guidelines for Multinational Enterprises,[39] are examples of international anti-discrimination policy. Groups and individuals increasingly appeal to the norms of international law to oppose state laws.[40]

Various kinds of laws may need to be enacted to effectively address discrimination against women in the workforce. These can range from equal access to education to tax laws that do not unduly penalize a second income in a household, and from family leave to adequate childcare. The most obvious are laws that ban discrimination in the workplace. One example is a law banning discrimination against married women. In Indonesia and Korea it is permissible to discriminate against married women.[41] Such discrimination not only prevents married women from getting jobs, it also affects the type of job an employer is willing to give women, if hired, and the type of training they are provided with. If an employer hires single women, it will tend to channel them into dead-end jobs, pay them lower wages, and lay them off first. Since most women will marry and, they assume, leave the workforce, there is little incentive to invest much in them.[42] Additionally, these laws affect the kind of education a family is willing to provide a girl.

Legislation, however, is only a beginning on the long road toward a solution. Several studies by social scientists in developing countries indicate that legislation mandating equality is not sufficient, at least in the short term, to change social norms.[43] For example, a study done in Indonesia after a Western legal system was implemented showed that the system operated at the formal, state level in a thin layer at the top, but that the traditional processes operated below that. The latter layers represent most of the issues faced on a daily basis.[44] Imposing rights was considered impolite because it would be contrary to harmonious communal life to consider the individual's interest before that of the community.[45] One of the results was that Toba Batak married women did not assert their right to inherit from their fathers' estates.[46] In India, women are persuaded out of asserting their legal rights.[47] Traditional legal rights are as interpreted by men from traditional texts.[48] The main property right of women emanates from marriage – labor markets are only a secondary source.[49]

Singapore and Malaysia have tried to address the resistance issue in implementing laws that conflict with cultural norms. Before adopting laws, an attempt is made to change people's perceptions, in preparation for the change.[50] Then, if laws have not become generally accepted after passage, implementation is deferred until the community accepts the laws.[51] Consequently, Malaysia has not adopted the Convention on Elimination of All Forms of Discrimination against Women,[52] and although various civil rights are mentioned in the constitution, no such right is mentioned with respect to gender equality.[53] In Thailand, women and family-related issues are seen as not being within the realm of the law.[54] Women, however, have been seen as good workers, obedient, and non-demanding.[55] But they are hindered from achieving greater parity with men because of their historical place as appendages to men, the cultural devaluation of manual labor, and the religious definition of women as polluting.[56] Women tend to hold themselves back in competition with men.[57] These are issues that are difficult to change through legislation.[58]

In addition to laws not being obeyed by individuals, governments may also ignore them and employers may purposely avoid them. For example, Mexico prohibits discrimination against women in the Mexican Federal Labor Law[59] and the Mexican Constitution.[60] These laws are commonly ignored, though, especially as they pertain to women.[61] In another example, when equal pay legislation was implemented in Canada, employers avoided the intended result by reclassifying jobs so that they were not comparable, or changed the wage rates for female and male jobs to light and heavy work.[62] Despite these barriers to effectiveness, law can play an important symbolic role[63] and can "educate a population to expect new forms of participation."[64]

An example of legislation that is counterproductive in terms of women's employment is protective legislation. China's labor legislation is illustrative. It emphasizes the biological differences between men and women, and protects women on the basis of some of those differences such as menstrual cycle, pregnancy, and nursing.[65] The result of such protective legislation reinforces traditional stereotypes, puts the burden of child rearing entirely on women, and leads to a preference for male workers.[66] It also hinders women's movement into nontraditional work roles.[67]

B. Other influences

Influences other than law such as nongovernmental organizations (NGOs),[68] the media, and the Internet,[69] can also lead to change.[70] However, the change may only occur in certain classes. For example, newspapers are influential,[71] but tend to reflect the concerns of the middle or upper classes.[72] Education can also play a role. Educating about rights at the elementary school level may eventually lead to a transformation.[73] However, multinational corporations (MNCs) operating within countries have the greatest potential to change existing norms through policies they implement in their generally large and desirable workplaces.[74]

C. What can business add?

MNCs can help by implementing what have been called *social rights*, such as the right to work and to a decent income.[75] MNCs can be particularly influential in developing countries which are anxious to get the developmental benefits of the companies' presence.[76]

1. Non-discrimination

Probably the most essential thing a company must have in order successfully to integrate women into the workforce is a nondiscrimination policy. As mentioned above, there are a large number of international treaties and compacts that call for such policies.[77] Additionally, MNCs operating in the USA will have a nondiscrimination policy. These policies will comport with the US federal nondiscrimination laws such as Title VII,[78] the Americans with Disabilities Act,[79] and the Age Discrimination Act,[80] and thus may be broader than the international mandates, and would largely be consistent in regard to the treatment of women. Clearly, in order for women to be hired in non-traditional workplaces, employers must begin with equal opportunity.

In many instances, as a practical matter, a nondiscrimination policy will not be enough. The organization will have to put incentives and oversight into effect to make sure the policy is implemented effectively. One important way to encourage compliance is to have the evaluations of those hiring and supervising be based, in part, on whether qualified women are brought into the workplace at appropriate levels and whether they receive appropriate training and promotion opportunities.[81] The evaluations should also be tied into pay raises. In economies where women are largely untrained to enter the workforce, the employer may need to make sure its training and educational efforts outside the workplace are nondiscriminatory for girls and women, as discussed below.[82]

a. Harassment

Once women are in the workplace, an essential component of a nondiscrimination policy is a ban on harassment. Harassment has typically been used by those in the majority group to send the message that the person being harassed is not welcome and to protect their territory.[83] For example, when women entered non-traditional jobs after the passage of title VII, harassment commonly followed. In the USA, harassment today is seen to be more about power than about sex.[84] In harassment law, it is an abuse of economic power to force demeaning and unwelcome behavior on women.[85] Besides reducing workers to sex objects, harassment reinforces sexual stereotypes, assaults individual dignity, and fosters a sense of degradation that can result in a loss of productivity, and physical and emotional problems.[86] It can also involve violence.[87]

In developing countries such as China, where women are moving from a rural area to a growing commercial area to get jobs, women must often be willing to sleep with the person doing the hiring or the supervising to get or keep a job.[88] This is seen by many as the dues one must pay to earn a living.[89]

MNCs which operate in the USA and other parts of the West are likely to have an anti-harassment policy. There are problems, though, with global application of a program developed to meet US law.[90] Two forms of sexual harassment are recognized in the USA: quid pro quo harassment and hostile environment sexual harassment. Quid pro quo harassment occurs when a supervisor offers or withholds a job or job benefit in exchange for sexual favors.[91] A hostile environment occurs when unwelcome sexual conduct from a supervisor or coworker unreasonably interferes with individual job performance or creates an intimidating, hostile, or offensive work environment.[92] These same theories have been adopted by other countries and trade organizations.[93] However, cultural and legal differences have resulted in the concept having different meanings and legal outcomes.[94]

The differences in the approaches of Japan, the Czech Republic, Australia, and the EU are illustrative. In Japan, there is no law specifically addressing sexual harassment, but courts have recognized harassing environment cases, and women have formed pressure groups to get organizations to address the problem.[95] In the Czech Republic, women have been reluctant to press or even recognize the issue,[96] but as the Czech Republic prepares to join the EU, changes may have to be made because the EU has taken a position against sexual harassment[97] and has adopted a program on gender equality.[98] There is currently no mechanism, however, to enforce the EU policy against harassment.[99] Australia statutorily bans both harassing environment and quid pro quo sexual harassment,[100] but if companies implement effective training programs, they cannot be sued.[101] The differences mean that MNCs must adjust their policies to meet local requirements. However, they would be legally safe and ethically correct to have a policy banning quid pro quo harassment wherever they operate.[102]

No country approves of the idea of a woman being forced to trade sexual favors for the right to employment and its benefits, of having her personal security threatened, or her human dignity under-mined. Evidence of this is reflected in global and regional declarations. These include the 1948 Universal Declaration of Human Rights,[103] the United Nations Convention on the Elimination of All Forms of Dis-crimination Against Women,[104] OECD Guidelines for Multinational Enterprises,[105] the Council of Europe's 1996 Social Charter,[106] and EC Directives and Codes of Practice.[107] Additionally, the laws, tenets, and philosophies of particular countries and religions support a ban on such behavior.

Ethically, the pervasiveness of coverage suggests there are three gen-eral rules, or *hypernorms*, that justify a ban on quid pro quo harass-ment. Hypernorms, principles "so fundamental to human existence that [they serve] as a guide to evaluating lower level moral norms," are usually reflected in global principles that are generally recognized in a variety of ways.[108] They are often cast in the language of rights. An examination of the global and regional declarations above sug-gests quid pro quo harassment involves the hypernorms of personal security,[109] respect for human dignity,[110] and nondiscrimination.[111] Professors Donaldson and Dunfee, in their integrative social contracts theory, recognize macrosocial and microsocial contracts.[112] They argue that hypernorms can be used to border or limit the cultural relativism of micronorms. If nonharassment is a hypernorm, then a MNC can ethically justify a global ban on harassment. This means that although quid pro quo harassment may be tolerated in China, for example, it is appropriate for a company operating there to ban it.

It is harder to justify a global ban on environmental sexual harass-ment. This type of harassment seldom involves personal security and there is no general consensus – even in the USA – as to what is included within the concept. Staring, verbal comments, jokes, and similar ac-tions are not perceived as harassment of women in many countries.[113] To the extent that such harassment erodes human dignity and is dis-criminatory, it violates two of the hypernorms. Thus, organizations can ban demeaning and discriminatory treatment. What constitutes such treatment, though, should be determined on a microsocial basis. Cul-tural imperialism, to be differentiated from insistence upon following universal norms, should also be avoided.[114]

It is appropriate for a MNC to have a uniform corporate culture[115] that stresses respect for individuals and equal opportunity. However, it would be necessary to have training and possibly some form of mentoring to effectively implement it. This is where cultural differences can be taken into account.[116] Exploration of what constitutes a harassing environment in a particular location should be addressed through seminars, focus groups, and by other means.[117] It is unrealistic to expect that the US standard for harassing environment sexual harassment would be accepted elsewhere. However, respecting cultural differences does not mean respecting the lowest common denominator. A minimum standard should be set by the MNC, and a chance to appeal outside the local organization should be provided.[118]

b. Equal pay and comparable worth

Another important part of a nondiscrimination policy is equal pay. Worldwide, no more than one-fifth of wages go to women.[119] This is partly due to women being concentrated in low-paying jobs, but it is also attributable to women often being paid less than men for the same work.[120] At a minimum, a company should have a policy of paying women the same wage as men for the same work. This would represent a big change in some developing countries where women are sought as workers because they are willing to work harder for less.[121] A more problematic issue is that of comparable worth. Although women's jobs are often lower paying than those where men are concentrated, the jobs that are predominately female are not necessarily of lesser value to the organization. Comparable worth is a means of addressing this inequity.

One basis for the doctrine of comparable worth emanates from the United Nation's Convention on the Elimination of All Forms of Discrimination Against Women, which was adopted by the United Nations General Assembly on December 18, 1979.[122] It entered into force on September 3, 1981, when it had been ratified by twenty states as provided by Article 27 of the Convention.[123] It is the most comprehensive Convention dealing with women's rights, and as of 1997, it has been ratified by 161 states.[124] The Convention requires signatories to "embody the principle of the equality of men and women" in their constitutions or appropriate legislations[125] and to "modify or abolish existing laws, regulations, customs and practices" that discriminate against women.[126] Article 11 explicitly mandates the doctrine of comparable worth by requiring signatories to "take all appropriate measures to eliminate discrimination against women in the field of employment"[127] and to ensure equality of men and women to "equal remuneration" and "equal treatment [for] work of equal value."[128]

In practice, the doctrine of comparable worth requires employers to pay workers in jobs traditionally held by women according to their worth to the employer.[129] Because male and female jobs are traditionally compared in terms of the skill, effort, responsibility, and working conditions of the job,[130] the doctrine would require, after a comparative evaluation of the jobs, employers to make equity adjustments if they find that jobs in which women predominate are valued by the employer, but are not paid according to this value.[131] The idea of comparable worth focuses on the requirement that men and women within the same organization be paid the same salary for work that is judged to be of equal value.[132]

Opponents of the comparable worth theory argue that "salaries are determined in large part by an assessment of the demand for, and the supply of the type of labor needed. Relying on prevailing market rates, they contend, is a neutral, non-discriminatory wage mechanism based on supply and demand."[133] In comparison, the doctrine of comparable worth assumes that women will continue to work in female-dominated occupations, but that they should be paid according to their worth to the employer rather than the value an imperfect labor market places on their services.[134]

Comparable worth has limited application in the USA,[135] but it is mandated in many other countries. Australia, Ireland, New Zealand, Switzerland, the UK, and Canada have implemented pay equity programs in one form or another.[136] As demonstrated by the GDI, the wage gap in Australia is much narrower than the wage gap in the USA, or other countries. This narrow gap has been attributed to "deliberate efforts by centralized wage-setting tribunals to promote equality for workers in jobs predominately held by women."[137] State and federal tribunals set minimum wages and other minimum terms of employment.[138] The tribunals, taking mandate from CEDAW, embraced pay equity principles as a natural part of the wage-setting process. Australia's wage-setting process is not market-based, workers in predominately female jobs benefit from pay equity without having to assert their individual rights, as litigation would require.[139]

In developing countries, especially, women who are in the labor force generally work in different sectors and perform tasks different from men.[140] For example, almost two-thirds of garment workers worldwide are female.[141] In some areas, women are the preferred workers because they are considered more submissive, they will work for lower wages, and are easier to fire.[142] Globalization increases the pressures on investment-hungry countries to "race to the bottom."[143] This type of exploitation must be avoided if women are to become meaningful members of the economy.

a. Pregnancy

Nondiscrimination on the basis of maternity and childcare issues is another important component of a discrimination policy. In some countries, women are confronted by sterilization certificate requirements, pregnancy tests, and single-status requirements.[144] Such screening devices keep large numbers of women outside the workforce.[145] Employer nondiscrimination is particularly important where young women are being hired for entry-level jobs in developing countries. Even if the laws prohibit such practices, they are still common. Mexico, for example, prohibits discrimination on the basis of maternity including discrimination against pregnant, and nursing women.[146] However, these laws are not enforced[147] and pregnancy tests before hiring, or firing on determination of pregnancy are common, especially in the border factories, or *maquiladoras*.[148]

The policies of the *maquiladoras* have been challenged by NGOs, the ILO, and lawsuits as being discriminatory and abusive.[149] Many of the *maquiladoras* are operated by MNCs who have policies against such discrimination in their US operations.[150] So far, they have successfully withstood the outside pressures to change their Mexican operations, arguing that if a company were to change, it would be at a competitive disadvantage vis-à-vis the other organizations, and that it cannot afford the "substantial financial liabilities in the social security system for maternity benefits."[151] The Mexican government has avoided forcing the issue because it is afraid that companies may move their operations elsewhere.[152] They claim that pregnancy testing of applicants is not illegal because their law speaks in terms of protecting employees, not applicants.[153] Even if this interpretation is accurate, it does not address the problem of the firing or constructive firing of employees who become pregnant. As the challenges to such policies continue to grow, as does the publicity, it becomes harder for the MNC to maintain such inconsistent policies. A feasible step in the right direction would be to ban firing of employees on the basis of pregnancy.

Protective legislation based on women's reproductive abilities present a barrier to equal treatment in some countries. China, for example, has regulations that limit a woman's work during menstruation and menopause.[154] During menstruation the level of physical exertion is regulated, and work in cold water, low temperatures, and high altitudes is prohibited.[155] More generally, Chinese Labor Law prohibits women from working in especially strenuous or dangerous jobs,[156] which are often the most highly paid, because such work is believed to increase the risk of dislocating the uterus.[157] Protective legislation and rules in the USA were seen as barriers to equal treatment decades ago, and as such have generally been eliminated.[158] China is a signatory to the Convention for the Elimination of All Forms of Discrimination Against Women, and the protective legislation is arguably in violation of this.[159]

Protective legislation based on pregnancy is more common, as is maternity leave. Over 120 countries have laws providing for paid maternity leave.[160] This does not solve the problem of (and indeed may contribute to)[161] discrimination against women "due to their reproductive roles"[162] because it is more expensive to hire women.

b. Childcare

One of the most difficult cultural norms to change is the idea that it is women who should bear the responsibility for children. Companies can address this by providing parental rather than only maternal leave. However, even in the USA where this is mandated by the Family and Medical Leave Act,[163] men seldom avail themselves of this option. Yet, they too need childcare. Over two million workers are single fathers; one in every six single parents is a dad.[164] Rather than fight against this norm, companies can better address the issue by providing childcare. Studies have indicated that providing childcare is not unduly expensive because it cuts down on absenteeism, increases employee loyalty, and contributes to a more stable workforce. The Families & Work Institute's (FWI) National Study of the Changing Workforce found that employees of companies that have implemented family-friendly programs were more likely to have "higher levels of job satisfaction, more commitment to their companies' success, greater loyalty to their companies, and a stronger intention to remain with their companies."[165]

Employee-sponsored childcare is a practice that enables employees to better integrate their work and personal lives. Research has shown that the difficulty of juggling work and personal lives can result in stress and fatigue, complaints about work demands, and more critically, the loss of valued employees or the sudden change in the performance of people who otherwise had great potential.[166] By providing childcare, companies make "an explicit link between people's personal needs and business goals."[167] As a result, companies both benefit the employees, and increase productivity and effectiveness in the business. Childcare "contributes to employees being at work and working productively."[168]

According to FWI's 1998 Business Work-Life Study, few companies have actually evaluated return on investment for work-life programs, including childcare assistance. However, the study notes a "perceived return on investment."[169] Two-thirds of employers reported that the benefits of childcare programs exceeded the costs or that the programs were cost-neutral.

Another study found that "when considering a job change, ninety-three percent of parents say work-site childcare is an important factor. In addition, twenty-six percent of management-level employees say they have turned down or failed to pursue a job opportunity because they valued their existing work-site childcare."[170] According to the charity Women Returners' Network, affordable childcare is still the main problem for women going back to work.[171]

Other studies have considered the cost of not providing childcare and found that employee absenteeism, due to childcare breakdowns, are estimated to cost US businesses $3 billion annually.[172] These breakdowns occur when parents are forced to rely on informal arrangements. "Forty percent of employees report missing one to five days of work annually due to childcare breakdowns."[173] This study concluded that better childcare, backed up in law, could save business up to 30 percent of the absenteeism and tardiness costs.[174] For example, one law firm reportedly spent $170,000 in one year to provide back-up childcare in emergencies, while realizing approximately $800,000 additional revenues from increased billable hours that the back-up childcare provided.[175]

Similarly, a review of JP Morgan Chase's back-up childcare program "showed that 98 percent of parents who use the program would have taken unscheduled time off from work to care for their children had the back-up program not been available. In just one year, the back-up program generated more than a 100 percent return on investment."[176] JP Morgan Chase tracked the savings from their program of back-up care centers at $803,000 annually. Moreover, a JP Morgan Chase work-life manager observed that when employees feel less torn between going back to work and staying home with their babies, the loyalty factor for the firm was tremendous. Their work-life manager has been quoted as saying that they "know that free infant care has made a big difference for people, and thus for the company."[177]

Whether to provide childcare and what may be needed varies across countries. For example, in societies where there are close, extended families as in the Philippines and Thailand, childcare may not be much of an issue for the employee.[178] A growing trend in this regard is to provide nursing areas and time off for mothers to nurse their children.[179]

Some countries mandate that companies provide childcare. In China, for example, regulations were created requiring employers to provide childcare centers and kindergartens.[180] The change in China from the government-provided subsidies for childcare due to economic reform and privatization, however, has resulted in many employers ignoring this requirement.[181]

2. Training

Training is particularly important for companies to implement for two reasons: to ensure compliance with company policies such as nonharassment, and to ensure a competent workforce, especially in developing countries.[182] Compliance with legal rules, without training, does not lead to success in fighting harassment.

Studies of workplace harassment in the USA show that the level of harassment has remained relatively consistent despite companies implementing bans.[183] Training, although not required for the safe harbor that companies seek through legal compliance, provides the necessary link between bans and results. It helps change perceptions and promotes understanding of the rules.[184] Social science studies show that training affects people differently. For example, women tend to be less affected by training than men.[185] Also, men with a high propensity to harass are affected more highly than men with a low propensity.[186] This suggests that training will be most effective when done in small groups of similar people.[187] Training is also likely to be most effective when it is clear that top management strongly supports it. This recommendation is consistent with the recommendation regarding mentoring for corporate norms. Additionally, it will probably be most effective when done by someone who thoroughly understands the cultural milieu.

The Philippines, in attempts to promote equality for women, implemented sensitivity training programs for males and females. The latter was thought necessary because women "tend to denigrate their own sex when it comes to making decisions."[188] Among the Toba Batak people, many families no longer think that investing in a girl's training or education is a waste because they can depend more on their daughters than their sons to be successful when they attend an institute of higher learning.[189]

Employers have an incentive to train women workers. Training makes them persistent workers as opposed to casual or secondary workers, which increases the stability of the workforce.[190] Computer work is an area where there may be less gender bias in terms of jobs. Training women to be "tech-savvy" not only gives employers a greater core of workers, it also means that women have portable skills and better chances for advancement and rehiring in times of economic downturns.

Some companies have recently been recognized for their training efforts. Motorola Malaysia, a winner of the US Department of State Award for Excellence in the Large Multinational category in 2000, has one of the largest private-sector workforces and a wholly Malaysian management team.[191] It supports a variety of training and educational opportunities at various levels in cooperation with different institutions.[192] If these training programs are open to women as well as men, their efforts will have a significant impact on women in the region. Xerox do Brasil, a winner in 1999, was cited for its significant training and education efforts, particularly at the local community level.[193] Several programs are aimed at teenagers. To the extent that such early intervention includes girls as well as boys, it can go a long way toward meaningful inclusion of women in the economy.[194]

3. Mentoring

When women enter the workforce, they often enter in jobs that are segregated by sex. One result of such segregation is a limitation in career opportunities.[195] In the USA mentoring "a developmental relationship between an individual and a more senior and influential manager or professional"[196] has long been recognized as a way to help individuals in underrepresented groups be successful in an organization.[197] In comparison to some of the other pro-equality measures mentioned above such as comparable worth, mentoring is relatively inexpensive for a company to implement.

Mentoring can provide visibility, access to information, and chances to gain experience and show competence that would otherwise not be available.[198] In countries where women have traditionally not been a part of the workforce or have only been involved at the lowest levels, company-provided mentoring programs are particularly important.[199] When women are seen as appendages to men,[200] and their decisions are suspect,[201] they cannot succeed in a male-dominated environment.[202] In addition to the mentoring benefits mentioned above, the relationship can also provide protection and help buffer the mentee from both overt and covert forms of discrimination[203] through "reflected power."[204] Further, mentoring can help the mentee develop a positive and secure self-image[205] and help to alter stereotypical perceptions.[206] However, in order for mentoring to be successful in an environment where there has been discrimination the mentor needs to be someone who has traditionally been seen as powerful within the organization.[207] In most developing societies, this will be a male, and often a male from a connected family,[208] or an older male.[209]

Studies in the USA suggest that male mentors can better confer organizational legitimacy because they are seen as having more power.[210] This includes both formal power, and informal power. Informal power gives holders better access to information and the social networks of organizations.[211] However, psychosocial mentoring may be better provided by someone who more closely matches the mentee.[212] Having a successful woman mentor a junior woman may give the mentee a model to emulate[213] and enable her to see that success is possible as well as how to achieve it. Additionally, peer mentoring may be successful if "pioneers" who have successfully worked in the organization for a while mentor newer female employees. This implies that there is not one model that will succeed in all settings, and that multiple mentoring relationships or programs may need to be established by a company.[214]

Some scholars have suggested that in collectivist societies, the mentoring relationship would likely be more focused on socializing mentees to the norms of the organization whereas in societies that have greater tolerance for individual differences, the mentoring relationship could foster career paths that could extend beyond the organization.[215] These studies rely on Hofstede's work in which he divided cultures along five dimensions including individualism, power distance, and whether a society tends to be dynamic or tradition-bound and resistant to change.[216] In situations where great emphasis is placed on organizational conformity and loyalty to the organization, support from leaders in the organization becomes critical if cultural norms are to change to include women as important members of the workforce.[217] A large number of the societies that have traditionally excluded women from the workforce fit within this profile.

In the USA, mentoring programs were often established as part of a formal affirmative action plan.[218] In societies where unattached men and women do not normally mix, a formal program is probably essential. It can be a part of a corporate nondiscrimination policy (discussed above). The company-sponsored mentoring activities should take place primarily, if not exclusively, in the workplace. This can help overcome negative connotations of cross-gender mentoring.[219] MNCs that operate in the USA are likely to have mentoring programs. Thus, they have an established base of experience to call on in setting up mentoring programs in their non-US operations.

For example, several of the companies that have received the US Department of State Award for Excellence have mentoring programs. Ford Motor Company, which received the award for its innovative HIV/AIDS program in South Africa,[220] has company-sponsored re-source groups such as the Professional Women's Network (PWN) and the Women In Finance Network (WIFN). PWN focuses on the professional development of women through promoting an environment that attracts, develops, retains, and advances talented women. An important part of this is mentoring programs. WIFN works to support diversity, among other goals. Another winner is Xerox do Brasil. In the USA, Xerox USA has a reputation as a good place for women to work, and it has a variety of programs to foster this atmosphere, including mentoring programs.[221] In the US operation, 21 percent of the people at the vice-president level and above are women.[222]

There is virtually no information on cross-cultural mentoring. Thus, it is unclear whether mentors from the USA who are sent overseas to work would be successful in mentoring women in that milieu. Some emerging work suggests that the relationship is especially susceptible to "conflicts in cultural values, work values, and gender expectations."[223] It would seem that the individual would be less successful at psychosocial mentoring and mentoring to the norms of the local organization. However, if that person is seen as having power within the organization, she or he is more likely to be successful in terms of women advancing within the organization.

Conclusion

Jeffrey Garten, the Dean of the Yale School of Management and a columnist for *Business Week*, argues that it is time for corporate officials to reassert their influence to work for global stability and peace. He visualizes this happening as part of the effort of companies to dig themselves out of their "reputational hole." It may be a byproduct of the increased vigilance of corporate America by the public, Congress, and more aggressive legislators.[224] Additionally, the heads of some MNCs have put forth the idea of an affirmative civic duty, the "duty to be doing good as opposed to avoiding doing bad."[225] Implementing these goals in conjunction with policies designed to better integrate women into the workforce as wage earners can have many positive effects. These include the ability to attract top people,[226] output gains and a reduction in poverty, and social stability.

Companies can most consistently, on a daily basis, often more than law, help effect change and bring women into the economy as wage-earners. Being a wage-earner leads to real power within the family. According to the World Report on Violence and Health, women becoming educated and economically empowered decreases the likelihood of violence within the family.[227] This power can also "expand out"[228] and create conditions that socialize and empower women outside of the workplace and "give them tools to interact more successfully in their society."[229] As indicated at the beginning of this chapter, there seems to be a correlation between involving women in the workforce and peace. The benefits to women, the employer, society, and global stability call for companies to implement inclusion policies.

Notes

This chapter is reprinted in large part from Terry Morehead Dworkin and Cindy A. Schipani, *Gender Voice and Correlations with Peace*, 36 VAND. J. OF TRANSN'L L. 527 (2003). Reprinted with permission.

1. The distinction between women working, and women as wage earn-ers, is important in data analysis. All women work. However, in many parts of the world, work in the fields and work in the home is not compensated through wages. The distinction is largely "socially

constructed" and affects a country's reporting of statistics. For example, when Sweden included agriculture work in its definition of women's work, the percentage of working women rose from about 8 percent to 52 percent. Zafiris Tzannatos, *Women and Labor Market Changes in the Global Economy: Growth Helps, Inequalities Hurt, and Public Policy Matters*, 27 WORLD DEVELOPMENT 551, 554–55 (1999).

2. Ibid., at 552.
3. Timothy L. Fort and Cindy A. Schipani, *The Role of the Corporation in Fostering Sustainable Peace*, 35 VAND. J. TRANSN'L L. 389, 394–399 (2002).
4. Partner violence is highest when women begin entering the labor force and fill non-traditional roles, challenging norms. WORLD HEALTH ORGANIZATION, WORLD REPORT ON VIOLENCE AND HEALTH, October 3, 2002, available at http://www5.who.int/violence_injury_prevention/main.cfm?p=0000000117(hereinafter cited as WORLD REPORT).
5. Ibid. The reason for the increase is that when women are at the low end of society, violence is not needed to demonstrate male superiority. With the attainment of status, gender norms change so that violence is not accepted. Ibid. This, of course, does not mean that it does not occur; it is merely reduced. For much of the 1990s, homicides were the leading cause of death of women in US workplaces. In 2000, 30 percent of the women who died on the job were homicide victims. *Workplace Violence*, 18 INDIV. RTS. RPTR. (BNA), August 6, 2002, at 70.
6. Tzannatos, above n. 1. Women entering the workforce does not have merely a redistributive effect; instead, the "size of the pie" grows, and women claim a bigger share. Men's wages do not necessarily decline in absolute terms. Ibid., at 560.
7. Ibid., at 555. In Vietnam, for example, the influence of Confucianism which is strong in Vietnamese culture tends to put women in a subordinate position in families and society, and awareness of gender equality issues is relatively low. This is despite Vietnam ratifying the Convention on the Elimination of All Forms of Discrimination against Women in 1982, and instituted a National Plan of Action for the Advancement of Women in 1997. Under this, all provinces and the central level of government have developed plans of action. The 1994 Labor Code mandates equality in the workplace and affirmative action in recruitment. UNICEF, *The Situation of Women and Children in Viet Nam* (2000).

8. Robert D. Baird, *Gender Implications for a Uniform Civil Code*, 28 LAW & SOC'Y REV. 145 (1994). "It is a common indictment of many if not most traditional texts, religious and otherwise, that they were written by men for men, that they express a man's point of view, and that the perspectives of women and other marginalized persons are systematically, if not consciously excluded." Ibid.

9. Ibid., at 149.

10. For example, Tahir Mamood, speaking on the Muslim law of *khul'*, states that the law of divorce is not widely understood by Indian Muslims. He states that a wife can dissolve a marriage that is irretrievably broken down, as can a husband. Most think, though, that this right only belongs to the husband. Ibid., at 155.

11. Ibid., at 157 (citing Mamood).

12. See Dexter Filkins, *Can Islamists Run a Democracy?*, N.Y. TIMES, November 24, 2002, at Sec. 4. "The Koran is inadequate as a basis for legislation. . . . There are too many places where it would conflict with the civil law [of Turkey]." Ibid. (quoting Nilufer Narli, a professor of sociology at Bogazici in Istanbul).

13. WORLD REPORT, above n. 4; Rachel Zimmerman, *Study Finds Violence Took 1.6 Million Lives in 2000*, WALL ST. J., October 3, 2002, at D5.

14. Zimmerman, above n. 13, at D5.

15. Heidelberg Institute for International Conflict Research, at http://www.conflict.com/hiik/manuel_en.html (last visited November 25, 2002).

16. Information on Transparency International can be obtained at http://www.transparency.de. See also Fort and Schipani, above n. 3, at 394–399.

17. Fort and Schipani, above n. 3, at 398.

18. Ibid.

19. Ibid., at 398.

20. Ibid.

21. See UNITED NATIONS DEVELOPMENT PROGRAMME, HUMAN DEVELOPMENT REPORT 14 (2001) (hereinafter HUMAN DEVELOPMENT REPORT).

22. Ibid.

23. Ibid.

24. Ibid.

25. Ibid.

26. Ibid., at 15.

27. Ibid.

28. Ibid., at 14. In relation to the World Development Report, the greater the disparity in basic human development, the lower is a country's GDI compared with its HDI. Ibid.

29. Ibid., at 14.

30. Ibid., at 213. The US GDI ranked it fourth of 144 countries. It fell behind Norway, Australia and Canada because of income disparity. In comparison, the USA had the greatest income disparity between men and women. Ibid., at 211.

31. Ibid., at 213.

32. Unfortunately, data were not available from the Heidelberg Institute for all countries for which a gender development index ranking was available. In total, we had 86 data points from the Heidelberg Institute data. See table 5.1.

33. Among the twenty-eight variables used to measure and rank countries by their levels of conflict are: region, participants, external parties, number of participating parties, initiator, political systems of the conflict initiator, political systems of the affected party, economic and political stage development, disputed issues in conflict, and political, territorial and military outcomes. Further information regarding these variables may be found at Heidelberg Institute for International Conflict Research, above n. 15.

34. Fort and Schipani, above n. 3, at 397 (citing the Heidelberg Institute for International Conflict Research, above n. 15).

35. Heidelberg Institute for International Conflict Research, above n. 15.

36. Tzannatos, above n. 1, at 563.

37. See below nn. 38–39 and accompanying text.

38. 19 I.L.M. 33 (opened for signature on March 1, 1980).

39. Clarification on Environmental Concerns in OECD Guidelines for Multinational Enterprises, 25 I.L.M. 494 (1986).

40. David Engel, *Concepts of Rights: Introduction*, 28 Law & Soc'y Rev. 489, 490 (1994).

41. Ibid., at 564.

42. While it is permissible to discriminate against married women in hiring in Korea, it is now illegal to discriminate against them in promotions and dismissal. Ibid.

43. See e.g. T. Omas Ihromi, *Inheritance and Equal Rights for Toba Batak Daughters*, 28 Law & Soc'y Rev. 525, 527 (1994) (citing the work of Max Weber, and of Sally Falk Moore).

44. Satjipto Rahardjo, *Between Two Worlds: Modern State and Traditional Society in Indonesia*, 28 Law & Soc'y Rev. 493, 494 (1994). Rahardjo further found that development did not proceed in the traditional way Weber's theory hypothesized, e.g., progressing from

the stage of traditional authority to charismatic authority to rational legal authority. The development of new nation-states in the second half of the twentieth century experienced "simultaneous waves of development." Ibid.

45. Ibid., at 500. Rahardjo asserts that this is true of Southeast Asian countries in general.

46. See Ihromi, above n. 43. Ihromi cites Sally Falk Moore's theory of semi-autonomous social fields. Falk argues that these fields generate internal rules, customs, and symbols. However, they are also vulnerable to forces coming from the surrounding world. Ibid., at 527.

47. Srimati Basu, *Indian Women and Inheritance Law*, 28 LAW & SOC'Y REV. (1994).

48. Ibid.

49. Ibid.

50. Ibid.

51. Ibid.

52. Ibid.

53. Ibid.

54. Juree Vichit-Vadakan, *Women and the Family in Thailand in the Midst of Social Change*, 28 LAW & SOC'Y REV. (1994).

55. Ibid.

56. Ibid.

57. Ibid.

58. See sources above n. 7. Ethiopia presents another example where "tradition and culture often prevail over civil and criminal law, and in practice women do not enjoy equal status with men." See AFROL, *Gender Profiles: Ethiopia*, at http://www.afrol.com; Cynthia Guttman, *When Girls Go Missing from the Classroom: Why Girls Are Not Being Educated in Parts of Africa, Afghanistan, and S. Asia*, UNESCO COURIER, May 1, 2001, at 13. Discrimination is worse in the rural areas where 85 percent of the population lives. Guttman, above. They cite the abduction of women for marriage despite its banning in the penal code. Ibid. "Culturally-based abuses including wife beating and marital rape are pervasive social problems." Ibid. In 1997, the government adopted a National Program of Action to enhance the status of women. This includes education and work opportunities for women. AFROL, above.

59. Ley Federal del Trabajo, arts. 3, 5, 56, 86, 164, 166.

60. Constitucion Political De Los Estados Unidos Mexicanos, art. 123, cited in Charles Hollon and Kathryn Culbertson, *Employment Discrimination Law in the U.S., Canada, and Mexico: A Comparative Overview*, 6 INT'L HUMAN RESOURCES J. 39 (1997).

61. See e.g. Baird, above n. 8, at 157–58 (discussing the Islamic law as it is practiced "on the ground" in India regarding women's rights, and as interpreted by scholars, and its relation to a civil code granting women's rights).

62. Tzannatos, above n. 1, at 566.

63. Law in Indonesia has been said to be an "expression of national aspiration," rather than an instrument of social change. Ihromi, above n. 43, at 536.

64. Joel Handler, *Legal Rights and Social Inclusion*, 28 LAW & SOC'Y REV. 504, 505 (1994).

65. See below nn. 154–59 and accompanying text.

66. Charles J. Ogletree and Rangita de Silva-de Alwis, *Gender Differences Become a Trap: The Impact of China's Labor Law on Women*, 14 YALE J. L. & FEMINISM 69 (2002).

67. Ibid. It also leads to women being seen as more expendable in economic downturns. This is reinforced by legislation requiring earlier retirement for females.

68. Sydney M. Cone, III, *Symposium: The Multinational Enterprise as Global Corporate Citizen*, 21 N. Y. L. SCH. J. INT'L & COMP. L. 1 (2001).

69. Kathleen Peratis, et al., *Markets and Women's International Human Rights*, 25 BROOK. J. INT'L L. 141 (1999).

70. Tourists can also be an agent for change toward global norms. See Engel, above n. 40, at 490.

71. The media have been important as a change agent in Southeast Asia. "Governments fear and respect the media and are sometimes inclined to capitulate rather than risk adverse publicity. The media are thus able to empower those groups within states whose causes they choose to report. . . . Indirectly, the media also play a significant role in disseminating ideas about law and politics across state boundaries." Engel, above n. 40, at 491.

72. Akin Rabibhadana, *Custom, State Law, and the Problem of Selective Enforcement*, 28 LAW & SOC'Y REV. 503, 504 (1994) (speaking of Thai society).

73. Handler, above n. 64, at 505 (citing Myrna Feliciano speaking of the Philippines' experience); Baird, above n. 8, at 147 (citing a study showing a lack of knowledge of the areas of law most significantly affected by a uniform civil code in India).

74. Engel, above n. 40, at 490. As states lose some of their predominance, the influence of multinational organizations including corporations becomes greater. See Dworkin, below n. 90, at 458, 486.

75. Handler, above n. 64, at 507 (citing T.H. Marshall). Marshall posited three types of rights important to the development of citizenship in Western society – civil rights (legal recognition of contracts, property rights, etc.), political rights (enfranchisement), and social rights. He viewed these as occurring by century, from the eighteenth to the twentieth.

76. James L. Gunderson, *Symposium: The Multinational Enterprise as Global Corporate Citizen*, above n. 68, at 15.

77. See above nn. notes 38–41 and accompanying text.

78. Civil Rights Act of 1964, Title VII, 42 U.S.C. § 2000e (1994).

79. Americans with Disabilities Act, 42 U.S.C. § 12111(5)(A) (1995).

80. Age Discrimination in Employment Act of 1967, 29 U.S.C. § 621 (1994).

81. Some developing countries such as Vietnam have instituted affirmative action requirements as a way to increase the number of women in the workplace. Labor Code of the Socialist Republic of Vietnam, available at www.ivietnam.com/eng/business/laws/labourcode/basic/chapterX.asp, Chapter X, art. 111.

82. See below nn. 83–111 and accompanying text.

83. See e.g. *Robinson v. Jacksonville Shipyards, Inc.*, 760 F. Supp. 1486 (M.D. Fla., 1991); *Horne and Another v. Press Clough Joint Venture and Another*, EOC 92-556 (Western Australia, 1994).

84. Note, *Sexual Harassment Claims of Abusive Work Environment Under VII*, 97 HARV. L. REV. 1449, 1449–51 (1984).

85. Terry M. Dworkin, et al., *Theories of Recovery for Sexual Harassment: Going Beyond Title VII*, 25 SAN DIEGO L. REV. 125, 127 (1988).

86. Ibid., at 127–28.

87. See e.g. *Meritor Savings Bank v. Vinson*, 477 U.S. 57 (1986); *Hunt v. State of Missouri*, 89 Fair Empl. Prac. Cas. (BNA) 867 (8th Cir., 2002); *Gaines v. Bellino*, 89 Fair Empl. Prac. Cas. (BNA) 886 (N.J., 2002).

88. In 1995, approximately 25 million Chinese were employed by foreign-owned export-processing firms, and the great majority of these workers were young female migrants from rural areas. United Nations Official Report, *Women Workers in China* 3 (1995), cited in Wiseman, below n. 143, at 198.

89. Young women working in the *maquiladoros* also feel compelled to tolerate harassment in order to keep their jobs. Arriola, below n. 148, at 781–83.

90. See Terry Morehead Dworkin, *Whistleblowing, MNCs, and Peace*, 35 VAND. J. TRANSNAT'L L.457, 478 (2002); *Highlights, Global*

HR, 89 Fair Empl. Prac. (BNA) 108 (August 29, 2002) (hereinafter *Highlights*).

91. See e.g. *Meritor Savings Bank* v. *Vinson*, 477 U.S. 57 (1986).
92. Ibid. The Supreme Court has recognized a defense to this type of harassment if the employer makes a reasonable effort to prevent and correct it, including effective policies and complaint procedures. The employer must also prove that the employee unreasonably failed to take advantage of employer-provided procedures. See e.g. *Faragher* v. *City of Boca Raton*, 524 U.S. 775 (1998); *Burlington Indus., Inc.* v. *Ellerth*, 524 U.S. 742, 744 (1998). Employers are strictly liable for quid pro quo harassment when a job benefit is denied.
93. See generally Michael Starr, *Who's the Boss? The Globalization of U.S. Employment Law*, 51 Bus. L. 635 (1996); Beverly H. Earle and Gerald A. Madek, *An International Perspective on Sexual Harassment Law*, 12 Law & Ineq. 43 (1993).
94. See Dworkin, above n. 90; *Highlights*, above n. 90.
95. Nancy Patterson, Recent Development, *No More Naki-Neri? The State of Japanese Sexual Harassment Law: Judgment of April 16, 1992, Fukuoka Chiiho Saibansho, Heisei Gannen (1989)(wa) No. 1872, Songai Baisho Jiken (Japan)*, 34 Harv. Int'l L.J. 206 (1993). This decision occurred at a time when harassment was dismissed as trivial by companies and businessmen. See Daniel Niven, *The Case of the Hidden Harassment*, Harv. Bus. Rev. 12 (March/April, 1992).
96. See Dworkin, above n. 90, at 479.
97. The European Commission prepared a Code of Practice after the Council of Ministers passed a resolution, *The Protection of the Dignity of Men and Women at Work*, which defined harassment in the same terms as those used in the USA. It did so after finding that harassment was a serious problem for many working women. See generally Michael Rubenstein, How to Combat Sexual Harassment at Work: A Guide to Implementing the European Commission Code of Practice (1993); Michael Rubenstein, The Dignity of Women at Work: A Report on the Problem of Sexual Harassment in the Member States of the European Communities (1987).
98. In 2000, in response to a proposal from the European Commission (2000 O.J. (E 337) 196), the Council issued a decision that established a program for a Community framework strategy on gender equality. It does not specifically mention sexual harassment. 2001 O.J. (L17/22) 19.1.
99. The Code is nonbinding on Member States and has no enforcement mechanism. See Anita Bernstein, *Law, Culture, and Harassment*, 142

U. Pa. L. Rev. 1227 (1994). Bernstein posits that the lack of sanctions resulted from sexual harassment not being widely viewed as a legal wrong in the EU Member States. Ibid. Because the Code was non-binding, the Member States were free to establish or maintain their own laws, and these vary from country to country. See Dworkin, above n. 90, at 478–79.

100. Sex Discrimination Act of 1984, 20 FCR 217, Div. 3, §§ 28A–28B (Australia). In addition to the federal legislation, Australia's six states and two territories have anti-discrimination legislation. See e.g. Equal Opportunity Act 1984, § 87 (S. Austl. Acts & Ord.); Anti-Discrimination Act 1991, § 118 (Queensl. Stat.). See generally Jeffrey Minson, *Second Principles of Social Justice*, 10 Law in Context 1 (1992).

101. "In any proceedings brought under this Act . . . it is a defence to prove that the person exercised all reasonable diligence to ensure that the agent or employee would not act in contravention of the Act." Equal Opportunity Act 1984, § 91 (3) (S. Austl. Acts & Ord.). The US Supreme Court has created a defense for hostile environment sexual harassment. See above n. 84.

102. Dana Deane, in-house counsel at Abbott Laboratories, argues for a global harassment and anti-discrimination policy so the organization can articulate a uniform policy and corporate culture. See *Highlights*, above n. 90.

103. UN GAOR, 3d Sess., 67th plen. Mtg., at 1, UN Doc. A/811 (1948). This document was part of the International Bill of Human Rights, UN GAOR, 3rd Sess., Supp. No. 1, at 71, UN Doc. A/565 (1948).

104. 19 I.L.M. 33 (opened for signature on March 1, 1980).

105. Clarification on Environmental Concerns in OECD Guidelines for Multinational Enterprises, 25 I.L.M. 494 (1986).

106. European Social Charter, Europ. T.S. No. 163, 36 I.L.M. 31 (1997).

107. See above n. 97.

108. Donaldson and Dunfee, below n. 112, at 265.

109. W.C. Frederick, *The Empirical Quest for Normative Meaning: Introduction and Orientation*, 2 Bus. Ethics Q. 91 (1992).

110. Donaldson and Dunfee, below n. 112, at 267.

111. Thomas Donaldson, The Ethics of International Business 87 (1989).

112. Thomas Donaldson and Thomas W. Dunfee, *Toward A Unified Conception of Business Ethics: Integrative Social Contracts Theory*, 19 Acad. Mgmt. Rev. 252 (1994). See also Thomas Donaldson and Thomas R. Dunfee, Ties that Bind: A Social Contracts Approach to Business Ethics 49–81 (1999).

113. See e.g. Sandra Orihuela and Abagail Montjoy, *The Education of Latin America's Sexual Harassment Law: A Look at Mini-Skirts and Multinationals in Peru*, 30 Cal. W. Int'l L.J. 323 (2000).

114. Richard T. DeGeorge, *International Business Ethics*, 4 Bus. Ethics Q. 1 (1994); Derek G. Barella, Note, *Checking the "Trigger-Happy" Congress: The Extraterritorial Extension of Federal Employment Laws Requires Prudence*, 69 Ind. L.J. 889, 913 (1994). Cf. Mark Granovetter, *Economic Action and Social Structure: The Problem of Embeddedness*, 91 Am. J. Soc. 481 (1985) (arguing that contractarianism and other business ethics arguments have a Western bias).

115. See *Highlights*, above n. 90, at 108.

116. Hofstede, below n. 216, at 276.

117. See Elletta Sangrey Callahan, et al., *Integrating Trends in Whistle-blowing and Corporate Governance: Promoting Organizational Effectiveness, Societal Responsibility, and Employee Empowerment*, 40 Am. Bus. L.J. 177 (2002).

118. The appeal could go to the person doing organizational compliance auditing, who would then be responsible for ensuring that local interpretations are not setting the bar too low. Dworkin, above n. 90, at 481. This may be easier now that companies are taking compliance more seriously and instituting oversight. See e.g. *ABA Task Force on Corporate Responsibility*, Bus. L., November/December, 2002, at 60–61; Carol Hymowitz, *Building a Board That's Independent, Strong and Effective*, Wall St. J., November 19, 2002, at B1.

119. Tzannatos, above n. 1, at 551.

120. Ibid.

121. See e.g. Arriola, below n. 148, at 765–782.

122. Convention on the Elimination of All Forms of Discrimination Against Women, opened for signature March 1, 1980, 1249 U.N.T.S. 13 (hereinafter CEDAW).

123. Ibid., art. 27, at 23.

124. Malvina Halberstam, *United States Ratification of the Convention on the Elimination of All Forms of Discrimination Against Women*, 31 Geo. Wash. J. Int'l L. & Econ. 49, 49 (1997).

125. CEDAW, art. 2(a), at 16.

126. Ibid., art. 2(f), at 16.

127. Ibid., art. 11(1), at 18.

128. Ibid., art. 11(1)(d), at 18.

129. See Andrea Giampetro-Meyer, *Resurrecting Comparable Worth as a Remedy for Gender-Based Wage Discrimination*, 23 S.w. U. L. Rev. 225, 226 (1994).

130. Value is determined by a detailed evaluation of jobs and considers the factors of skill and knowledge, mental and physical effort, responsibility and working conditions. Ibid., at 229.
131. Ibid.
132. Ibid., at 229.
133. SUSAN G. MESEY, IN PURSUIT OF EQUALITY PAY 99 (1992).
134. Giampetro-Meyer, above n. 129, at 229.
135. See ibid., at 230–31. Comparable worth has mainly been adopted through union efforts, and primarily in the public sector. The primary argument against its adoption is that it does not let the marketplace determine wages.
136. Ibid., at 236. When the EC was established, France insisted on the adoption of comparable worth because it had already implemented the concept, and was concerned that it would be at a competitive disadvantage if all the countries did not adopt it.
137. Ibid., at 238.
138. Ibid.
139. Ibid.
140. Tzannatos, above n. 1, at 555.
141. Ibid., at 556. These female workers account for nearly one-fifth of all women in the labor force in manufacturing. Ibid.
142. See Arriola, below n. 148, at 783–87.
143. Lesley J. Wiseman, Note, *A Place for "Maternity" in the Global Workplace: International Case Studies and Recommendations for the International Labor Force*, 28 OHIO N.U. L. REV. 195 (2001).
144. Ibid., at 562.
145. In the Arab world, there is often a tension at the national level between a desire to further development and to preserve the traditional family unit. This results in explicitly pro-natalist policies such as unavailability of effective contraception which, of course, inhibits women in becoming members of the labor force. Valentine M. Moghadam, *The Political Economy of Female Employment in the Arab Region*, in GENDER AND DEVELOPMENT IN THE ARAB WORLD: WOMEN'S ECONOMIC PARTICIPATION: PATTERNS AND POLICIES 6 (Nabil F. Khoury and Valentine M. Moghadam eds., 1995).
146. Hollon and Culbertson, above n. 60.
147. Chinese labor laws protecting women are also commonly not enforced. Ogletree and Silva-de Alwis, above n. 66.
148. See HUMAN RIGHTS WATCH, *No Guarantees: Sex Discrimination in Mexico's Maquiladora Sector*, August, 1996; Elvira R. Arriola, *Voices from the Barbed Wires of Despair: Women in the Maquiladoras, Latina Critical Legal Theory, and Gender at the U.S.-Mexico*

Border, 49 DePaul L. Rev. 729, 784 (2000); Reka S. Koerner, Note, *Pregnancy Discrimination in Mexico: Has Mexico Complied with the North American Agreement on Labor Cooperation?*, 4 Tex. F. on C.L. & C.R. 235 (1999).

149. See Koerner, above n. 148; Wiseman, above n. 143, at 213–15.
150. See Wiseman, above n. 143, at 214–15. General Electric is one of the companies cited.
151. See Arriola, above n. 148, at 785 (quoting Zenith Corporation's policy on pregnancy screening).
152. Wiseman, above n. 143, at 215.
153. Koerner, above n. 148, at 247.
154. Woo, below n. 180, at 157.
155. Ibid., at 157.
156. Labor Law of the People's Republic of China, art. 58-65, translated in China L. & Prac. 21 (1994).
157. Woo, below n. 180, at 158.
158. See e.g. *UAW v. Johnson Controls, Inc.*, 499 U.S. 187 (1991).
159. Wiseman, above n. 143, at 206.
160. International Labor Organization, *More than 120 Nations Provide Paid Maternity Leave: Gap in Employment Treatment for Men and Women Still Exists*, ILO Press Release, February 16, 1998, http://www.ilo.org/public/english/bureau/inf/ pr/1998/7.htm.
161. Wiseman, above n. 143.
162. Ibid.
163. 29 U.S.C. § 2601 et seq. (1993).
164. Bureau of Labor Statistics, *Household and Family Characteristics from the March 1998 Current Population Survey* (as cited in Hawaii Community Foundation – Biz Kids, *It's Good Business to Invest in Child Care*, http://www.hcf-hawaii.org/hcf/ bizkids/employers/good_business.htm).
165. Ellen Galinsky and James T. Bond, *Executive Summary*, in The 1998 Business Work-Life Study: A Sourcebook (Families and Work Institute, 1998).
166. Lotte Bailyn, Joyce Fletcher and Deborah Kolb, *Unexpected Connections: Considering the Employees' Personal Lives can Revitalize Your Business*, Sloan Management Review (Summer, 1997).
167. Ibid.
168. Phyllis Hutton Raabe, *Constructing Pluralistic Work and Career Arrangements* in The Work and Family Challenge: Rethinking Employment (Susan Lewis ed., 1996).
169. Combining Human Resource professionals' personal views with reported findings from evaluations, the study derives the *perceived*

return on investment. "Among companies offering any childcare benefit, 24 perceive negative returns on their investments, seven to eight percentage points higher than the percentages reported for flexible work arrangements and family leave policies. Another 40 percent perceive childcare assistance programs to be cost-neutral and 36 percent think the benefits of these programs outweigh their costs." Ibid.

170. Lindsay Wood, *Workplace Childcare Centers Increasing in Numbers*, THE GALT GLOBAL REVIEW, Business News, at http://www. galtglobalreview.com/business/workplace_childcare.html.

171. Galinsky and Bond, above n. 165.

172. Sheri A. Mullikin and Anthony B. Taddeo, Jr., *Balancing a Legal Career and Child Care in a 24/7 World*, http://www. milesstockbridge.com/ articles/parentrap.html, also appearing at FOR THE DEFENSE RESEARCH INSTITUTE, FOR THE DEFENSE (January 2001); see Landsman, *Juggling Work and Family*, BUS. INS. 28 (1994); Friedman, *Child Care for Employees' Kids*, HARV. BUS. REV. (March/April 1986).

173. Mullikin and Taddeo, Jr., above n. 172; see Families & Work Institute, *National Study of the Changing Workforce* (1997).

174. Mulliken and Taddeo, Jr., above n. 172; see Landsman, above n. 172; Friedman, above n. 172.

175. Mulliken and Taddeo, Jr., above n. 172; see *Big Washington Law Firm to Offer On-Site Child Care to Ease Stress for Parents*, CHIC. TRIB., March 29, 1995, at C2 (citing increased morale and productivity as additional benefits of its back-up childcare services).

176. Bright Horizons, *Benefits of Employer-Sponsored Care*, at http://www.brighthorizons.com/pages/frameset.asp?side=employer. html&content=benefits_employer.html (last visited December 2, 2002).

177. Child Care Information Exchange, *JP Morgan Chase Offers Free Infant Care*, EXCHANGE EVERY DAY 492, October 22, 2002, http://mail.ccie.com/eed/issue.php?id=142 (last visited December 2, 2002).

178. Ibid., at 565.

179. Chinese regulations require two thirty-minute nursing periods per day. Woo, below n. 180, at 159.

180. Margaret Y.K. Woo, *Biology and Equality: Challenge for Feminism in the Socialist and the Liberal State*, 42 EMORY L.J. 143, 159 (1993). These were part of a large set of regulations aimed at addressing health and other issues of women workers. The regulations are provincial regulations.

181. Wiseman, above n. 143, at 202.
182. Training helps break the vicious cycle of women's low initial human capital endowments and inferior labor market outcomes compared to men's. Tzannatos, above n. 1, at 551.
183. Joanna Grossman, *Sexual Harassment in the Workplace*, FINDLAW's WRIT, at Justice.com /MY FindLaw (November 11, 2002). Grossman is an Associate Professor of Law, Hofstra University.
184. Ibid.
185. Ibid.
186. Ibid.
187. See Callahan, et al., above n. 117.
188. Myrna Feliciano, *Legal Rights and Social Inclusion*, 28 LAW & SOC'Y REV. 507, 508 (1994). Cf. Ihromi, above n. 43, at 535 ("A convention on an international level, made into law, and equating the rights of men and women in cases of inheritance . . . cannot work for the Batak people. The women themselves would not be willing to accept such a matter." (quoting the reaction of the Toba people to the United Nations Convention on the Elimination of Discrimination Against Women)).
189. Ihromi, above n. 43, at 536.
190. Tzannatos, above n. 1, at 562. Viewing women as persistent workers means that employers are more likely to invest in them in terms of training.
191. See http://www.state.gov/www/about_state/business/cba_00award_motorola.html (last visited December 2, 2002).
192. The company supports programs such as school adoption, local university internships, scholarships, and support for university and industrial training collaboration through joint development of curriculum, research, and cross-training. It also hosts an ethical practices workshop. Ibid.
193. See http://www.state.gov/www/about_state/business/cba_99award_xerox.html (last visited December 2, 2002).
194. Much of the training is aimed at high-risk teens and less privileged groups. One of the programs helps teenagers learn in the workplace by combining work with training for personal and professional life and reaches beyond Xerox permanent staff. Ibid.
195. Tzannotos, above n. 1, at 556. The segregation also negatively affects wages.
196. George F. Dreher and Taylor H. Cox, *Race, Gender, and Opportunity: A Study of Compensation Attainment and the Establishment of Mentoring Relationships*, 81 J. APPLIED PSYCHOL. 297 (1996).

197. R.J. Burke, *Mentors in Organizations,* 9 GROUP & ORG. STUD. 353 (1984); E.A. Fageson, *The mentor advantage: Perceived career/job experiences of protégés vs. non-proteges,* J. OF ORG. BEHAV. 309 (1989). In one study, employees with extensive mentoring relationships received more promotions, higher income, and experienced more satisfaction with their pay and benefits. George F. Dreher and Ronald A. Ash, *A Comparative Study of Mentoring Among Men and Women in Managerial, Professional, and Technical Positions,* 75 J. APPLIED PSYCHOL. 539 (1990).

198. Ibid., at 298. The mentee is referred to as a *protégé.*

199. Ragins, below n. 203, at 348, states that mentoring is "essential for women" in order to achieve success within an organization. Catalyst reported that 91 percent of female executives they surveyed had mentors. Ibid. Newcomers to organizations are at a particular disadvantage in interpreting the organizational cues "because they have no history and limited contacts for making sense of the context." Jane E. Dutton, et al., *Red Light, Green Light: Making Sense of the Organizational Context for Issue Selling,* 13 ORG. SCI. 355, 356 (2002).

200. Juree Vichit-Vadakan, *Women and the Family in Thailand in the Midst of Social Change,* 28 LAW & SOC'Y REV. 515522–24 (1994). Vichit-Vadakan, cites Thailand, where women have made gains in entering the paid workforce. However, their advancement toward parity with men is hindered by the "beauty culture" and the traditional notion of their being appendages to men.

201. Feliciano, above n. 188.

202. They are also at greater risk when trying to raise potentially controversial issues such as gender-related issues. Dutton, et al., above n. 199, at 356.

203. Belle Rose Ragins, *Gender and Mentoring Relationships,* in HANDBOOK OF GENDER & WORK 347, 348 (Gary N. Powell ed., 1999). "Cultural patterns of interaction influence every aspect of an organization and give information about what is collectively valued and how people typically behave and react." Dutton, et al., above n. 199, at 365.

204. Ibid., at 348.

205. Dreher and Cox, above n. 196, at 298.

206. Ragins, above n. 203, at 348. They help women overcome the "male managerial model." Ibid.

207. In a study by Dreher and Cox, above n. 196, mentees mentored by white males earned an average of $16,840 more than those who had women or minorities as mentors. In another study of

African-American graduates of traditionally black colleges, the graduates with white male mentors had higher pay. George F. Dreher and Josephine A. Chargois, *Gender, Mentoring Experiences, and Salary Attainment among Graduates of an Historically Black University*, 53 J. VOCATIONAL BEHAV. 401 (1998).

208. There is very little research on mentoring outside the USA. Ragins, above n. 203, at 369. Ragins cites Hofstede's work on cultural differences to note that effective mentoring relationships in cultures which have collectivist orientations may differ from the Western model. Ibid., at 369–70.

209. Older may be more persuasive in societies where age rather than a youth culture is valued. Ragins, above n. 203, at 370.

210. Dreher and Cox, above n. 196, at 298, citing Belle Rose Ragins, *Barriers to mentoring: The female manager's dilemma*, 42 HUMAN RELATIONS 1 (1989).

211. Ibid.

212. Ibid., at 299. Ragins found that women may provide more psychological or supportive mentoring functions. Ragins, above n. 203, at 357. Additionally, there is some evidence that same gender mentoring yields psychosocial and career development functions. Ibid., at 362.

213. Belle Rose Ragins and D. McFarlin, *Perceptions of mentor roles in cross-gender mentoring relationships*, 37 J. VOCATIONAL BEHAV. 321 (1990).

214. Ragins, above n. 203, at 349, notes that mentoring can take a variety of forms, but identifies three forms as particularly relevant to the effects and outcomes of mentoring women. The most important of these is the distinction between formal and informal mentoring. In formal mentoring, mentors are matched with or assigned to their mentee, and the relationship typically lasts about a year. Informal mentoring arrangements happen spontaneously, and tend to last two to five years.

215. H.C. Triandis, *The self and social behavior in differing cultural contexts*, 96 PSYCHOL. REV. 506 (1989). Triandis described "tight" cultures with clear norms and low tolerance for deviation, and "loose" cultures with greater tolerance for individual differences.

216. GERT HOFSTEDE, CULTURE'S CONSEQUENCES: INTERNATIONAL DIFFERENCES IN WORK RELATED VALUES (1980).

217. Dworkin, above n. 90, at 474. One US study indicates that the most crucial cue that women relied on regarding whether to push a gender-related issue within their organization was the openness of male managers to the raising of issues. This was more important than

the number of women in management positions and changes in demographic composition. Dutton, above n.199, at 366–68.

218. Ibid.

219. In the USA, this is usually due to the perception of a romantic relationship. J.G. Clawson and K.E. Kram, *Managing cross-gender mentoring*, 27 Bus. Horizons 22 (1984). Of course, the incidence of intimate *relationships* may also increase. Conversely, woman-woman mentoring can have the negative consequence of being viewed as "plotting a revolution." Ragins, above n. 203, at 359.

220. The award was given to Ford Motor Co. South Africa in 2001. The CEO of this organization is a woman, and two of the six members of the board of directors are women. http://www.gov/r/pa/prs/ps/2002/7288.htm.

221. For example, Xerox has an Assent Management Program which includes mentoring. The CEO of Xerox is Anne Mulcahy, has been identified by Fortune as one of the "*Most Powerful Women,*" at http://www.xerox.com/go/xrx/template/display2X.jsp?url=about_xerox/about_xerox_detail. Another company cited for its employee development efforts, especially with minority Maori, is Rayonier New Zealand.

222. Ibid.

223. Ragins, above n. 203, at 370.

224. Jeffrey E. Garten, *A Foreign Policy Harmful to Business*, Bus. Wk., October 14, 2002, at 72–73. Garten cites a long history of companies influencing foreign policy. He argues that the national policy pendulum has swung too far in the direction of force of arms, and needs to swing back to a focus on long-term economic and social issues.

225. Gunderson, above n. 76. Gunderson is Secretary and General Counsel of Schlumbger Limited.

226. Ibid.

227. World Health Organization, World Report on Violence and Health (2002).

228. See Dworkin, above n. 90, at 486.

229. Ibid.

6 | The ecological challenges of war: the natural environment and disease

"[E]NVIRONMENTAL forces transcend borders and oceans to threaten directly the health, prosperity and jobs of American citizens.... [A]ddressing natural resource issues is frequently critical to achieving political and economic stability, and to pursuing our strategic goals around the world," according to then US Secretary of State Warren Christopher, in the spring of 1996.[1] "The next war in our region will be over the waters of the Nile, not politics," observed Boutros Boutros-Ghali in 1988, then Egypt's Minister of State for Foreign Affairs.[2] "Business is business, and capital, money, is a coward. It is drawn to places which have the rule of law, places where there is an accountability of government, educated healthy workforces, secure working conditions. Capital will flee – money will flee from corruption, bad policies. It will flee from conflict. It will flee from sickness," according to US Secretary of State Colin Powell in fall of 2001.[3]

From the pronouncements of these foreign policy leaders, it seems that businesspeople have a profound interest in a stable allocation of natural resources as well as an environment relatively free from violent conflict.[4] The consequences of war involve the destruction of both human life and natural resources and directly impact business. For instance, in the conflict between East Timor and Indonesia that began in the mid-1970s, the Indonesian Air Force's use of napalm was not only a psychologically effective weapon against guerilla forces, it also destroyed forests, crops, and livestock, poisoned land and water, and started forest fires.[5] In the 1991 Gulf War, smoke and pollution from sabotaged oil wells reduced the life expectancy of at least 50,000 people, and between 1990 and 1992 infant mortality increased by 100 percent.[6] The destruction of water purification and sewage facilities resulted in raw, untreated sewage and chemicals being dumped into rivers and streets. As a result, incidences of hepatitis increased from 1,816 cases in 1989 to 13,776 cases in 1992.[7] Thirty percent of hospital water was also contaminated.[8] Thus, human and natural resources vital for the operation of business were destroyed.

In Kashmir, extensive deforestation resulted from skirmishes between India and Pakistan and 150,000 Kashmiri Hindus were relegated to refugee camps with limited healthcare.[9] The refugee situation was even more pronounced in the conflict in Mozambique from 1980–1992, where over 5 million people were displaced internally and 1.7 million others fled to other countries.[10] Deforestation has been a problem here too as has the destabilization of coastal mangroves and coral ecosystems.[11]

Location and disruption of public health infrastructures can have further devastating impacts on the rise of diseases; this may be a central aim of combatants. In the Sudan, for instance, retreating troops intentionally destroyed hospitals and other health facilities.[12] With depleted medical care, incidents of malaria, typhoid, TB, and meningitis have now become common in southern Sudan.[13] The destruction of infrastructure generally has left people with no other choice than to turn to wood as a fuel, thus prompting deforestation; this also accelerates desertification of soil, and with fewer windbreaks, more topsoil is blown away by desert winds.[14]

Of course, the results of warfare do not create the kind of conditions in which businesses typically flourish and the loss of economic vitality in each of these areas has been documented.[15] Yet, the connection between problematic social effects, violence, and economics runs deep because industrialization of the global economy exacerbates social tensions.[16] Not surprisingly, the fastest growing industry around the world is security and private police protection; this was true even before the terrorist attacks of September 11, 2001.[17] Security systems may provide a measure of stability and protection from violence, but the dynamics driving tensions around the globe are much deeper than can be controlled by adding additional (private or public) police officers. At least in liberal societies, which most of the richest countries of the world emulate,[18] extra security measures are likely to be a necessary but insufficient component of a solution toward the kind of stability needed for business to thrive.

Indeed, research reported by Thomas Homer-Dixon characterizes five social effects that can significantly increase the likelihood of violence in the world, and are more complex than can be controlled by security forces: (1) constrained agricultural production, often in ecologically marginal regions; (2) constrained economic productivity, mainly affecting people who are highly dependent on environmental resources and who are ecologically and economically marginal; (3) migration of these affected people in search of better lives; (4) greater segmentation of society, usually along existing ethnic cleavages; and (5) disruption of institutions, especially the state.[19] These kinds of social effects create tensions that can erupt in violent expression. It is difficult to envision how additional security forces will solve the embedded social problems that link violence with economic, social, ethnic, and even religious frustrations.

This chapter seeks to address these concerns. Section I elaborates ways in which these issues of violence manifest themselves in a globalized economy. Section II discusses the business implications of these tensions and suggests a way in which business can be a mediating actor to lessen these tensions. Section III addresses a related issue concerning war and disease. The chapter concludes with a suggestion for a recharacterization of the corporation in a way to sensitize it to the ecological issues necessary to address the potential issues of violence in societies.

I. The relationship between the physical environment and war

This section describes four ways in which ecological issues connect with warfare and directly impact violence. These involve: (1) resource scarcity resulting in competition for resources; (2) exacerbation of identity-based tensions, resulting from either competition for scarce resources or from ecological degradation; (3) the impact of disease either as a weapon in its own right or as a consequence of the degradation of infrastructure; and (4) broader issues of sustainability in the face of increasing populations and increasing industrialization.

A. Resource scarcity and implications for business

Contests among nations and states for valuable resources are nothing new. Much of colonial history resonates with the drive for acquisition of material goods, whether gold, spices, fur, or other items. The days of European conquests of the New World may have abated, but violent contests for natural resources still occur throughout the world.

Consider in Africa,[20] the Democratic Republic of the Congo, where six countries are fighting to control gold, copper, diamonds, and timber.[21] Although Western interests in Middle Eastern oil tend to be more concerned with protecting access to petroleum rather than controlling it to the exclusion of other countries, it is not inconceivable that disputes for oil could turn into battles over controlling the resource.

The raw contest for control of resources by nation-states who simply need or desire wealth is one example of how the physical environment connects with potential conflict. Michael Klare names three other kinds of conflict, where the control over the natural resource is connected to genuine sovereign claims of nation-states.[22] The first of these occurs when the supply of a natural resource extends across the boundaries of adjoining sovereign states. This is the case, Klare says, with an underground oil basin or a large river system.[23] As noted in the opening quotation from Boutros Boutrous-Ghali, Egypt's insistence on controlling the waters of the Nile has historically put it at odds with upstream African nations, such as Ethiopia and the Sudan.[24] Similarly, the concern that an adjoining country that shares a resource might make excessive use of it was one of Iraq's complaints against Kuwait in 1990.[25] A second point of contention can arise with respect to an offshore mineral resource where, by exercising sovereign rights of up to 200 miles under the United Nations Convention on the Law of the Sea,[26] multiple states may claim ownership of minerals located in relatively small bodies of water, such as in the Caspian Sea.[27] Third, disputes over control of bodies of water, such as the Persian Gulf or the Suez Canal, may cause conflict as well.[28]

Disputes over any of these four resource-based issues may well spill over into other contests relating to ethnic tensions, as will be described later, but they are important in their own right. In particular, consider the potential problems with respect to the resources of oil and water.

1. Mixing oil and water: the economization of foreign policy

Oil and water are critical for industry.[29] Moreover, oil and water are also finite resources that can foreseeably become exhausted in the twenty-first century. Estimates of global oil supplies suggest that there is enough oil to sustain global requirements into the middle part of the century with potentially significant shortages occurring in the second or third decade of this century.[30] Similarly, although the earth has vast quantities of water, only 3 percent is fresh water, including a significant amount of that in polar icecaps and glaciers.[31] With population growth and higher standards of living, the middle part of the twenty-first century may also see 100 percent usage of the available supply of fresh water.[32]

Similarly, petroleum-based fuels currently account for 95 percent of the world's consumed transportation energy.[33] There is every reason to believe that the demand for oil, for both transportation and other energy uses, will increase substantially in the future, particularly in Asia and Latin America.[34] In China and India alone, countries home to almost half of the world's population, oil consumption is projected to rise 3.8 percent annually.[35] From 1990 to 1996, the Chinese economy expanded by 93 percent.[36] The Department of Energy expects energy consumption to grow by 3.4 percent annually in Brazil, 3.0 percent in Mexico, and 3.7 percent in India between 1997 and 2020.[37] It is estimated that by 2020, these four countries will require 151 quadrillion BTUs of energy, or three times the amount needed in 1990.[38] With such increasing demands, pressure will likely be applied to the supply of petroleum. Based on studies done by BP Amoco, there are 1,033 billion barrels of oil in existing reservoirs that could be extracted under "existing economic and operating conditions."[39] Others estimate additional "unproven" reserves of 200 to 900 billion barrels. If the unproven reserves are averaged so as to expect a supply of 1,600 billion barrels being consumed at a current rate of 73 million barrels a day (as of 1999), the current supply would only satisfy demand for sixty years.[40] This estimate itself places exhaustion of oil supplies within the life expectancies of children born at the turn of the millennium, but if the Department of Energy's projection that worldwide oil consumption will rise by 1.9 percent per year between 1998 and 2020 is correct, the resulting consumption of 113 million barrels of oil a day would result in depletion of world oil stocks by 2040 rather than by 2060.[41]

This supply-demand dynamic places the reliance on fuel for industrialization and transportation within sight of exhaustion.[42] This could mean that countries will develop other sources to fuel economic development. It also could mean that the intensity of competition for oil could increase. Because of this dynamic, it is not surprising that many countries have now announced "the economization of foreign policy."[43]

Without undertaking a long historical analysis of the connection between economic gain and foreign policy, three important moments in the last sixty years – 1941, 1973–74, and 1989 – demonstrate why countries tend to consider natural resources a cornerstone of their foreign policy. In World War II, for instance, Japan's attempt to gain control over the Dutch East Indies oil-producing region triggered the 1941 US oil export embargo on Japan, which in turn led Japan to conclude that war with the USA was inevitable.[44] Meanwhile, Germany's need for oil prompted, at least in part, its 1941 invasion of the Soviet Union.[45] The 1973–74 disruption of oil supplies to the West by oil-exporting countries in the Middle East not only prompted the West to look for other oil supplies (such as in the North Sea and Alaska), but also led to pronouncements by Secretary of State Henry Kissinger in 1975 and by President Jimmy Carter in 1980 that the USA would go to war to protect Persian Gulf oil supplies.[46] Since the end of the Cold War in 1989, emerging and post-communist countries have tried to adapt to the free market and, in doing so, faced the issue of the need for resources to support economic development. Thus, Russia's President Putin, in 2000, announced a doctrine in which one of the purposes of the country's military would be the "creation of the conditions for the security of economic activity and protection of the Russian Federation's national interests in the territorial seas, on the continental shelf, and in the exclusive [offshore] economic zone of the Russian Federation and on the high seas."[47] Similarly, China has focused more of its military attention on the South China Sea, with its reserves of petroleum and natural gas, and Japan has adopted a defense program to protect shipping lanes around the country.[48] In part, these efforts are simply a continuation of any sovereign's attempt to protect resources important to a given political entity, but when economic development becomes central to a country's foreign policy, then protection of resources necessary for that development becomes critical.[49]

This economization of foreign policy has two particularly significant consequences. First, competition is increasingly acute because the supply of oil is concentrated in a few places, a concentration sometimes called the "Strategic Triangle."[50] Second, the competition is not simply among nation-states, but businesses, particularly multinational corporations, are also enmeshed in the competition among countries.

2. Oil flashpoints: The Strategic Triangle

The Strategic Triangle refers to a region stretching from the Persian Gulf to the Caspian Sea and then to the South China Sea.[51] These areas possess huge, significantly undeveloped sources of oil and natural gas as well as numerous, unresolved territorial disputes.[52]

The issues surrounding the Persian Gulf need little elaboration. The region has been the site of two major interventions by the West, led by the USA and Great Britain, in the past twelve years, as well as the feature of disputes between powers in the region including between Iraq and Kuwait (and various other parties in the 1991 Persian Gulf War),[53] Iraq and Iran,[54] Turkey and Syria,[55] and Turkey and Iraq.[56] In addition, because of the unequal distribution of oil revenues benefiting royal or business elite, there is resentment within Middle Eastern countries, often linked with religious dimensions, even though the governments of such countries have provided relatively generous benefits to the general population in terms of education, healthcare, food, and housing.[57] Connected with the interests of Western countries that have intervened in the region, the volatility of the region is well known. Because of the dangers of relying upon oil from the Middle East, the USA and other countries have sought to diversify by shifting their sources to other regions.[58] As a result, new areas of development, in regions such as Africa, the Caspian, and Latin America, have become more prominent suppliers of US petroleum needs.[59] Yet, events suggest that these new locales are not panaceas for stable extraction. The Sudan oil industry, for instance, has become a $1 million per day profit-maker for the Sudanese government, but the profits seem to have sponsored government war-making capability and activity.[60] Venezuela, South America's major oil-producing nation, has been gripped by social and labor unrest.[61] Two additional potential sources for oil and natural gas – the Caspian Sea Region and the South China Sea Region – merit further exploration.

a. The Caspian Sea Basin

The Caspian Sea Basin may hold the world's second or third largest reserve of oil along with a significant amount of natural gas.[62] Projections of its size are ambiguous, but according to some estimates, it holds as much as 270 billion barrels of oil, approximately 20 percent of the world's proven petroleum reserves, an amount second only to the Persian Gulf's 675 billion barrels.[63] In addition, the region holds

665 trillion cubic feet of natural gas – about 12 percent of the world's total reserves.[64]

The region's attractiveness as a supplier of oil as an alternative to the Middle East has garnered the attention of the USA, but US interests are also of concern to Russia, which considers the Caspian region to be part of its traditional sphere of influence.[65] Beyond the US-Russian contest for influence, there are "contests boundaries and territorial disputes, the prevalence of authoritarian regimes, severe economic disparities, long-standing regional rivalries, and a cauldron of ethnic and religious strife."[66] These animosities have produced fighting in Uzbekistan, Kyrgyzstan, and Dagestan as well as conflicts between Russia and Chechnya.[67]

Interestingly, however, competition for influence in the Caspian region does not so much involve jockeying among the USA, Russia, local governments, Turkey and Iran,[68] but among the companies that will do the actual work of drilling, refining, and selling the oil. After all, although governments gain influence and revenues, whether through taxes and fees or, more sinisterly, via bribery and kickbacks, precious few governments actually engage in the oil business. In the Caspian region, the companies seeking to negotiate contracts include BP-Amoco, Chevron, Exxon-Mobil, Royal Dutch/Shell, Elf Aquitaine of France, Agip of Italy, Stat-oil of Norway, Lukoil of Russia, and the China National Petroleum Corporation, and most attempt to partner with state-owned local concerns.[69] To succeed, however, the companies and the governments must be able to work without an established framework for determining who has rights to offshore drilling in the Caspian Sea.[70] Perhaps more significantly, there are also issues concerning how to transport the oil and natural gas to port because the Caspian Sea is landlocked.[71] As a result, the oil and natural gas will need to pass through pipelines.[72]

Passing oil through pipelines is not a benign decision. Indeed, in Afghanistan, the decisions made to determine where Russian oil should pass had dark consequences. After the Soviet Union withdrew from Afghanistan, the country fell into chaotic struggles for control, with no clear authority in the country.[73] In 1994, some ex-mujahideen fighters allied with Mullah Mohammed Omar challenged the stronger warlords. In the meantime, several oil companies wished to build a pipeline across Afghanistan to carry oil to Pakistan, seeing the potential for revenue from shipping and transportation if the oil were transferred from Pakistani ports to tankers headed to oil dependent countries. All the while the success of Mullah Omar did not go unnoticed.[74] Impressed by Omar's success, the Pakistani government provided aid for Omar's group, which the Pakistanis named "the Taliban," to expand its control from Kabul and Kandahar to the rest of the country to secure the corridor necessary for the pipeline.[75] The subsequent history of the Taliban is now, unfortunately, well known after its support of Osama bin Laden and his Al Qaeda terrorist organization was unearthed.[76] The interesting feature, however, is that in business's desperate, and to use Secretary of State Colin Powell's term, cowardly,[77] need for stability it may seek governmental assistance from sovereigns uninterested in providing justice. In other words, the choices corporations make in maximizing their profitability, particularly in areas of the world where there are major risks of violence, are not benign. The choices to be made by both governments and businesses, in building pipelines, for example, have proven to have significant negative spillover effects.

b. The South China Sea

As noted above it is anticipated that Asia's economic development will spur additional demand for energy.[78] China's energy needs are expected to double between the years 2000 and 2020 and Japan's needs are expected to increase by 25 percent within the same time period.[79] Together, this would result in these two countries consuming 20 percent of world energy by 2020 – an amount that is equivalent to the amount of consumption of all of Western Europe and Latin America combined.[80] China can turn to coal, which it possesses in abundance, but burning coal results in significant air pollution as well as major contributions to greenhouse gases.[81] Given China's desire to be the dominant Asian power, as well as its desire not to become dependent on foreign sources of energy, one would expect it to turn its attention to the South China Sea, which it has.[82] In 1992, China formally claimed two islands – the Spratley (a collection of a few hundred rocks, reefs, and inlets covering over 80,000 square miles, scattered throughout the Sea, and claimed by five other nations)[83] and the Paracel Islands – demonstrating *de facto* authority over the South China Sea.[84] In turn, China then provided drilling contracts to several Western companies off of the coast of Vietnam and expanded its military force in the region.[85] That region, bordered on the north by Taiwan and China, on the west by Vietnam, on the south by Indonesia and Malaysia, and on the east by

the Philippines, is a vibrant region of burgeoning economic development, as is nearby oil-dependent Japan and South Korea, with their
own thirst for crude oil and gas.[86] In addition, shipping from other
areas, such as the Persian Gulf and the Caspian Sea, generally cuts directly across the South China Sea so that control of the Sea implies not
only extractive, but also transport sovereignty.[87] It may well be that
countries such as Japan, South Korea, and Taiwan wish to benefit from
the extraction of oil from the South China Sea, but regardless, control
of that sea creates potential difficulties for each of these countries.[88]
The explosive part of this scenario involves the overlapping claims for
economic development rights in this region and the military means
to enforce those claims.[89] A clash already occurred in 1995 between
China and the Philippines over a small islet called Mischief Reef.[90]

   One question for South China Sea development involves the potential willingness of various countries to go to war for the zones they
claim. Although with respect to all oil development involving unsettled claims of sovereign control, whether in Africa, the Caspian Sea,
the Middle East, or the South China Sea, the actions taken by corporations to contract with various governments affects geopolitical resolu-
tions of power and influence. Oil, in short, is not simply about governmental decisions, but also about competition among oil companies.

3. Competition for water

Related to the issues presented by competition for oil are the similar
and perhaps more volatile issues surrounding competition for water.
With almost 300 river basins crossing national boundaries[91] and a
six-fold increase in worldwide water use between 1900 and 1995,[92]
it is not surprising that many commentators predict that contests for
water will be a source of violent conflict in the twenty-first century.[93]
Like oil, water crosses boundaries, giving rise to potential disputes over
its use.[94] Additionally, water supply is finite and once readily known
supplies are depleted, it is very costly to obtain additional amounts.[95]
And with the use of water so dramatically increasing, flashpoints are
bound to occur. An additional unknown factor is the potential impact
that may result from changes in the global climate.[96]

   More specifically, flashpoints revolve around increasing needs for
water as a result of increasing populations. These include both needs
for drinking water and water for industrial and agricultural use.[97] The
World Bank estimates that each person requires 36 to 72 cubic meters

of water annually to survive.[98] This number does not include agricultural, industrial, and energy-related production; together, these additional uses dramatically raise each person's needs to approximately 1,000 cubic meters per year, or as much as 70 percent of the world's fresh water supply with the largest use being for agriculture.[99]

The combination of increasing population and inaccessibility of much of the fresh water supply complicates its efficient distribution. Increasing populations mean that more people need water to drink, and more land devoted to agriculture. Yet, most of the world's arable land is already under cultivation, so that to make additional land productive, irrigation will be required. Irrigation is dependent on accessing remote water supplies.[100] To make matters worse, human beings are able to access less than 1 percent of the world's fresh water supply because most of the earth's water is trapped in the polar regions and glaciers.[101] After precipitation, evaporation and transpiration, the balance of the annual replenishment of the earth's water supply amounts to 40,000 cubic kilometers.[102] Half of this is currently lost through flooding and another 20 percent is carried off into inaccessible locations, such as Siberia.[103] This leaves only 12,500 cubic kilometers of water annually renewable for various human uses, an amount that is probably double existing population needs.[104] Yet, affluence tends to increase water use; for instance, the world's population doubled between 1950 and 1990, but water use (resulting from indoor plumbing, appliances, and the consumption of meat) increased by 300 percent.[105] It is foreseeable that, with increased population and increased affluence, human beings could fairly quickly reach all of the renewable fresh water and, although underground aquifers are available, once they are used, they – like oil reserves – cannot be replenished.[106] Desalinization is a possibility but is currently very costly. An additional perhaps more significant difficulty is that water availability is not evenly dispersed, but shortages are instead concentrated in areas that are either already impoverished or also struggling with potential conflicts regarding oil.[107] The Middle East, North Africa, and South Asia are particularly prone to water shortages and huge population increases. They are also already the subject of territorial disputes, some connected with petroleum.[108]

With many groundwater resources traversing existing national boundaries and with predictions that by 2025 two-thirds of humanity will suffer from moderate to severe water stress, the opening quotation from Boutros Boutros-Ghali[109] that future wars will be fought over water may bear some truth. In addition to the Nile, which is shared by several countries, four countries share the Tigris-Euphrates system and the Jordan River is shared by three countries and the Palestinian Authority.[110]

In contrast to Boutros-Ghali's assertion that future wars will not be about politics, but water scarcity, it is important to see that politics is inherently a part of the water conflict. First, water conflict tends to exacerbate ethnic tensions that already exist within a given region or country.[111] Second, the nature of water flow, particularly with respect to rivers, tends to favor the upstream states that control the flow.[112] Disputes occur not only among countries, but also within countries such as in India, where farmers in adjoining states have fought over irrigation rights to the Cauvery River and even in the USA, when in the 1920s farmers in eastern California sabotaged the aqueduct system carrying water to Los Angeles.[113]

Launching hostilities over water historically has occurred as a result of concerns over prestige, security, and survival. Certainly, the canals and irrigation systems of Egypt, Mesopotamia, and China contributed heavily to each country's economic development and security,[114] but spectacular projects – such as the building of the Aswan Dam in Egypt – also enhanced the prestige and power of the rulers.[115] The need to control water supplies remains crucial to each country's security and survival. Egypt's President Anwar el-Sadat, for instance, threatened to bomb water facilities in Ethiopia, where the main contributor to the Nile, the Blue Nile, originates, if Ethiopia diverted water for irrigation projects.[116] Similarly, with Egypt, Sudan, Uganda, and Ethiopia all needing to feed burgeoning populations in an arid region of Africa, the danger of conflict grows significantly.[117]

Tensions also exist in the basins of the Tigris-Euphrates and the Indus rivers. These rivers, which provide the only significant amounts of water for their basins, supported a population of approximately 500 million people in 1998 with 1 billion people expected by the middle of the twenty-first century.[118] The people living in these regions are divided ethnically and religiously and the rivers themselves often have deep symbolic meaning, suggesting that disputes over the rivers are likely to take on additional elements beyond that of the access to the water.[119] In addition, while the Nile features only one power, Egypt, with significant military might, these other basins feature many nation-states with substantial military capability.[120] Fortunately, these regions have made efforts to negotiate shared water agreements, but there are major demographic and ethnic pressures that could push disputes over water into explosive problems.[121]

Countries sharing the Tigris-Euphrates River, for instance, are heavily dependent on the river for their fresh water needs, given the common aridity of the region. The rivers are responsible for approximately 30 percent of Turkey's needs, 85 percent of Syria's needs, and 100 percent of Iraq's requirements.[122] In response to this dependence, several countries have constructed dams in order to control floods, generate power, and irrigate land.[123] Turkey has built three dams on the Euphrates and has plans for others in the Tigris; Syria has built one dam on the Euphrates with plans for another; and Iraq has built dams on both the Euphrates and the Tigris Rivers.[124] Constructing these dams creates potential for reduced water flow and subsequent disputes for downriver countries heavily dependent on water from the rivers. A dispute of this kind broke out in 1990 when Turkey essentially cut off the Euphrates from Iraq and Syria in order to fill the Ataturk Dam Reservoir.[125] Because the cutoff was taken in the winter before the growing season, practical impacts were minimized, but the capability to control these waters raised serious concerns in downstream Iraq and Syria.[126] Linked to demands by Turkey for Syria to exercise greater control over groups troublesome to Turkey, this control has resulted in a general sense of unease and potential conflict.[127] Moreover, greater needs for water to satisfy growing populations suggests the potential for ongoing conflict over the control of water flow.[128]

The Jordan River basin has seen more than its share of violent conflict over the past fifty years. Water stress is a hovering reality in all of the conflicts between Israel and its Arab neighbors. Steps have been taken to attempt to minimize the water-related aspects of this conflict, although there are open questions regarding whether they have satisfactorily taken place. Like the Nile, Tigris, and Euphrates basins, the Jordan basin has also seen tremendous population growth. Nearly seven times the number of people lived in the Jordan basin in the 1970s as did in the 1920s with additional significant growth expected.[129] In the 1970s, the region as a whole began a period of water deficit, where more use was being made of water than was being replenished annually.[130] Israel in particular, has adopted a water management plan through the importation, rather than the growing, of food. If 90 percent of an individual's 1,000 annual cubic meters of water needed[131] is for cereals, it makes sense to import rather than to grow food.[132]

Yet, flashpoints remain because of the basic problem of a growing population in an arid climate. Moreover, as in other cases, the distribution of water is not even. A central point of contention in the basin is the Israeli strategy of protecting the annual recharge of the Mountain Aquifer in the West Bank, from which Israel obtains some of its water. Israelis require Palestinians to obtain permission to sink wells on the West Bank land – where precipitation runoff flows to the Mountain Aquifer and thereby limits Palestinian use of water.[133] The result of this and other policies is that Palestinians have access to 105 million cubic meters of groundwater while Israel makes use of 450 million cubic meters.[134] Without making judgments as to the relative merits of various allocations, the perception created by this difference fuels animosity in the basin.

4. Business complexities

In recognizing the collisions between resource availability, population growth, and geopolitical quests for power, it is tempting to simply characterize these as issues of concern for nation-states. Yet, this characterization would be simplistic. It is true, for instance, that the contest for the extraction of oil from the Caspian Sea region pits Russia, the USA, Iran, Turkey, and other nations against one another.[135] Many disputes in the region center around disputed interpretations of the United Nations Convention on the Law of the Sea (UNCLOS).[136] For example Russia and Iran claim that the Caspian is a lake for which there are Soviet-Iranian treaties from the 1940s that control exploitation and distribution of resources.[137] However, if the Caspian is a sea it is under the jurisdiction of UNCLOS.[138] But nation-states are not the only parties involved. Russian energy firms such as Lukoil and Gazprom and Western companies such as BP-Amoco, Chevron, Exxon-Mobil, Royal Dutch/Shell, Elf Aquitaine, Agip, Stat-oil, and China National Petroleum are also involved.[139] Pakistan's support of the Taliban in Afghanistan as a way to secure oil transportation was borne of pressures and opportunities presented by oil companies.[140] Geopolitical control over natural resources provides security in making oil available to fuel tanks, jeeps, and airplanes. Thus, the contest for control over resources is also very much one among business entities as well as governments.

The situation in Africa provides an example of the complexity of business-and-government relationships. Although Africa is rife with innumerable disputes, major energy companies have not been prevented from working with local warlords to obtain agreements to extract oil.[141] In this respect, Colin Powell's claim that business will run away from dangerous situations[142] may not be as compelling as one might expect. Or, to put it otherwise, businesses value stability, but when faced with an opportunity to secure a valuable resource, businesses, like governments, may resort to the methods necessary to benefit their own interest. If this is true, however, there is reason to hold businesses accountable for their actions that contribute to the likelihood of violence; in short, contests for natural resources are not only governmental responsibilities.

The same may be true with respect to water, such as with attempts to privatize water distribution. In Latin America and the Caribbean, for instance, there have been efforts to turn water services over to private ownership.[143] These efforts are not always warmly embraced, in part because of the specter of trying to profit from a resource that is essential to human survival. In other words, market-oriented solutions may not be perceived as appropriate for a public good, such as clean water.

Oil and water are obvious resources to examine because of their importance to human survivability and economic development. But other natural resources, such as gold, diamonds, timber, and minerals, are valuable.[144] From the receipts generated by the sale of diamonds, for instance, the governments of Liberia and Sierra Leone are able to pay wages to young boys to fight in civil wars equipped with inexpensive guns.[145] This is significant in light of a World Bank study that has found a twenty-fold increase in the likelihood of a civil war in countries where the primary export is a single undifferentiated commodity.[146] In Sierra Leone, up to fifty thousand people have been killed since 1991 with hundreds of thousands becoming refugees.[147] Multinational corporations are in the midst of this problem because of their desire for the commodity; thus DeBeers has been the target of considerable criticism for allegedly buying "blood diamonds."[148] Not insignificantly, Liberia exported almost 300 million dollars worth of diamonds to Belgium in 1998.[149]

Contests for lootable resources often entail significant ecological damage, such as with the case of clear-cutting valuable, old-timber forests.[150] Seventy-two percent of Liberia's 2000 timber trade was done in conjunction with French and Chinese companies.[151] This exploitation of natural resources was made possible through the arms trade; although not through the sale of fighter jets, AWACS surveillance systems, or nuclear know-how, but from the trade of 640 million small arms and light weapons.[152] There is nearly one weapon for every person of Mogadishu's 1.3 million population and an AK-47 in Mogadishu can be purchased for merely 200 dollars.[153] In Aceh, Indonesia, an automatic rifle can be bought for the equivalent of US $6.[154] With hundreds of millions of dollars being gained by the extraction and export of natural resources, with cheap weapons readily available, with impoverished populations having little alternative means of income, it is unrealistic to lay the issue of war and peace at the feet of only nation-states. Many more actors are involved and the very nature of geopolitical balances of power may be changing in response to the growing influence of multinational corporations.[155]

Thus, contests for natural resources are one example of how violence may erupt. Often, however, it is not simply the possession of resources that gives rise to conflict. As already noted, for instance, river basins that are shared by populations with different ethnic and religious memberships also make it possible for contests over natural resources to have a flavor of identity-based conflict.[156] The Caspian Sea area has long had deep ethnic divisions; and the arrival of competing oil companies has exacerbated those divisions.[157] The same is true of contests for lootable resources, such as diamonds and timber, which are embedded within historic antagonisms.[158] As a result, it is also important to examine how ecological issues can inflame identity-based tensions.

B. Exacerbation of identity tensions

In his research on environmental scarcity and its connection to violence, Thomas Homer-Dixon concludes that scarcity itself does not cause violent conflict, nor rarely does violence have a single cause.[159] Yet a great deal of violence, particularly with respect to violence occurring within preexisting borders, is causally related to environmental scarcity.[160] This includes violence that has occurred in Chiapas, Mexico, South Africa, Pakistan, the Philippines, and Haiti.[161] Homer-Dixon suggests that scarcities of cropland, fresh water, and forests contribute to violence by generating social stress that fosters "subnational insurgencies, ethnic clashes, and urban unrest" and that developing countries are particularly prone to these disturbances because they are typically dependent on natural resources.[162] Thus, apart from the specific competition for a particular resource, it is also important to see how competition, or the spillover effects from such contests, can contribute to identity-based tensions that, in turn, can result in violence.

1. Uneven distribution of resources

Just as energy and water resources provide an initial lens through which to examine competition over natural resources, it is helpful to contextualize the issues that can arise from identity-based conflicts. Homer-Dixon notes that 40 percent of the people on the planet use fuel-wood, charcoal, straw, or cow dung as their main source of energy and up to 60 percent rely on these fuels for at least a part of their primary energy needs.[163] More than 1.2 billion people do not have access to clean drinking water.[164] The allocation of valuable resources is highly desired and the potentially increased marginalization of those mired in this level of poverty is likely to breed resentment. There are at least two ways in which the distribution of resources can exacerbate simmering identity-based tensions.

The first maldistribution concerns resource capture or structural scarcity.[165] This occurs when some groups in a given society are able to recognize the value of scarce resources and then act to control large percentages of those resources.[166] Frequently, these powerful groups also manipulate the power structure of society to access further resources.[167]

Amy Chua argues that the opportunities presented by free markets have been seized upon by minorities in many countries to significantly enrich themselves, but that majorities in those countries remain impoverished.[?] Market-dominant minorities may be able to establish and to maintain power in a country[169] – apartheid in South Africa would be an extreme example – and they exist, she argues throughout the world.[170] She cites the role of the Chinese in the Philippines and elsewhere in Southeast Asia.[171] In Indonesia, for example, Chinese Indonesians comprise only 3 percent of the population, but control 70 percent of the economy.[172] Similar situations exist in Brazil, Ecuador, Guatemala, West Africa, Nigeria, the former Yugoslavia, and Russia.[173] The concentration of wealth, however, engenders hostility within countries that can be expressed when majority rule democracy comes with it; the majority then has the capability of scapegoating the wealthy minority, almost always with strongly ethnic overtones.[174] Chua argues further that this dynamic has consistently resulted in actions of mass murder by the minority against the market-dominant majority; Rwanda is another case in point as are actions in Zimbabwe against white farmers and actions against Chinese in Indonesia.[175] Even more controversially, Chua argues that the same dynamic is at work with respect to Arab resentment of the regionally market-dominant power in the Middle East, Israel,[176] and against the USA as a globally market-dominant power in the attacks of September 11, 2001.[177] Thus, according to Chua, governments frequently take on the character of a privileged minority group in the position to benefit itself, at least as long as they can effectively control power and make arrangements to minimize opposition.

Environmental scarcity adds to this dynamic. It is one thing to observe that another ethnic group has better cars or homes. It is another if that other group has clean water while one's children suffer from dysentery caused by drinking dirty water. As already demonstrated, this is one of the problematic perceptions articulated in the ongoing disputes between Palestinians and Israelis on the West Bank.[178] Given the expected population increases in those countries where access to a critical, basic resource such as water is expected to become even harder to obtain, the prospects that environmental scarcity will provoke increased ethnic hostilities exists. Adding to the potential is the visual connection provided by contemporary telecommunications and the Internet, where impoverished, suffering populations can see the glitter of the West.

A second maldistribution concerns what is done with the leftovers of resource use; that is ecological marginalization.[179] This scenario occurs when the structural distributions already in place join with population growth so that the poor, again typically from the same impoverished ethnic groups, are forced into ecologically marginal living quarters such as upland hillsides, land subject to desertification, and tropical rain forests.[180] This psychological resentment is not necessarily different from that of resource distribution generally, but living in a marginalized area contributes to ethnic resentments that can lead to uncontrollable eruptions. As is the case with the location of petroleum and water, these resentments tend to be found in critically important areas of the world.[181] These places include South Africa, Mexico, Pakistan, India, and China, the latter two countries comprising over 40 percent of the world's population.[182]

In both of these cases, the distribution of either benefits in terms of desired resources or costs in terms of living in degrading conditions does not typically happen across a demographically neutral board. Instead, certain groups tend to be favored while others tend to be disfavored. Environmental scarcity thus sharpens the potential grievances of rivalries that may often already be simmering in a given country.

2. Struggle to control identity

A related but distinguishable category is the struggle to control identity. The previous discussion on the distribution of resources concerned primarily material costs and benefits as well as the social psychological reaction to them; this second category relates to threats to more spiritual identities. These too, can create the conditions for ethnically related violence.

Rivers often are imbued with spiritual significance.[183] Whether it be a large river like the Nile,[184] or the Kunene River separating Angola and Namibia,[185] bodies of water, like other natural resources, often embody a deep manifestation of the identity of people. These identifications are critically important. Thomas Friedman characterizes those things that anchor human beings to a rooted identity as "olive trees" and writes, "[o]live trees are important. They represent everything that roots us, anchors us, identifies us and locates us in this world – whether it be belonging to a family, a community, a tribe, a nation, a religion or, most of all, a place called home."[186]

Although globalization allows for greater interaction among people to cooperate on a range of things that bordered-up societies previously could not have allowed, it also means that within countries, there remains the tug of the olive tree.[187] Re-routing and damming of rivers, clear-cutting forests, and punching holes in the ground can challenge the identities of people for whom these natural things have spiritual significance. Globalization also challenges cultures in that things that were familiar are now gone, replaced by something strange. To the extent this causes consternation in France about the prevalence of Big Macs and Mickey Mouse, this may not be a huge issue.[188] At the same time, as Friedman argues, when there is a sense that a community has lost control of its economic vitality, as has been the case when financial markets move money in and out of a country virtually overnight,[189] one is left with the feeling that no one is in charge except for an arbitrary, faceless market.[190] But, as Israeli political theorist Yaron Ezrahi notes:

The most arbitrary powers in history always hid under the claim of some impersonal logic – God, the laws of nature, the laws of the market – and they always provoked a backlash when morally intolerable discrepancies became glaringly visible. The Enlightenment was really the globalization of science and rationality and the backlash came when every thief, crook, exploiter and fraud claimed that whatever he was doing was necessitated by science and logic. The same could happen with globalization.[191]

It is noteworthy that since the end of the Cold War, fewer than 10 percent of contemporary wars have begun as interstate conflicts, but issues of religious, ethnic, or national identity have spurred two-thirds of wars.[192] In the West, where since the Enlightenment, it has been common to hear concerns raised about religious wars,[193] statistics that show that over half of the wars had a religious dimension may not be surprising. Yet, it is surprising that religious belief systems, which always venerated peace, are so intimately connected with contemporary conflict.

Scott Appleby, a leading authority on fundamentalist religious groups, addresses one aspect of this. Appleby concedes that raising the specter of violence is not normal for most religions, but argues that often the justification for resorting to violence is an argument that the times are not normal.[194] Indeed, evidence suggests that many times this characterization is made by groups faced with new threats. Appleby argues that religious extremists typically do not mobilize orthodox believers; instead, they concentrate on the young and untutored during a time when outside pressures threaten traditional ways of life.[195] Thus, by shrinking time and space through communications and transportation technologies, modernity has made it much more likely that Sikhs, Buddhists, Christians, Jews, Hindus, Muslims, and nonbelievers live in close proximity to one another, especially in large urban areas around the world. In this globalized milieu, religious extremism – with the violent intolerance of outsiders – has become the response of choice for a disproportionately influential minority within traditional religious communities that feel threatened by the new pluralism.[196] If believers, again typically the young and untutored, think they are threatened, then there is an obligation to fight the enemy by any means.[197] The threat is that orthodoxy has not adequately responded to the secular, pluralistic, materialist, feminist West.[198] Fundamentalist leaders who are often charismatic mold an attitude of absolute devotion to the will of God, demonizing the infidel, focusing almost exclusively on a very narrow subset of religious doctrine as being the key to religious truth and connecting that truth to political goals.[199] "Thus the religious Zionists of the Ichud Rabbanim and their counterparts in the Gush Emunim emphasize one of the 613 Torah mitzvoth and subordinate the remaining 612 religious duties to its observance – the commandment to settle the land is tantamount to all other commandments."[200] In short, believers can latch on to a particularly important dimension of religious tradition – in the quoted example, physical real estate – and use adherence to that tradition to express rebellion against a cultural change. Religion can thus be linked to ecological resources and thereby foster additional, militant violence.

Appleby's account is respectful of religion as a whole, noting how religion can also be militantly devoted to peace.[201] In his account of fundamentalism, extremists distort a religious tradition that might otherwise be a force for nonviolence. A more cynical view of religion, consistent with Vayrynen's and Chua's analysis of how a minority group can seize control of government and orient policies for personal benefit, is presented by anthropologist Jared Diamond.[202] Diamond argues that, historically, human beings tended to live in relatively small bands comprised of between five to eighty people, most of them closely related to each other.[203] Although there were differences among the relative authority of individuals within these groups, a common feature was that the groups were relatively egalitarian.[204] There were no formal stratification of class hierarchy, no formal legal institutions, such as the police or even codes of law, and no monopolies of information or decision-making.[205] Yet human beings, beginning in the last few tens of thousands of years, also lived in tribes (usually populated by hundreds of people), clans, and chiefdoms.[206] Tribes,[207] like bands, also tended to be relatively egalitarian with little institutional formality.[208]

When chiefdoms arose 7,500 years ago, there was potential for greater conflict because people lived in close proximity with others they did not know.[209] One solution was for the chief to hold a monopoly on force; ideally, that force would be used for the welfare of all members of the chiefdom, but realistically the chief could also be a thief.[210] A kleptocracy could only flourish if there were reasons for common people to tolerate the transfer of wealth to the elite.[211] Historically, those reasons were to: (1) disarm the common people and arm the elite; (2) make the common people happy through redistribution of resources; (3) use force to create satisfaction through maintenance of a safe, public order; and (4) create an ideology or religion justifying the theft.[212] The last solution typically came in the form of a notion of the divine connection of royalty.[213] Moreover, the state ideology was able to bind non-kin together in conjunction with a common good that would justify even death for the welfare of others.[214] The idea of dying for the state, however Diamond argues, was unthinkable for bands and tribes.[215] Patriotism, he argues, was an unknown commodity.[216] Diamond argues that fanaticism in war was probably unknown until about 6,000 years ago, the time when the great world religions emerged.[217]

Regardless of Diamond's conclusions about kleptocracy, the anthropological data concerning bands and tribes on the one hand and chiefdoms (and even larger organizations) on the other suggests potential for violence in a couple of ways. First, within any large religious organization, there may be disaffected members who are reachable by those who articulate the dangers of a materialistic, secular threat. Second, this threat may be articulated in some way by designating an ecological entity as paradigmatic of either that threat or the essential meaning of the religion. This means that natural resources and landmarks which play a prominent role in most religious traditions of any size can be pulled into ecological conflict.

Thus, identity-based conflict can result from ecological issues. This can occur through the sharpening of ethnic grievances resulting from one ethnic group obtaining more of the benefits of natural resources and fewer of the costs of environmental degradation. It can also occur through the symbolic associations that the natural environment may carry, which become important for various reasons to religious believers. Those adherents, whose faith may or may not be associated with a particular organized religion, may have their beliefs molded by attention to a natural, ecological resource.

An overarching issue with respect to sustainability is the extent that a consumption-driven economy can be supported by the natural environment. Evidence mounts daily that humanity will be confronted this century with major consequences resulting from climate change.[218] Fossil fuels are thought to be the major cause of the greenhouse gas problem.[219] A central threat of climate change is a potential partial melting of polar icecaps, which would raise sea levels and cause severe coastal flooding.[220] This connection of fossil fuel and flooding presents an entirely different dimension of the issues of oil and water described above.[221] Not only may oil and water be depleted, but there are also impacts on cropland scarcity, tropical deforestation, and depleted fish stocks.[222]

The world is faced with a complicated, difficult ecological condition which could provide the breeding ground for many kinds of violence, justified by those who believe that the current system has not treated them fairly.[223] It may be comforting to believe that these issues are the province of governments. It seems somewhat unrealistic to believe that governments can solve these issues without the engaged thoughtfulness of the business sector.

II. Business implications

Regardless of whether the evidence is sufficient to insist on the accountability of business to the connection of war and peace, many places around the world are already making the connection. As we have already noted, Shell Oil Co., a company currently recognized for its social responsibility efforts, was once vilified for its alleged complicity in the oppression of the Ogoni people in Nigeria and its alleged involvement in the assassination of rebel leader Ken Saro-Wiwa.[224] Exxon has faced protests from human rights organizations for not confronting human rights abuses perpetrated by security forces protecting Exxon's pipeline in Indonesia.[225] Apart from ecological examples, chapter 1 reported how disgruntled consumers attacked McDonald's restaurants by breaking windows and smearing the walls with cow dung after it was learned that, contrary to previous announcements, its French fries were cooked in oil containing beef tallow rather than in vegetable oil.[226] Hindus who had inadvertently violated religious precepts by eating these fries as well as vegetarians were outraged.[227] In January, 2002, Argentine protestors ransacked a McDonald's restaurant in Buenos Aires[228] and the McDonald's in Quebec City simply closed and removed all identifying signs in advance of the 2001 Summit of the Americas to avoid attracting the interest of demonstrators.[229] Protests against banks in Argentina[230] and Wal-Mart stores in Bonn[231] are additional examples of how corporations are increasingly targeted as responsible parties for a variety of perceived social injustices.

It may or may not be fair for businesses to be targets for protests and it also may be true that governments are responsible for managing the resulting conflicts. But business is involved in all of these issues. Although it may not be a moral requirement for corporations to take responsibility for the issues connected with violence, it would benefit both business and society if they did. As Thomas Friedman puts it, "Arab nationalism, socialism, fascism or communism – while they may have made no economic sense, had a certain inspirational power. But globalization totally lacks this. When you tell a traditional society it has to streamline, downsize and get with the Internet, it is a challenge that is devoid of any redemptive or inspirational force. And that is why, for all of globalization's obvious power to elevate living standards, it is going to be a tough sell to those millions of people who still say a prayer before they ride the elevator."[232]

It is plausible that business can do something to contribute to sustainable peace, a peace that endures because it is just. Engaging that connection could well be the free market's way of addressing the social void[233] that transactional economics cannot. Businesses are engines of economic development that can be beneficial to social harmony. On one hand, through globalization, businesses consistently reach across borders to allow people from faraway places to gain understanding of each other by working together in ways that would otherwise not be possible. Businesses can do this in creating diverse work forces where members of different ethnic groups may work together for a common project – even if that project is simply that of economic profitability – for the first time. Businesses may be able to, on occasion, mediate conflicts between governments. On the other hand, if businesses are viewed as being exploitative, culturally undermining, greedy, or socially insensitive, they can sow the seeds for potential violence.

Thomas Homer-Dixon[234] argues that protection from the dilemmas concerning environmental scarcity depends on having better governance to protect the environment, human rights, labor standards, and financial transactions despite no global government.[235] Solving these problems requires, he argues, technical ingenuity. That kind of creativity depends on social ingenuity together with adequate background institutions to support public and semi-public goods such as markets, funding agencies, educational and research institutions, and effective governments.[236] Other commentators have argued further that the natural world provides business models, such as biological mimicry, that can be a source for ecologically sensitive management.[237] Out of the natural environment, therefore, are models for thinking about how businesses can make significant contributions to sustainable peace.

Regardless of the particular source, approaching issues of ecology and war draw upon the approach we have articulated. That is, preventing war is not about one thing. It is about many things. Business finds itself in the midst of most all of them and, as a result, has some contribution to make to all of them. A balanced approach of economic development, openness to external evaluation, building community (including ecological citizenry), and track two diplomacy, can mediate many of the tensions exacerbated by natural resource stresses.

III. Disease and war

As products of nature, human beings are also directly affected by ecological and biological elements. Just as human beings need natural resources, particularly water, in order to exist, so also a disruption in biospherical equilibrium can make life impossible. Thus, the issue of disease and war is not neutral when it comes to the lethal nature of disease; war enhances it and sometimes promotes it. Nor is business neutral to disease. Outbreaks of disease, such as sudden acute respiratory syndrome, can wreak havoc on economic affairs. So here again, business has an interest in the containment of disease and because war works against that containment, disease can be seen as something of the ultimate ecological challenge to human life – the challenge to our physical bodies.

War can foster deadly diseases as an incidental weapon and by undermining the capability of societies to control their spread. Jared Diamond argues that Europeans were able to have military success and dominance over native populations because Europeans had guns, the nastiest germs, and steel.[238] In the Spanish conquest of the Incas, Francisco Pizarro's band of 168 soldiers were able to rout an Incan army of 8,000 without *any* Spanish casualties.[239] The use of horses, the sharpness of Spanish weapons, and the protective armor provided against Incan clubs turned the Battle of Cajamarca into a spectacle.[240] Even so, the Spaniards may not have succeeded had not the Incan Empire already been stricken with an epidemic of smallpox for which the Incans had no resistance.[241] This, according to Diamond, captures one of the essential reasons for European imperial success: "diseases transmitted to peoples lacking immunity by invading peoples with considerable immunity."[242] Smallpox was also crucial in South Africa in 1713.[243] In Hawaii, after being discovered by Captain James Cook in 1778, the native population shrunk from approximately 800,000 to 135,000 in just forty-five years and further shrunk to just under 40,000 by 1896 due to the spread of venereal disease, tuberculosis, measles, mumps, whooping cough, smallpox, cholera, leprosy, and a disease resembling typhoid fever, all introduced by Westerners.[244] Between 1520 and 1618, Mexico's population is estimated to have dropped from 20 million to 1.6 million from disease.[245] For the New World as a whole, the native population is estimated to have been reduced by as much as 95 percent within two centuries following Columbus's landing.[246] More than swords and spears, most of the killings came from smallpox, measles, influenza, typhus, diphtheria, malaria, mumps, pertussis, plague, tuberculosis, and yellow fever.[247]

A possible reason for the lack of immunity of native peoples and the robust immunity of Europeans is the prevalence of domesticated animals. Diamond argues that, with agriculture, a smaller amount of land was able to feed larger groups of people who lived in nomadic hunter-gatherer bands.[248] Larger societies possessed their own military advantages over small bands in terms of manpower, but in addition, the domestication of animals led to their trained use. This increased the possibility for specialization once animals were trained and fewer hands were needed to provide food; people could instead make weapons and build buildings and larger governments.[249] Moreover, because domesticated animals, including household pets such as dogs and cats, carry disease, the resulting density of human and animal populations allowed their immune systems to develop, even in the face of highly mutated diseases such as smallpox, measles, and flu.[250] These mutated diseases may have been frustrated by the immunities of Europeans and their animals, but the diseases faced no resistance from native populations.[251] Agricultural societies then, with their specialization of labor, their stores of food to feed armies, their ability to support large populations, and their ability to build up resistance to diseases were at a tremendous advantage over populations of native peoples.[252] As Diamond rather colorfully puts it, a naked farmer has no advantage over a naked hunter-gatherer, but because the farmer breathes out nastier germs (excluding the possibility that he may also have armor and horse), the farmer is more likely to prevail.[253] The densities accompanying urban life make the immunity issue even more pronounced.[254]

Globalization and its associated mobility puts people into contact with each other at a rate previously unimagined.[255] And, not surprisingly, fatal diseases such as AIDS have been linked to infections that seem to have jumped from animals (specifically monkeys in Africa) to human beings and have spread very quickly around the world due to mobility and the lack of immunity to the disease.[256] Disease thus represents a major ecological threat to the physical well-being of human beings and that threat is one that has been part of violent conquests of other peoples. The basic threat to ecological devastation as a part of warfare has an unfortunately deep history.[257]

Even in warfare, at least until World War II, and probably continuing in wars in emerging countries, more soldiers die as a result of disease than wounds.[258] The reason for battlefield deaths through disease is that battlefields do not posses public health infrastructures. Battlefields are not designed for providing safe drinking water, shelter from the elements, and pristine latrines. What occurs on the battlefield can be a spillover effect from war itself insofar as public health infrastructures are destroyed as battles are fought or, in an age where the separation between civilian and military populations may not be valued, attacking the infrastructure may even be a tactical decision.

"War [is] not healthy for children and other living things."[259] The actual collision with weaponry can be fatal, but war also loosens diseases. Once disease outbreaks, as in the case of AIDS, for instance, it is difficult to control it. Disease itself wreaks human ecological destruction in ways sometimes even more devastating than fighting battles.

Conclusion

In his interviews with leading CEOs, former Yale Business School Dean Jeffrey E. Garten concludes that CEOs should take "a broader agenda" that goes beyond philanthropy and beyond the typical commissions, trade, associations, and lobbying.[260] That this has not been done is not a criticism of CEOs, he argues, but a missed opportunity.[261] Similarly, it seems that not engaging business in a quest for sustainable peace is also a missed opportunity.

Businesses have power and influence. They are functioning, productive institutions. Corruption seems to be linked to violence. Gender equity seems to be correlated with less violence. Poverty resulting from lack of economic opportunity is linked to violence. Democratic kinds of participation and voice can be linked to peace. Corporations can help reduce corruption by being transparent. They can provide more equitable treatment of women. They can contribute to economic development and in ways that are widely distributed. They can be managed in a participatory way that embraces the voice of employees and other stakeholders and thus demonstrate democratic values.

Disease and war are linked. Diseases can be used as a weapon of war and can be a consequence as well. Disease has also served as a metaphor for war as well. Nobel Laureaute Albert Camus analogizes the isolating, suffocating and dehumanizing dimensions of the bubonic plague to the scourge of Naziism and war.[262] Although many actors – governments, health authorities, and others – had primary responsibility for battling the plague, Camus's heroes were ordinary people who did their job the best they could each day and in doing so, made a continuous dent in the brutality of the disease.[263] These bookkeepers, doctors, reporters, and others preserved a humanity threatened by disease.

Businesspeople too can make contributions daily to contribute to sustainable peace and reduce the potential of violence. Individually, no one person nor no one business is likely to prevent a war but businesspeople can make contributions that matter. Camus once wrote that "perhaps this world is one in which children suffer, but we can reduce the number of suffering children. And if you do not do this, then who will do this."[264] Today that can be paraphrased. Perhaps this is a world in which there is warfare. But businesspeople can reduce the amount of violence in the world. And if they do not do this, then who will?

We propose sustainable peace as an aim to which businesses should orient their actions both for reasons of avoiding the activities that contribute to the spilling of blood as well as for the promotion of sustainable economic enterprises, which are fostered by stable, peaceful relationships. Thus, business must do what it does best and address economic development, even in terms of the extraction of natural resources. But it must also be attentive to the rights of others, to the development of community and meaning, and to stop violence when it is likely. Given the dangers ecological stresses pose for the planet, it is difficult to think of a more compelling reason to reorient business behavior.

Notes

This chapter originally appeared as Timothy L. Fort and Cindy A. Schipani, *Ecology and Violence: The Environmental Dimensions of War*, 29 COLUM. J. OF ENVTL. L. forthcoming (2004).

1. Quoted in PAUL HAWKEN, AMORY LOVINS AND L. HUNTER LOVINS, NATURAL CAPITALISM: CREATING THE NEXT INDUSTRIAL REVOLUTION 20 (1999).
2. Quoted in MICHAEL T. KLARE, RESOURCE WARS: THE NEW LANDSCAPE OF GLOBAL CONFLICT 12 (2001).
3. Quoted in Ted C. Fishman, *The Myth of Capital's Good Intentions*, HARPER'S MAGAZINE, August 2002, at 34 (Fishman rejects Powell's statement, arguing that business makes a great deal of money from war and instability).
4. Because the term "environment" can also refer to legal, governmental, cultural, and social issues in addition to those relating to ecology, we primarily use the word "ecological" rather than "environmental" to designate the connection of violence, business, and the natural world.
5. Ian Robinson, *The East Timor Conflict*, in THE TRUE COST OF CONFLICT: SEVEN RECENT WARS AND THEIR EFFECT ON SOCIETY 10–11 (Michael Cranna ed., 1994).
6. Gregory Quinn, *The Iraq Conflict*, in THE TRUE COST OF CONFLICT, above n. 5, at 26.
7. Ibid., at 29.
8. Ibid., at 33.
9. Nils Bhinda, *The Kashmir Conflict*, in THE TRUE COST OF CONFLICT, above n. 5, at 64–65.
10. Shaun Vincent, *The Mozambique Conflict*, in THE TRUE COST OF CONFLICT, above n. 5, at 93.
11. Ibid., at 92 (stating that the area of mangrove forest has declined 70 percent, and coastal erosion threatens the livelihood of 55,000 families dependent on the fishing industry).

12. Nicholas Shalita, *The Sudan Conflict*, in THE TRUE COST OF CON-
FLICT, above n. 5, at 138 (finding that government troops destroyed
the equipment and buildings of the only two functioning hospitals in
1992).

13. Ibid., at 139.

14. Ibid., at 145.

15. See generally THE TRUE COST OF CONFLICT, above n. 5 (discussing
several world conflicts and how they have depressed the economies
of countries around the world).

16. HAWKEN, ET AL, above n. 1, at 8.

17. Ibid.

18. See generally AMY CHUA, WORLD ON FIRE: HOW EXPORTING FREE
MARKET DEMOCRACY BREEDS ETHNIC HATRED AND GLOBAL INSTA-
BILITY (2003) (arguing that the simultaneous adoption of majority-
rule democracies and free markets is a recipe for violent, ethnic
clashes in developing countries).

19. THOMAS HOMER-DIXON, ENVIRONMENT, SCARCITY, AND VIOLENCE
80 (1999).

20. See e.g. GEORGE B.N. AYITTEY, AFRICA IN CHAOS 5–6 (1998) (noting
the vast material wealth of the African continent and the interest of
countries in exploiting that wealth).

21. Fishman, above n. 3, at 37.

22. See generally KLARE, above n. 2.

23. Ibid., at 19.

24. See ROBERT O. COLLINS, THE NILE (2002) (for a history of the ecological dimensions of the Nile River, particularly as effected by various hydroelectric projects, the attempts to control the river, and the
geopolitical rivalries spawned by issues of such control).

25. Ibid., at 22. See also Philip K. Verleger, *Understanding the 1990 Oil
Crisis*, THE ENERGY J., October, 1990, at 15 (asserting that preceding
Iraq's invasion of Kuwait, Iraqi President Saddam Hussein claimed
that Kuwait was stealing oil from the disputed Rumaila field and
producing in excess of its OPEC quota).

26. United Nations Convention on the Law of the Sea, December 10,
1982, 21 I.L.M 1261.

27. KLARE, above n. 2, at 22. See also Paul Thomas, *Geopolitics Around
the Caspian*, ENERGY ECONOMIST, September 1993, at 16 (explaining
the various regions surrounding the Caspian and Aral Seas and the
conflicts and politics therein).

28. KLARE, above n. 2, at 22.

29. Ibid., at 19.

30. Ibid. See also James J. MacKenzie, *Heading Off the Permanent Oil Crisis*, Issues in Sci. and Tech., June, 1996, at 48 (finding that the rate of production of oil producing countries will decline rapidly in the coming years as crude oil supplies are consumed).

31. Klare, above n. 2, at 19. See also Barry James, *Less Water and Less to Eat*, Int'l Herald Tribune, October, 2002, at 1 (asserting that only 1 percent of fresh water is available for human use, as the remainder is trapped in the icecaps and glaciers).

32. Klare, above n. 2, at 19.

33. Ibid., at 36–37.

34. Ibid., at 38 (Asia and Latin America are particularly susceptible to increases in need for fuel due to development and rapid industrialization).

35. Ibid.

36. Ibid., at 16.

37. Ibid., at 17; see also International Energy Outlook, available at http://www.eia.doe.gov/oiaf/ieo.

38. Klare, above n. 2, at 17.

39. Ibid., at 41.

40. Ibid., at 42 (noting that this is a conservative estimate that assumes a static rate of global consumption).

41. Ibid.

42. Ibid., at 42–43.

43. Ibid., at 10 (this economization is a result of giving more strategic significance to economic and research concerns, i.e. US protection of critical resources and trade routes).

44. Ibid., at 31. See also Eric Black, *Why Did Japan Decide to Attack Pearl Harbor?*, Star Trib. (Minneapolis-St. Paul), May 25, 2001, at 11A (asserting that Japan had no intention of attacking Pearl Harbor until the US embargo drove them to seek out the Dutch East Indies region and to try and stop the US Navy from interfering with the plans).

45. Klare, above n. 2, at 31.

46. Ibid., at 33 (Kissinger stated to *Business Week* magazine that the USA would be willing to go to war over oil supplies, although he was reluctant to use force, while Carter asserted that the USA would use any means necessary to protect its interests in the Gulf, including military force).

47. Cited in Klare, above n. 2, at 11.

48. Ibid. See also Ben Barber, *Beijing Eyes South China Sea With Sub Purchase*, Wash. Times, March 7, 1995, at A13 (stating that China

intended to buy twenty-two submarines from Russia in order to pursue its interests in the South China Sea).

49. KLARE, above n. 2, at 14.
50. Ibid., at 49 (the Strategic Triangle is the region stretching from the Persian Gulf in the west, to the Caspian Sea in the north, and to the South China Sea in the east).
51. Ibid.
52. Ibid., at 49–50 (the Strategic Triangle accounts for about half of the current world oil production and three quarters of the currently identified reserves).
53. John Omicinski, *U.S. in for the Long Haul With Persian Gulf Mission*, THE SEATTLE TIMES, October 17, 1997, at A2 (stating that in 1990 Saddam Hussein invaded Kuwait and instigated the Persian Gulf War).
54. Jay Tolson, *Iraq: After Sadaam*, U.S. NEWS & WORLD REP., April 28, 2003, at 27 (chronicling the history of Iraq and the eight-year war that began in the 1990s).
55. Scott MacLeod, *Syria: The Peace Conflict*, TIME, October 18, 1999, at 56 (stating that Syria has a crucial dispute with Turkey, since Turkey controls Syria's main water source, the Euphrates).
56. Jeffrey Fleishman, *Turkish-Kurdish Rift Muddles War Plans*, L.A. TIMES, February 25, 2003, at A10 (outlining the history of the troubled relationship between Iraq and Turkey).
57. KLARE, above n. 2, at 53.
58. Ibid., at 46.
59. Ibid. (quoting the National Security Council as saying Venezuela has become the number one source, and Africa supplies 15 percent, of oil in the USA).
60. Fishman, above n. 3, at 36.
61. Scott Wilson, *Political Deadlock Bolsters Chavez; Venezuelan Leader Exploits General Strike to Remake Institutions, Opponents Say*, WASH. POST, January 20, 2003, at A15.
62. KLARE, above n. 2, at 81.
63. Ibid., at 2 (citing US Department of Energy figures).
64. Ibid.
65. Ibid., at 83.
66. Ibid., at 81.
67. Ibid., at 82. See also *Chaos in the Caucasus*, THE ECONOMIST, October 9, 1999, at 23 (quoting newspaper columnists in Moscow as describing the fight between Russia and Chechnya as a war between "civilization and barbarism").

68. KLARE, above n. 2, at 84.
69. Ibid., at 86–87.
70. Ibid., at 81–82.
71. KLARE, above n. 2, at 88.
72. Ibid.
73. Nazif M. Shahrani, *War, Factionalism, and the State in Afghanistan*, 104 AM. ANTHROPOLOGIST 715, 720 (2002).
74. Ibid.
75. Ibid.
76. Michael Elliot, *Special Report: The Secret History*, TIME, August 12, 2002, at 28 (explaining the history of the disputes for control of Afghanistan and the history of Al Qaeda).
77. Fishman, above n. 3, at 34.
78. KLARE, above n. 2, at 36–38.
79. Ibid., at 113.
80. Ibid.
81. Ibid., at 114 (there are already dangerous levels of air pollution throughout the country, and China's percentage of world carbon emissions is expected to rise from 13 to 21 percent over the next twenty years).
82. Ibid., at 117. See also Stephen B. Young, *China Holds the Indochina Key*, FAR EASTERN ECONOMIC REVIEW, June 6, 2002, at 24 (describing the takeover of the islands from Vietnam).
83. KLARE, above n. 2, at 120. See also Young, above n. 82, at 24.
84. See KLARE, above n. 2, at 116.
85. Ibid.
86. Ibid., at 117.
87. See ibid., at 111–112 (since countries such as Japan and South Korea are dependent, they need to seek to prevent the continued flow of resources through the sea, and whichever country controls the flow has transport sovereignty).
88. Ibid., at 119–120 (the coastal irregularities and the numerous islands make determining boundaries in the South China Sea extremely difficult).
89. Ibid., at 118.
90. Ibid., at 125. See also *China and the Philippines: Reef Stricken*, THE ECONOMIST, May 29, 1999, at 36.
91. HUSSEIN A. AMERY AND AARON T. WOLF, WATER IN THE MIDDLE EAST: A GEOGRAPHY OF PEACE 64 (2000).
92. Ibid., at 2 (citing 1997 report from the Commission on Sustainable Development).

93. Ibid., at 64.
94. KLARE, above n. 2, at 142.
95. Ibid.
96. Ibid., at 140 (noting that the greenhouse effect will cause temperatures to rise and rainfall patterns to change in different areas of the country – the impact is as yet unknown).
97. Ibid., at 142–143.
98. Ibid.
99. Ibid. (citing World Bank statistics).
100. Ibid., at 143–44.
101. Ibid., at 143.
102. Ibid. See also Sandra Postel, *Dividing the Waters*, TECHNOLOGY REVIEW, April 1, 1997, at 54.
103. KLARE, above n. 2, at 143–144.
104. Ibid., at 144.
105. Ibid.
106. Ibid. See also Nicolaas van Rijn, *What We Have is All There is*, THE TORONTO STAR, September 25, 1999 (comparing an underground aquifer to a bank account that is used for withdrawals and never deposits).
107. KLARE, above n. 2, at 144–45.
108. See ibid., at 140, 145.
109. Ibid., at 12.
110. Ibid., at 145–46.
111. See KLARE, above n. 2, at 161–64.
112. AMERY AND WOLF, above n. 91, at 6.
113. KLARE, above n. 2, at 147.
114. Ibid., at 141.
115. Ibid. See also Robert L. Pollock, *Mideast Peace? Let's Start With the Rule of Law*, THE WALL STREET JOURNAL, November 27, 2002, at A10 (stating that the dam was Nasser's way to "economic salvation").
116. KLARE, above n. 2, at 153.
117. Ibid., at 156–57 (this population in total is likely to grow by approximately 300 million in the next fifty years).
118. Ibid., at 161.
119. Ibid., at 162.
120. Ibid., at 164 (The Jordan River basin includes Israel, Jordan, Syria, and the Palestinian Authority; the Tigris-Euphrates includes Iran, Iraq, Syria, Turkey, as well as Kurdish areas; the Indus includes Afghanistan, China, India, Pakistan, and Kashmir).
121. Ibid., at 162–64.

122. Ibid., at 175.
123. Ibid., at 176. See also Louis Jacobson, *Back to Eden: Restoring the Marshes of Iraq*, WASH. POST, April 28, 2003, at A11.
124. KLARE, above n. 2, at 176.
125. Ibid., at 177.
126. Ibid., at 177–78.
127. Ibid., at 180.
128. Ibid., at 161–64.
129. AMERY AND WOLF, above n. 92, at 21.
130. Ibid., at xii.
131. Ibid., at xiii.
132. Ibid., at xii.
133. Ibid., at 34.
134. Ibid., at 36.
135. KLARE, above n. 2, at 90–92.
136. Ibid., at 99.
137. Ibid.
138. Ibid.
139. Ibid., at 86–90.
140. Ibid.
141. Ibid., at 14.
142. Fishman, above n. 3, at 34.
143. See e.g. Terence R. Lee and Andre Jouravlev, *Private Participation in the Provision of Water Services: Alternative means for private participation of water services* (1997), at http://www.thewaterpage.com/PPP% 20Debate%20Lee2.pdf.
144. KLARE, above n. 2, at 190.
145. See Fishman, above n. 3, at 37–38.
146. Paul Collier, *Economic Causes of Civil Conflict and Their Implications for Policy* 6 (June 15, 2000), at http://econ.worldbank.org/files/13198_EcCausesPolicy.pdf.
147. KLARE, above n. 2, at 192.
148. Ibid., at 191–92. See also Thomas W. Dunfee and Timothy L. Fort, *Corporate Hypergoals, Sustainable Peace, and the Adapted Firm*, 36 VAND. J. TRANS. L. 563 (2003) (providing an in-depth analysis of the blood diamonds controversy).
149. Fishman, above n. 3, at 38.
150. KLARE, above n. 2, at 193–94.
151. Fishman, above n. 3, at 38.
152. Ibid., at 39.
153. Ibid.
154. Ibid.

155. See generally PHILIP BOBBITT, THE SHIELD OF ACHILLES: WAR, PEACE AND THE COURSE OF HISTORY (2002).
156. Ibid.
157. KLARE, above n. 2, at 97.
158. Ibid., at 190.
159. HOMER-DIXON, above n. 19, at 7.
160. Ibid., at 7.
161. Ibid.
162. Ibid., at 12.
163. Ibid., at 13.
164. Ibid.
165. Ibid., at 15.
166. Ibid.
167. Ibid.
168. CHUA, above, at 6–7.
169. Ibid.
170. Ibid.
171. Ibid.
172. Ibid.
173. Ibid.
174. Ibid.
175. Ibid., at 231.
176. Ibid., at 211.
177. Ibid., at 230–31.
178. Ibid.
179. HOMER-DIXON, above n. 19, at 16.
180. Ibid.
181. Ibid., at 18–19.
182. Ibid.
183. See COLLINS, above n. 24 (discusses the religious significance of the Nile River to the communities through which the river flows).
184. See ibid.
185. Carol Ezzell, *The Himba and the Dam*, SCI. AM., June, 2001 at 81.
186. THOMAS L. FRIEDMAN, THE LEXUS AND THE OLIVE TREE 31 (2000).
187. Ibid., at 31.
188. Barbara Robinson, *Disney Displayed Cultural Ignorance in Planning Paris Park*, LAS VEGAS REVIEW-JOURNAL, September 3, 1993, at 11B.
189. *Is it at Risk? Globalisation*, THE ECONOMIST, February 2, 2002, available at 2002 WL 7245017.
190. FRIEDMAN, above n. 186, at 191.
191. Ibid., at 191.

192. R. SCOTT APPLEBY, THE AMBIVALENCE OF THE SACRED: RELIGION, VIOLENCE, AND RECONCILIATION 17 (2000).

193. See Timothy L. Fort, *Religion and Business Ethics: The Lessons from Political Morality*, 16 J. BUS. ETHICS 263, 268–69 (1997) (describing the consequentialist concerns of philosophers and legal scholars with respect to the incendiary dimensions of allowing religion to play a part in politics).

194. APPLEBY, above n. 192, at 88.

195. Ibid., at 17.

196. Ibid., at 58.

197. Ibid., at 90–91.

198. Ibid.

199. Ibid.

200. Ibid.

201. Ibid., at 7.

202. JARED DIAMOND, GUNS, GERMS, AND STEEL, THE FATES OF HUMAN SOCIETIES (1999).

203. Ibid., at 267.

204. Ibid. at 269.

205. Ibid.

206. Ibid., at 270–71.

207. Ibid., at 271.

208. Ibid., at 271–73.

209. Ibid., at 273.

210. Ibid., at 273–76.

211. Ibid., at 276.

212. Ibid., at 277.

213. Ibid., at 277–78 (specifically citing the example of the kings and gods of Hawaii).

214. Ibid., at 278, 281.

215. Ibid., at 281.

216. Ibid.

217. Ibid., at 281–82.

218. *Climate Panel Reaffirms Major Warming Threat*, N.Y. TIMES, January 23, 2001, at F8, cited in Donald O. Mayer, *Corporate Governance in the Cause of Peace: An Environmental Perspective*, 35 VAND. J. TRANSN'L L. 585, 609 (2002).

219. Ibid.

220. Clare Nullis, *UN Report Warns of Global Climate Changes*, CHI. TRIB., February 20, 2001, at 4.

221. Mayer, above n. 218, at 617.

222. HOMER-DIXON, above n. 19, at 63.
223. Mayer, above n. 219, at 618.
224. William E. Newberry and Thomas N. Gladwin, *Shell and Nigerian Oil*, in ETHICAL ISSUES IN BUSINESS: A PHILOSOPHICAL APPROACH 522 (Thomas Donaldson and Patricia H. Werhane eds., 7th ed., 2002).
225. Jane Perlez, *Indonesia's Guerilla War Puts Exxon Under Siege*, N.Y. TIMES, July 14, 2002, International Section, at 1.
226. Laurie Goodstein, *For Hindus and Vegetarians, Surprise at McDonald's Fries*, N.Y. TIMES, May 20, 2001, at A1.
227. Ibid.
228. Anthony Faiola, *Argentine Peso Quickly Sinks After Government Lets it Float: Protests Against Economic Changes Turn Violent in Capital*, WASH. POST, January 13, 2002, at A23.
229. *Protestors in Quebec Tear Down Part of Barricade, Throw Objects at Police*, ST. LOUIS POST-DISPATCH, April 21, 2001, at 6.
230. Faiola, above n. 228, at A23.
231. Toby Helm, *Bush Protests Off to Early Start*, LONDON DAILY TELE-GRAPH, May 22, 2001, at B1.
232. FRIEDMAN, above n. 186, at 341.
233. See Lee A. Tavis, *Corporate Governance and the Global Social Void*, 35 VAND. J. TRANS. L. 487 (2002).
234. See HOMER-DIXON, above n. 19, at 28–31.
235. Ibid., at 206–07. Human beings are simply biologically predisposed to work in small groups. Diamond above n. 202. It may be the case that this predisposition has frequent negative consequences, but it is an aspect of human nature that must be acknowledged and, can be utilized for positive outcomes.
236. Ibid., at 110.
237. HAWKEN, ET AL., above n. 1, at 15. As an example of the possibilities of biomimicry:

"[b]usiness is switching to imitating biological and ecosystem processes replicating natural methods of production and engineering to manufacture chemicals, materials, and compounds, and soon maybe even microprocessors. Some of the most exciting developments have resulted from emulating nature's life-temperature, low-pressure, solar-powered assembly techniques, whose products rival anything human-made. Science writer Janine Benyus points out that spiders make silk, strong as Kevlar but much tougher, from digested crickets and flies, without needing boiling sulfuric acid and high-temperature extruders. The abalone generates an inner shell twice as tough as our best ceramics,

and diatoms make glass, both processes employing seawater with no furnace."
HAWKEN, ET AL., above n. 1, at 15.

238. DIAMOND, above n. 202, at 23.
239. Ibid., at 75.
240. Ibid., at 76.
241. Ibid., at 77.
242. Ibid., at 77.
243. Ibid., at 78.
244. LILIKALA KAME'ELEIHIWA, NATIVE LANDS AND FOREIGN DESIRES: PEHEA LA E PONO AI 141 (1992).
245. DIAMOND, above n. 202, at 210.
246. Ibid., at 211.
247. Ibid., at 211–12.
248. Ibid., at 88–90.
249. Ibid., at 89–91.
250. Ibid., at 92.
251. Ibid., at 92.
252. Ibid., at 92.
253. Ibid., at 195.
254. Ibid., at 195, 206–07. Diamond further argues that literacy also provided competitive advantages because literate societies were able to transmit knowledge that could make them more effective on any political endeavor that native peoples often could not duplicate through oral traditions. Thus, along with better weapons, nastier diseases, and central political organizations, literacy also contributed to military superiority. DIAMOND, above, note 202, at 215–16.
255. Caroline Baum, *Global Economic Ties Solid, but Boycotts Still Worrisome*, THE LOS ANGELES BUSINESS JOURNAL, April 7, 2003, at 12 (stating that globalization causes the free flow of labor and information to increase).
256. Matt Wickenheiser, *Idexx Begins Search for Mad-Cow Marker*, PORTLAND PRESS-HERALD, June 15, 2003 (using mad-cow disease as an example of how a disease has jumped to humans from the consumption of animals, and the body does not recognize it as a disease and thus has no immunity to it).
257. See generally THE TRUE COST OF CONFLICT, above n. 5.
258. DIAMOND, above n. 202, at 197.
259. See e.g. George Packer, *The Way We Live Now: Recapturing the Flag*, N.Y. TIMES, September 30, 2001, Section 6 (Magazine), at 15.
260. JEFFREY C. GARTEN, THE MIND OF THE CEO 221 (2001).

261. Ibid., at 222.
262. ALBERT CAMUS, THE PLAGUE (1947). See also JEAN KELLOGG, DARK PROPHETS OF HOPE 103–04, 117–18 (1975).
263. Timothy L. Fort, *Who Will Clean Up the Mess?*, CHI. TRIB., June 15, 1990, Section 1, p. 25.
264. CAMUS, above n. 262.

Conclusion

WAR and terrorism, economic distress, and corporate scandals have dominated the news in the first two and a half years of the new millennium. It is not hard to link economic distress to unease over terrorist attacks and concern about the war against Iraq. It is also not hard to link economic distress with the corporate scandals and their resulting impact on the trustworthiness of corporate USA. This book goes further and suggests that there might also be a link between positive corporate behavior and a more secure, safe world.

On the one hand, it would seem that corporations are well positioned to do exactly this. Corporations, after all, are the engines that produce jobs and with them the economic and social benefits that follow employed engaged individuals. Corporations also have the capability of reaching across borders to engage individuals who might otherwise be in conflict with common enterprise. On the other hand, to the extent that corporations are perceived to be exploiting local populations and dominating valued cultures, they can also sow the seeds for unrest. From this, we posit that a particular kind of company, a company that provides economic development with a sensitive eye to the concerns of affected stakeholders, might be able optimally to contribute to sustainable peace, a peace that endures because it is just.

These concepts warrant an exploration of how ethical business behavior might be a force for positive social change. That change might be measured by the extent to which bloodshed is reduced. As the world confronts environmental challenges, increased crowding, global migration, and border-transcending technologies, it may not be enough to rely on only the nation-state for a secure and safe world. We conclude, as noted throughout this book, that there are at least four contributions corporations can make toward that end.

The first, and probably the most obvious contribution corporations can make toward stability involves providing jobs and economic development. Businesses bring with them jobs. Moreover, not all economic benefits come from direct employment. Companies may also train and educate the local workforce as well as the companies' suppliers. In so doing, companies provide a transfer of managerial expertise that may spill over to other productive enterprises in the economy. Additionally, the transfer of expertise may also extend to technological transfer. Corporations also often become involved in social and charitable activities in the areas where they do business. And not insignificantly, corporations pay taxes and, provided that the governmental system is reasonably just – an admittedly large assumption – these resources can reinforce the public infrastructure necessary for social progress.

The second contribution corporations can make to sustainable peace is being open to external evaluation. That is, corporations can practice transparency, avoid corruption, and discourage political systems that practice corruption. This is important when considering a recent study suggesting a possible link between corruption and violence, described in chapter 1.[1]

No one company, of course, is going to solve a country's corruption problems. Yet, companies can try to limit the corruption endemic to a country and also work toward changing laws. Indeed, this is the recommendation of the Organization for Economic Cooperation and Development (OECD) for promoting efficient markets. Moreover, if there is also a correlation between corruption and violence, then the cause of peace could be beneficially supported by corporate efforts to limit or eliminate corruption.

This commitment to support laws that reduce or eliminate corruption leads to a second kind of evaluative commitment: support of the rule of law itself. One of the lessons from the emerging economies of central and Eastern Europe is that those countries that quickly established a commitment to a rule of law, particularly in terms of contract and property protection, flourish more those that do not.[2]

The third contribution corporations can make relates to the building of communities. This means both building a sense of corporate community as well as corporate attentiveness to the needs and sentiments of the communities in which they work. More specifically, companies can become mediating institutions. As argued elsewhere, there are both moral and neurobiological reasons for why human beings develop their values in relatively small groups – mediating institutions – such as family, neighborhood, religious groups, and voluntary associations.[3] Large bureaucratic companies do not necessarily lend themselves to being communities, but creating a sense of connectedness among members of an organization can provide a sense of security and identity to the people who work there.

As part of this process, companies can encourage the use of "voice" by those in the company. Having a voice in the promulgation of rules is a critical, identifying characteristic of a democracy. Although subtle, it is plausible that when a company committed to quality processes insists that its employees speak up when they recognize a product defect, they have learned something about participatory governance and this knowledge may spill over into the country itself. This could be significant, as several studies show that democratic countries rarely, if ever, go to war with each other.[4]

A corporation can also contribute to the psychological security and identity of a country by investing in the people of that country. To the extent that companies can develop and empower leaders in the countries where their plants are located, the less likely, it would seem, that those plants would be seen as a threat to local culture.

Acting a bit more subtly, corporations can mediate some of the contests for power between people for whom either power or security is at stake through what has become known as "track two" diplomacy. We have already suggested how this occurred in conflicts between India and Pakistan. In addition, corporations can act as good citizens. Corporations acting as good citizens can be ambassadors for their countries. In doing so, a more positive vision of the country may emerge.

Similarly, an extension of building corporate community involves providing the opportunity for different people to work together for a common goal. Sometimes this is explicit; other times it is implicit. Either way, work provides a place where people of different backgrounds can meet each other.[5]

This is not to claim that corporations are the magic key to sustainable peace. But what it does suggest is that in a complex world with many actors, multinational corporations can have an influence on geopolitical developments. With that influence comes at least an opportunity for corporations to take actions that are likely to lead to longer-term stability. Businesses benefit from stability. After all, in an increasingly crowded world with populations migrating to every part of the world, technological linkages affecting all corners of the earth, and with the resulting tensions that come with some changes, any opportunity to reduce violence needs to be seriously explored.

Notes

This section is reprinted in part from Timothy L. Fort and Cindy A. Schipani, *Scandals and Sustainable Security*, 10 CORPORATE ENVIRONMENTAL STRATEGY – INT'L J CORPORATE SUSTAINABILITY (October, 2003) and from a paper presented at Rutgers University in November 2002 as the Prudential Lecture in Business Ethics. Reprinted with permission.

1. Timothy L. Fort and Cindy A. Schipani, *The Role of the Corporation in Fostering Sustainable Peace*, 35 VANDERBILT J. TRANS. LAW 389 (2002).
2. Thomas W. Dunfee and Timothy L. Fort, *Corporate Hypergoals, Sustainable Peace, and the Adapted Firm*, 36 VANDERBILT J. TRANS. L. 563 (2003).
3. TIMOTHY L. FORT, ETHICS AND GOVERNANCE: BUSINESS AS MEDIATING INSTITUTION (2001).
4. See e.g. SPENCER R. WEART, NEVER AT WAR: WHY DEMOCRACIES WILL NOT FIGHT EACH OTHER (1998) (arguing that once adjusted for stable democracies that have endured at least a minimal test of time, no two democratic countries, defined as having two-thirds of male citizens voting, have ever gone to war); see also ARIE M. KACOWICZ: ZONES OF PEACE IN THE THIRD WORLD: SOUTH AMERICA AND WEST AFRICA IN COMPARATIVE PERSPECTIVE (1998) (arguing that democratic regimes tend to affect the quality of peace more than being a necessary and sufficient cause of peace itself). Cf. AMY CHUA, WORLD ON FIRE: HOW EXPORTING FREE MARKET DEMOCRACY BREEDS ETHNIC HATRED AND GLOBAL INSTABILITY (2003) (opposing the view that democracy is essential for peace and instead suggesting that the combination of majority democracies and free market economies tend to exacerbate ethnic tensions. Chua's argument, however, relates more to intrastate violence as opposed to interstate violence and she relies on a certain kind of majority rule democracy without safeguards for minority rights).
5. RONALD TAKAKA, A DIFFERENT MIRROR: A HISTORY OF MULTICULTURAL AMERICA (1993).

Index